SUMMERS BROTHERS

Dedicated to
Bob & Bill Summers - American Speed Kings

The author would like to acknowledge that three generations of his extended family put tremendous effort into the production of this book: daughter Tamara Donahoe contributed a great book design and beautiful art direction, grandson Scott Lozano did many of the illustrations and photo compositions and everyone, including family friend Heather Palermo, participated in photo cleanup and restoration. My thanks to all of them for taking this as seriously as I did.

The author would further like to acknowledge the extraordinary contribution by Mike and Penny Cook, whose tireless efforts ensured the timely completion of this landmark project.

On July 14, 2018, the Summers Brothers were inducted into the Mopar Hall of Fame, recognizing their world record achievement. The author was privileged to speak on their behalf at the induction ceremonies, highlighting their extraordinary accomplishments with Chrysler Hemi engines.

GOLDENROD

The Resurrection of America's Speed King

© 2018 by John Baechtel

LANDSPEED MEDIA GROUP
www.landspeedmedia.com

The GOLDENROD
WORLD LAND SPEED RECORD HOLDER FOR WHEEL-DRIVEN AUTOMOBILES

Official World Land Speed Records (2-way average)
  1 mile: 409.277 mph
  1 kilometer: 409.695 mph
Set Nov. 12, 1965, Bonneville Salt Flats, Utah
Owners, designers and builders: Bob and Bill Summers, Ontario, Calif.
Driver: Bob Summers

First American car to hold the wheel-driven mile record since 1928.

Best Wishes
Bob Summers
Bill Summers

Summers Brothers
Builders of World Land Speed Record Streamliners
R. S. (BOB) SUMMERS
(714) 986-5362
909 W. Mission Blvd.
Ontario, California

Summers Brothers
Builders of World Land Speed Record Streamliners
BILL SUMMERS
(714) 986-5362
909 W. Mission Blvd.
Ontario, California

Summers Brothers
Builders of World Land Speed Record Streamliners
JIM CROSBY
Crew Chief
(714) 986-5362
909 W. Mission Blvd.
Ontario, California

Published by Landspeed Media Group

www.goldenrodbook.com

© **2018 by John Baechtel**

All rights reserved. No part of this publication may be reproduced or utilized in any form or by any means, electronic or mechanical, including photocopying, recording, or by any information storage and retrieval system, without prior permission from the Author. All text, photographs, and artwork are the property of the Author unless otherwise noted or credited.

The information in this work is true and complete to the best of our knowledge. However, all information is presented without any guarantee on the part of the Author or Publisher, who also disclaim any liability incurred in connection with the use of the information.

All trademarks, trade names, model names and numbers, and other product designations referred to herein are the property of their respective owners and are used solely for identification purposes. This work is a specialty publication of the Landspeed Media Group, and has not been licensed, approved, or endorsed by any other person or entity.

BOOK DESIGN AND ART DIRECTION:
Tamara Donahoe

PHOTO RESTORATION:
Tamara Donahoe, Scott Lozano, Heather Palermo

SPECIAL CONSULTANTS:
Dennis Dean - President
FIA Land Speed Records Commission

Dave Petrali - USAC
United States Auto Club

Tom Burkland - FIA Record Holder
200 MPH Club - 400 MPH Chapter

"Landspeed" Louise Ann Noeth
LandSpeed Productions
www.landspeedproductions.biz

Dr. Charles Jenckes, Ph.D.
F1 Aerodynamicist

First Edition

ISBN 978-1-7321761-0-2

Printed in China

Crew chief's snapshot of Hot Rod Magazine® cover shoot, September 1965.

FRONT COVER:

Main: Goldenrod with Bob and Bill Summers (Greg Sharp)

Left: Goldenrod front suspension (David Freers)

Center: Bob Summers routing ignition wires (John Veenstra)

Right: Goldenrod cockpit (David Freers)

BACK COVER:

Top Right: Author removing dummy engine to begin restoration. (Leann Furgerson)

Lower Right: Mike Cook and Billy Hodges trial-fitting repaired lower body panel. (Joe Pettitt)

Lower Left: Tom Clarke repainting the Summers Brothers logo on the nose of the newly restored Goldenrod. (Joe Pettitt)

TITLE PAGE:

Author conducting initial examination. (Bob Casey)

TABLE OF CONTENTS

Introduction 1

    Meet the Record Setters 3
    Defining the World Land Speed Record 5

1. Humble Beginnings 7

    Project Goldenrod 13
    Engine Overview 16
    Driveline Overview 21
    Body Overview 22
    Goldenrod Specifications 24

2. The Summers Brothers 25

    The Roadster Years 29
    The Pollywog 33

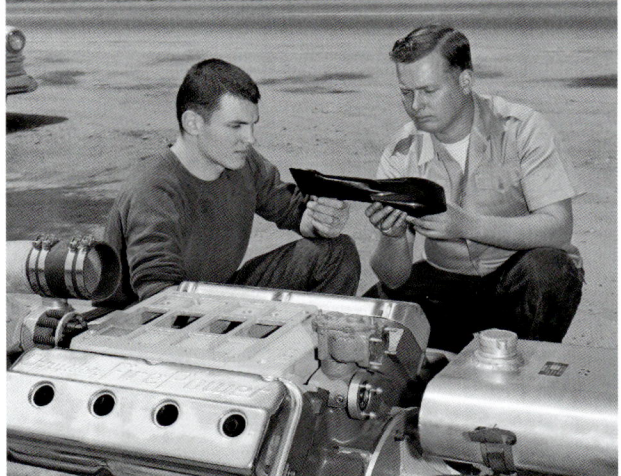

3. Building a Record Holder 37

    Front Upper Control Arm Detail 45
    Rear Upper Control Arm Detail 46
    Front Suspension 47
    Jim Crosby - Crew Chief (1937 - 2017) 53
    Crosby Family Album 54

TABLE OF CONTENTS

4. Aerodynamics 61

Fundamentals of Aerodynamic Drag 66
Inside the Goldenrod Wind Tunnel Program 75
The Air Scoop Controversy 89
Jack "Willie" Sutton - Master Fabricator 95
Record Busters in the News 101

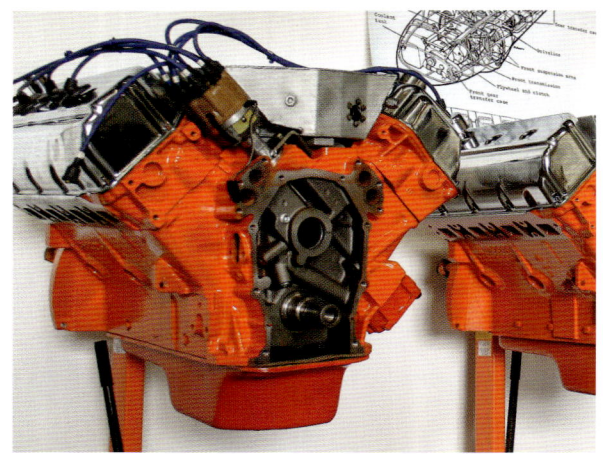

5. The Chrysler Race Hemi 103

Goldenrod Race Hemi Engine Specifications 106
Chrysler Race Hemi Engine Specifications 112
Dry Sump Oiling System 113
Fuel Injecting the Race Hemi 115

6. Grasping for Glory 121

Riverside Raceway Test 123
Chasing the Record at Bonneville 137
Record Run 409.277 MPH - November 12, 1965 151
FIA Record Certificate 157
The Goldenrod Crew 158
Goldenrod Record Documentation 159
Parting Shot: 425.99 MPH - November 13, 1965 167

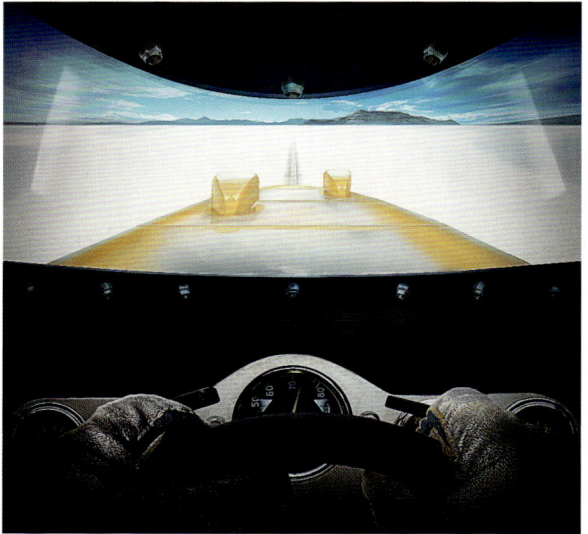

7. A Fine Mess 169

The Tear Down Blues 183
Bulkhead Replacement 205
Transfer Case Restoration 209
Header Repair 211
Some Assembly Required 213

TABLE OF CONTENTS

8. Goldenrod Reborn 215

Front Transmission Install 217
Rear Transmission and Drive Hub Install 221
Moving to Cook Motorsports 231
Overview 255
Firestone Tire Restoration 265
Museum Bound 269

9. The Legend Lives 273

10. Special Events 279

Goodwood Festival - United Kingdom 283
European Tour 285

Team Players 287

Mike Cook 287
Restoration Team 288
Goldenrod Volunteers & Crew 289

Tribute 291

400 Club Salutes Goldenrod 291

Photo Credits & Acknowledgements 294

INTRODUCTION

The Summers Brothers' Goldenrod is the best known and most significant LSR car to ever challenge the legendary Bonneville Salt Flats. On November 12, 1965, builder and driver, the late Bob Summers, established a new land speed record by streaking to a two-way record average of 409.277 mph in the flying mile and 409.695 in the kilometer; establishing an FIA record that stood for nearly 45 years. Bob Summers, or Butch as most people knew him, and his brother Bill brought the full potential of the American hot rodder's ingenuity to bear in their quest for the land speed record. Campbell had been the first to achieve a 400 mph record with a multi-million-dollar effort backed by British industry. And while the Brothers' car benefited from the donation of four 426-cubic-inch Chrysler Hemi engines, specially-designed Firestone high-speed tires, and the backing of the Hurst Corporation, it was nonetheless built by hot rodders in a small backyard shop and raced on a shoestring budget of about $100,000. The Goldenrod achieved a faster one-way pass at 425.99 mph the next day, but it did not make a return run for the average, hence the long-standing 409.277 mph record.

For almost four decades after that the car was stored and sometimes displayed at various shows and events, including the prestigious Goodwood Festival of Speed in Britain where it was displayed beside Campbell's Bluebird. Years of outdoor storage had not been kind to the Goldenrod and it had suffered alarming corrosion and deterioration issues. The original engines were removed and returned to Chrysler only to find new homes in drag cars and other projects. Shamefully, the car was re-fitted with four incomplete display engines with no internals.

As a former editor at *Hot Rod Magazine*, 200 MPH Club member and a land speed record enthusiast, I set out several years ago to compile an in-depth technical book about wheel-driven land speed record cars. Needing a credible hook to help convince the British museums to help me partially disassemble many of their treasured record cars for photography, I chose to begin my effort with the Goldenrod since it was nearby at the NHRA Museum. I figured that if I could demonstrate a factual and well-written technical chapter about the Goldenrod, the British museums might be more inclined to help me with the rest of the book. After speaking with my friend Bill Summers and Greg Sharp at the NHRA museum, I learned that the car had been purchased by The Henry Ford Museum and was still awaiting transportation to Dearborn, MI.

Accordingly, I contacted Bob Casey, Curator of Transportation at the museum and gave him my pitch. He agreed to let me take the Goldenrod back to my shop and remove the body panels to photograph the technical details. But once I began to disassemble the car I discovered that near-fatal salt corrosion had taken a severe toll. The aluminum bulkheads holding the

engines in place were delaminating, and several had already begun to collapse. It was immediately clear that the car required a complete restoration if it was ever going to survive for display in a museum environment. Casey and museum officials agreed, and plans were made to initiate the restoration. After a lengthy period of time and a superbly written grant proposal by Casey, the museum obtained a federal grant under the Save America's Treasures program, and the recovery program got underway. There were no plans to make the car run again. The intent was to restore it as closely as possible to the condition it was in when it made its record runs. By the end of May 2005, the dummy engines were removed from the car, and the nearly bare frame was prepared for sandblasting and repair. Many items were missing from the car, but enthusiasts and volunteers stepped forward with parts and assistance. SCTA president Mike Cook provided substantial assistance with locating missing components and volunteer workers assisted in carefully disassembling the car and cataloging the components for reassembly.

One of the more difficult tasks facing the restoration team was locating the missing parts. Through vague references from Bill Summers, I traced the original wind tunnel model, the record-setting air scoops, center fuel bladder and the only surviving tail cone to Stuart Thompson, an avid collector in Britain. Bob Casey negotiated their return, and he was able to purchase them back to help complete the car. Additionally, several early Prestolite ignition boxes were missing, as were all of the original coils, oil pans, and oil pumps. Each engine was originally equipped with a stack of three modified factory oil pumps to create a unique dry sump lubrication system. One intake manifold was missing, but Stu Hilborn still had the original pattern, and he offered to cast and outfit a replacement. The engines were also missing timing covers and the Hilborn front-drive fuel pumps and fuel filter systems.

Following the May 2005 *Hot Rod Magazine* article announcing the restoration plans, representatives of Firestone expressed interest in looking at the original tires and wheels, all of which were subsequently sent to them. Based on the tire numbers, they were able to pull the original mold drawings and completely restore the tires and wheels in their facility. Bill Summers and crew chief Jim Crosby consulted on the project and numerous people worked on various parts of the car such as the body panels and the engines. *Hot Rod Magazine* supplied original photos to work from and for use in this book.

Hot rodders and salt flats racers take great pride in the record-setting accomplishment engineered by the Summers Brothers. Based on their experience with previous cars like the 300+ mph Pollywog, the brothers approached the task with a hot rodder's zeal for innovation and workmanship. Unique answers to difficult problems are found everywhere on the car. When a simple approach was deemed appropriate, it was applied without hesitation. Nothing was complicated beyond necessity. The Summers Brothers' achievement was staggering at the time and remains so today. The Goldenrod will never set tire to salt again, nor should it. But it wears its glory proudly as the most extraordinary example ever of hot rodding ingenuity at its finest.

Meet the Record Setters

Bob "Butch" Summers

Robert Sherman Summers (1937 - 1992)

Bob Summers, better known as "Butch" was born in Omaha, Nebraska, on April 4, 1937. As a child he moved to California with his parents. He attended Chaffee High School in Ontario, California, where he graduated in 1955 as an Industrial Arts major. After high school, he attended Mt. San Antonio College and has since worked as a machinist and certified welder; skills that have served him well in the major construction of the Goldenrod land speed record contender.

In 1962, Bob joined the Naval Air Reserve and is currently assigned to one weekend a month as a sonar operator on an anti-sub warfare helicopter in the active reserve. Virtually all his spare time activities have been built around cars and hot rodding. From a Model A Ford roadster which he acquired as a youngster, Bob collaborated with his brother Bill on their first serious hot rod; a '36 Ford with a Chrysler engine which they ran at Bonneville in 1954.

Since then there has been a succession of cars and records set by Bob who is the driver in the brother team. Bonneville, El Mirage Dry Lake (Calif.) and local drag strips have seen the Summers Brothers' cars set records with Bob at the wheel. Bob is a member of the exclusive 200 MPH club for which he qualified by setting a two-way record average (221.06 mph) at Bonneville when he was 21.

In 1962 at the Bonneville National Speed Trials he drove their single-engine Chrysler-powered streamliner 322.79 mph. The following year he set National and International Class C records with the same car at Bonneville. Speeds were 1 kilometer - 283.71 mph; 1 mile - 279.74. Bob is single and lives with his brother in Ontario near their shop where the Goldenrod is under construction. The shop is located at 909 West Mission Boulevard, Ontario.

Bill Summers

William Ray Summers (1935 - 2011)

Bill Summers is a native of Omaha, Nebraska, born December 18, 1935. He came to California as a child with his parents, attended local schools and was graduated from Chaffee Union High School, Ontario, California, as an Industrial Arts major in 1953. Although deeply involved in racing, his interest has tended to the mechanical side and he leaves the driving to his brother Bob.

Before the Goldenrod became a full-time project, Bill was a truck driver for Chet Base Transportation, Pomona, California, driving large rigs all over the United States. Bill was in the Army from 1959 to 1961, then was recalled for the Berlin crisis in 1961, discharged in 1962. His military duties also involved truck driving. He dates his first serious try at hot rodding to the Chrysler-powered '36 Ford coupe that he and Bob built for Bonneville in 1954. Since that year, the brother team has participated in the Bonneville National Speed Trials each season with time in between at California's El Mirage dry lake speed strip and on local drag strips. Bill calls rebuilding and riding motorcycles his hobby although the Goldenrod project leaves him little time for it. Bill is single, shares an apartment in Ontario with Bob. They call their shop at 909 West Mission Boulevard in Ontario their headquarters, at least until the Goldenrod is completed.

These original bios are reproduced word for word from the Summers Brothers press releases written by their close friend and press agent Wayne Thoms.

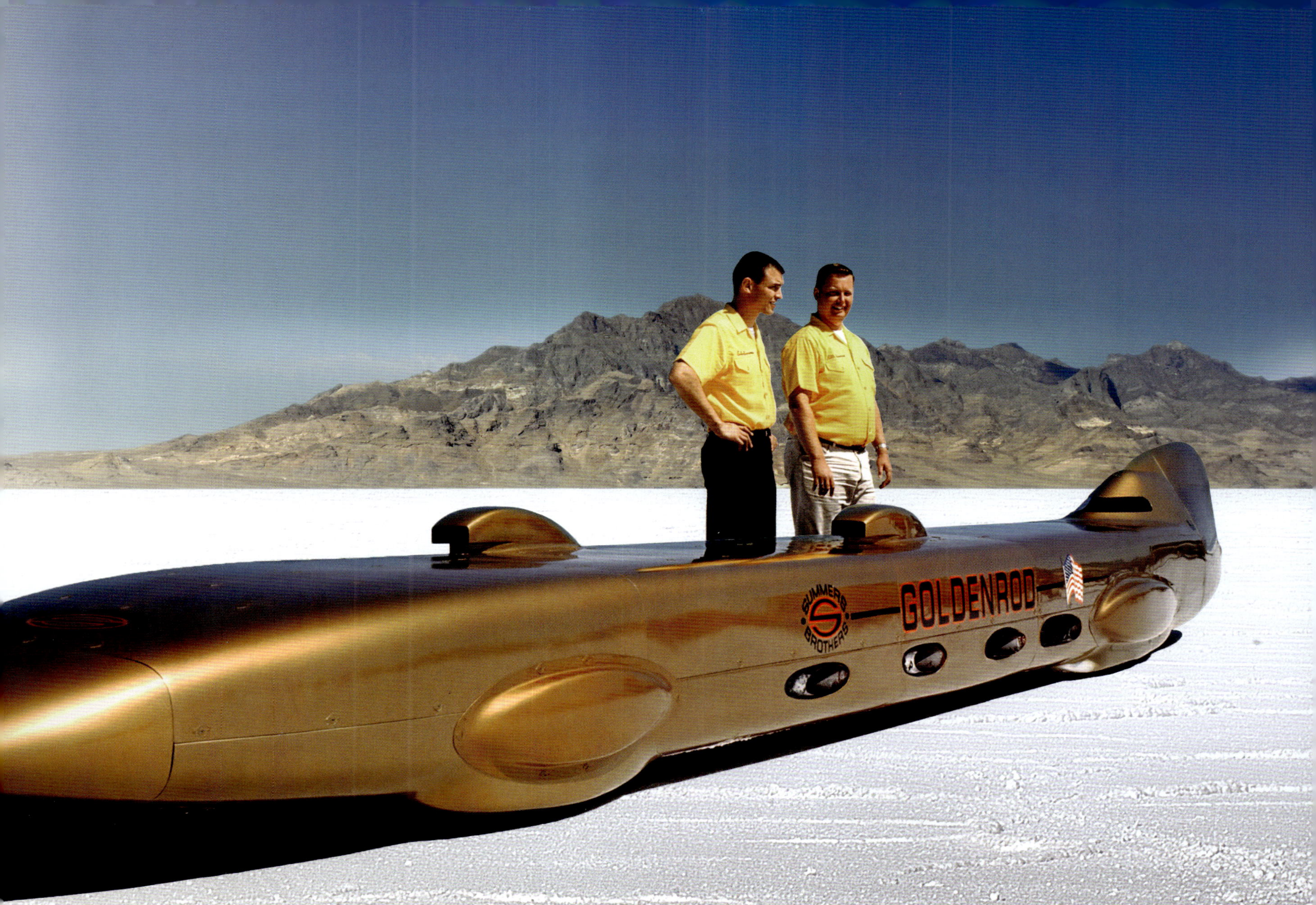

409.277 MPH

November 12, 1965 - Bonneville Salt Flats

- First 400 MPH Wheel-Driven Record Set at Bonneville
- First 400 MPH Record with Automotive Engine Power
- First 400 MPH Record with a Multi-Engine Car
- First 400 MPH Record with an Unsupercharged Car
- First 425 MPH Wheel-Driven Run at Bonneville
- Longest-Standing Record in Land Speed Racing History

An FIA World Land Speed Record is not a singular entity. However, there is only one Outright World Land Speed Record, and it is held by Thrust SSC; a twin-jet, thrust-powered vehicle that established the world record and broke the sound barrier on both runs for the average record speed of 763.035 mph in 1997. Until the advent of jets and rockets in the mid-sixties, the Outright World Land Speed Record was held by wheel-driven vehicles primarily powered by reciprocating airplane engines.

WORLD RECORD: Best performance accomplished in a determined class or group. There are World Records for Automobiles and Special Automobiles. Automobiles are Categories A and B; Special Automobiles are Category C.

ABSOLUTE WORLD RECORD: A record recognized by the FIA as the best performance achieved for a recognized distance or time by an Automobile irrespective of category, class or group.

OUTRIGHT WORLD RECORD: A record recognized by the FIA as the best flying start kilometer or mile result obtained with an automobile, irrespective of category, class or group. It is important to note that the Outright World Record can be in either the kilo or the mile.

Defining the World Land Speed Record

The FIA made no particular distinction prior to 1970 when they established specific categories consisting of:

- Category A (special construction)
- Category B (production vehicles)
- Category C (thrust)

Thrust-powered cars were accepted in 1964, but confusion flourished until the categories were clearly defined in 1970. All categories except Category C are wheel-driven. Category A and B vehicles are further divided into groups by engine type (internal combustion, electrical, turbine, steam, and hybrid) and fuel type (carbon fuel, hydrogen, electricity, and solar). All groups are divided into classes according to cylinder capacity or vehicle weight.

The Goldenrod falls under Category A in the normally-aspirated Group 2, Class 11. At one time that was also listed as with or without supercharger, but was later changed. While it's commonly thought that the Goldenrod broke Donald Campbell's 403.100 mph record, that is only partially correct. It surpassed Campbell's record speed but actually broke John Cobb's 394.196 mph record set in 1947 because both were powered by reciprocating engines, and Campbell's Bluebird was turbine-powered. Until the rules were modified to include thrust power in 1964, Campbell was officially the absolute land speed record holder.

Campbell set a new record by exceeding Cobb's speed and achieved the first ever record with a turbine car. John Cobb had actually exceeded 400 mph one-way in 1947, running 385.645 mph and 403.135 mph respectively, hence he remains the first man to actually travel over 400 mph on land. Data indicated that he reached 415 mph terminal speed which suggests he was still accelerating. The two runs were averaged to set the record.

When thrust-powered cars were first accepted in 1964, the Goldenrod no longer stood any chance of ever holding the Outright World Land Speed Record; hence, it and subsequent cars hold wheel-driven world land speed records within the FIA's category structure.

The FIA did not clarify all this until January 1, 1970, when it officially established its groups, categories, and classes; hence the common misconception that the Goldenrod broke Campbell's record based on a chronological progression of speeds. Nonetheless, Goldenrod was officially the record holder for its class until its record was exceeded by Charles Nearburg in 2010 with a 414.316 mph normally-aspirated average. Al Teague's single-engine streamliner advanced a supercharged world record of 409.978 mph in 1991, but it did not eclipse the Goldenrod's normally-aspirated record.

The late Don Vesco set the absolute Category A record in 2001 when his Turbinator streamliner averaged 458.481 mph and exceeded 470 mph terminal speed. This is the fastest wheel-driven land speed record. The Terminator record resides under Category A, Group 9, Class 3.

Being supercharged entries, Cobb, Teague and Tom Burkland all fall under the Category A, Group 1, Class 11 which further distinguishes their record performances. In similar fashion, George Poteet's Speed Demon currently holds the fastest unlimited supercharged record in Group 1, Class 10 at 439.024 mph.

The accompanying chart details relative speed records since 1947. These are all FIA certified World Land Speed Records. Note the last three are FIA records, but not absolute land speed records because they do not exceed Vesco's speed. Honorable mention also to Nolan White whose 413.156 mph SCTA/BNI record in 2002 was not FIA certified. Nolan's fastest speed exceeded 438 mph.

Other vehicles have exceeded 400 mph, but none of them have established SCTA national records or FIA World Land Speed Records, except for Danny Thompson's Challenger II, which ran 406.769 mph in the SCTA's AA/Unblown Fuel Streamliner class.

For the purpose of this book, the terms World Land Speed Record and/or land speed record are used with respect to Category A, Special Construction vehicles and with the full acknowledgment that the Outright World Land Speed Record is currently held by Thrust SSC. And of course, Don Vesco holds the absolute wheel-driven record, returning that glory back to the United States by eclipsing Campbell's 1964 record speed, although the FIA does not currently use that record terminology.

Driver	Car	Speed WLSR	Year	Power	Fastest Speed
John Cobb	Railton	394.196	1947	Piston	403
Donald Campbell	Bluebird CN7	403.100	1964	Turbine	429
Bob Summers	Goldenrod	409.277	1965	Piston	425
Al Teague	Spirit of '76	409.978	1991	Piston	432
Don Vesco	Turbinator	458.481	2001	Turbine	470
Tom Burkland	Burklands	415.896	2008	Piston	450
Charles Nearburg	Spirit of Rett	414.316	2010	Piston	422
George Poteet	Speed Demon	439.024	2012	Piston	462

GOLDENROD

Humble Beginnings

The Summers Brothers' Goldenrod is quite arguably one of the most revered record holders in land speed racing history. It held the world land speed record for longer than any car in land speed history and remains today an iconic symbol of innovation in man's unending pursuit of speed. If the land speed record is forever a moving target, the Goldenrod redefined the bullet and the bullseye. Conceived in the visionary mind of young Bob Summers and painstakingly created from scratch by Bob and Bill Summers, crew chief Jim Crosby and a small group of generous and talented contributors, it remains one of the most interesting and technically innovative racing vehicles to ever achieve an official FIA World Land Speed Record. Bob, or Butch as most people knew him, and his brother Bill brought the full unbridled potential of American hot rodding ingenuity to bear in their bold quest for the land speed record.

On November 12, 1965, builder and driver Bob Summers eclipsed the existing speed previously set by Donald Campbell's Bluebird by streaking to a two-way record average of 409.277 mph in the flying mile and 409.695 mph

This converted fruit stand at 909 W. Mission Blvd. in Ontario, CA, was the birthplace of the legendary land speed record holder, the Summers Brothers' Goldenrod.

8

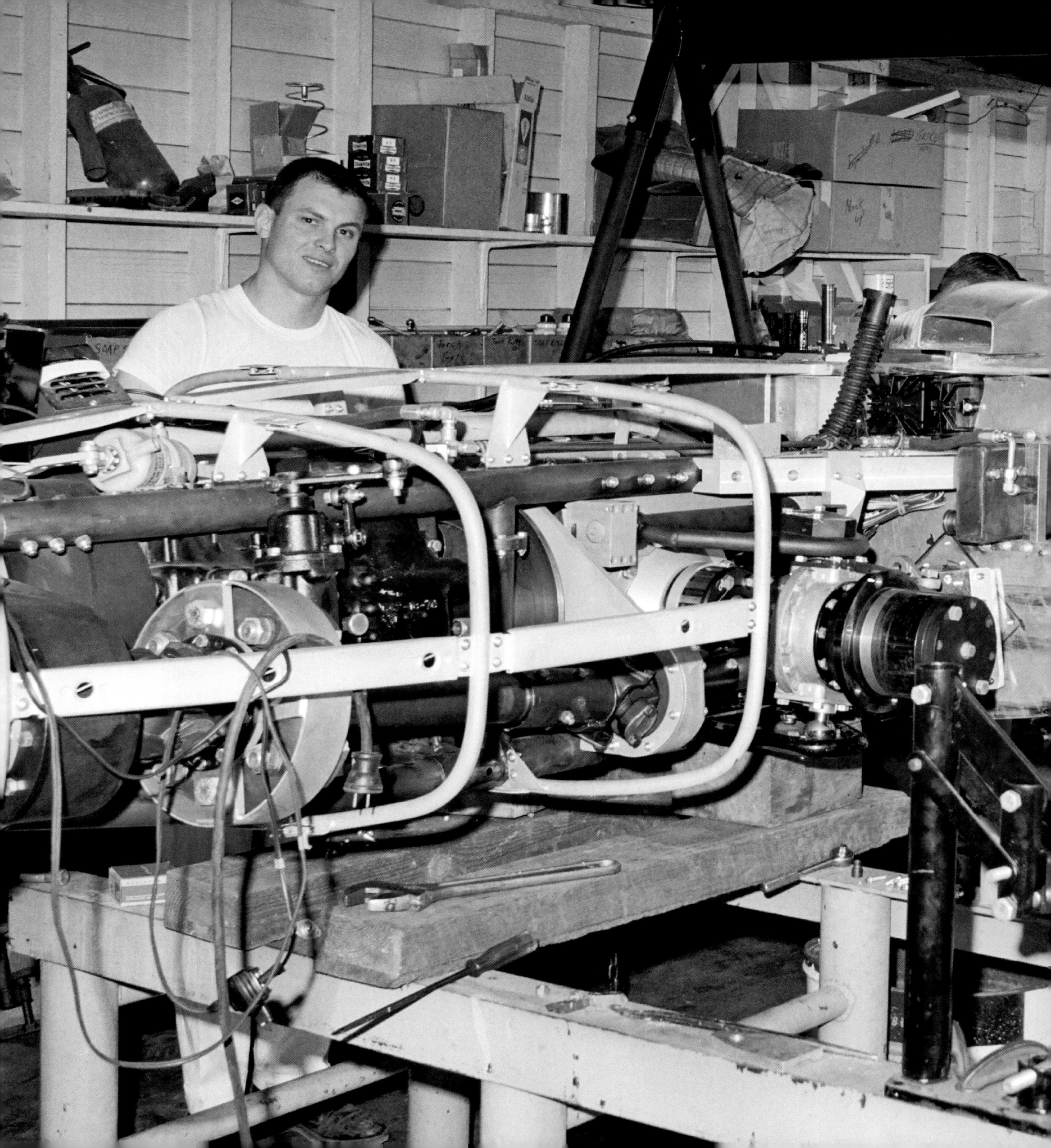

GOLDENROD

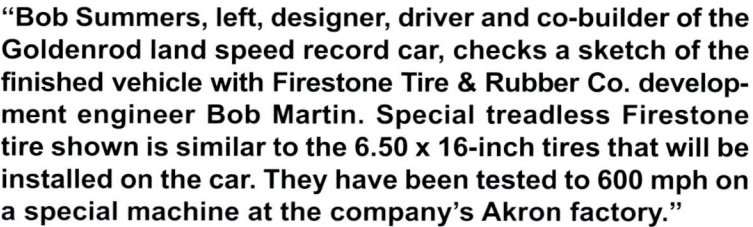

"Bob Summers, left, designer, driver and co-builder of the Goldenrod land speed record car, checks a sketch of the finished vehicle with Firestone Tire & Rubber Co. development engineer Bob Martin. Special treadless Firestone tire shown is similar to the 6.50 x 16-inch tires that will be installed on the car. They have been tested to 600 mph on a special machine at the company's Akron factory."
- Wayne Thoms, Summers' Press Agent

"Bob Summers, 28, examines one of the differential units for his land speed record streamliner Goldenrod during the car's early stages of construction. Bob engineered the car, is doing much of the major construction along with his brother Bill and will drive it during record attempts on the Bonneville Salt Flats." - Wayne Thoms

in the kilometer, thus establishing a new FIA international record that held for nearly 45 years. This extraordinary feat made Bob Summers the first American to hold the land speed record since Ray Keech established a 207.552 mph record at Daytona Beach, FL, in 1928.

Donald Campbell had been the first racer to achieve an official 400-plus mph land speed record in a wheel-driven vehicle. His fantastic multi-million-dollar machine was backed by a who's who consortium of British industrial supporters. While the Goldenrod clearly benefited from the donation of four modified 426-cubic-inch Chrysler A-864 Hemi engines, specially-designed Firestone high-speed tires, aerodynamic design and wind tunnel testing by a renowned Lockheed aeronautical engineer and the generous backing of the Hurst Corporation, it was nonetheless, hand-built by a small group of very talented and relentlessly determined hot rodders in a cramped backyard shop and raced at Bonneville on a shoestring budget of about $100,000.

The Summers Brothers were no strangers to record setting on the Bonneville Salt Flats, having previously campaigned a very successful rear-engined T-roadster that raised the E/Modified roadster record from 204.896 mph to a swift 221.062 mph, ushering Bob Summers into the prestigious 200 MPH Club. Despite a spin and

GOLDENROD

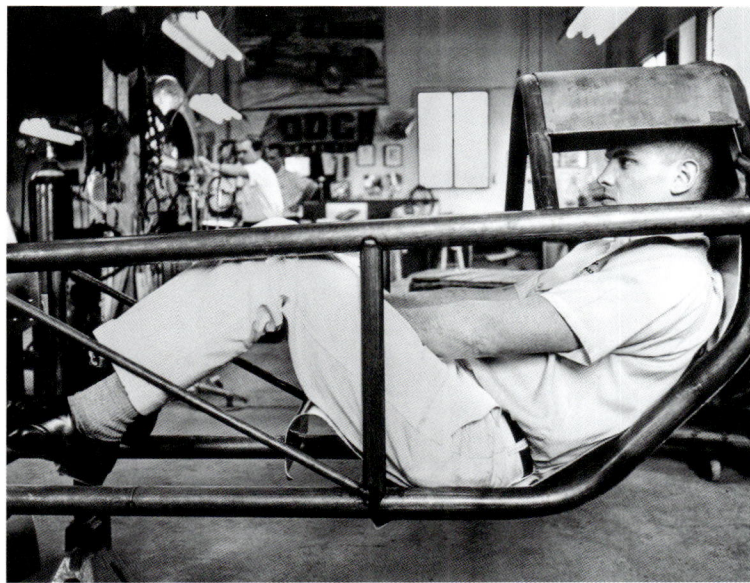

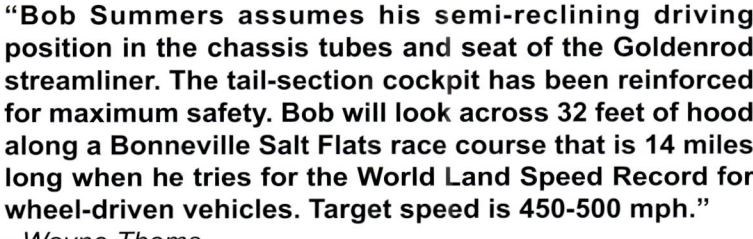

"Bob Summers assumes his semi-reclining driving position in the chassis tubes and seat of the Goldenrod streamliner. The tail-section cockpit has been reinforced for maximum safety. Bob will look across 32 feet of hood along a Bonneville Salt Flats race course that is 14 miles long when he tries for the World Land Speed Record for wheel-driven vehicles. Target speed is 450-500 mph."
- Wayne Thoms

"George Hurst, left, one of the Goldenrod land speed record car's primary sponsors, looks over a wind tunnel model of the 32-foot-long, four-engined streamliner with Bob Summers, designer, co-builder and driver of the car. Hurst, whose Hurst Performance Products, Inc. manufactures custom aluminum wheels and shifters, will furnish special wheels and a shifting linkage for the automobile. The car is designed for 500 mph, will attempt to break the World's Land Speed Record for wheel-driven cars (excluding jets) at the Bonneville, Utah, Salt Flats late this summer. Existing record is 403.1 mph." - Wayne Thoms

a flip the following year Bob Summers again raised the record to 225.078 mph. Shortly after, the inherently unstable rear-engined roadsters were summarily banned, and the brothers immediately decided to build a streamliner.

The Summers' remarkable creativity quickly surfaced. They set out to build a front-wheel-drive configuration cloaked in a strikingly beautiful, aerodynamic teardrop-shaped body that achieved its unique shape by placing the undriven rear wheels in tandem, one behind the other. The innovative new single-engine front-wheel-drive Pollywog ran over 302 mph on only its second pass, making it the fastest single-engine car ever at that time. The car ultimately ran 322 mph in 1962, and no doubt spurred the subsequent notion to challenge the land speed record with an all-new car specifically designed to exceed 400 mph. The Pollywog's ultimate success patently reinforced the need for aerodynamic efficiency, and the brothers determined that the new car would have to be the slipperiest car ever built for speed record attempts.

In 1963, after many years of attacking class records, a plan to challenge the unlimited land speed record was finalized, and they set out seeking sponsorship. They found it very time consuming and exceedingly difficult. It took the

PROJECT GOLDENROD

409.277 MPH — NOVEMBER 12, 1965
WHEEL DRIVEN WORLD LAND SPEED RECORD

**USAC TIMED
FIA SANCTIONED**

GOLDENROD... THE FIRST AMERICAN AUTOMOBILE TO HOLD THE WHEELDRIVEN WORLD LAND SPEED RECORD SINCE 1928 WHEN RAY KEECH DROVE HIS "WHITE TRIPLEX" TO A RECORD OF 203.55 MPH. *It is interesting to note that after only six runs of the GOLDENROD, the land speed record fell.*

OBJECTIVE TO:

I. RESEARCH & DEVELOP A NEW CONCEPT OF A WORLD LAND SPEED RECORD CAR.

II. DESIGN & CONSTRUCT THE CAR USING COMPONENTS OF UNITED STATES MANUFACTURE.

III. DRIVE THIS CAR AT BONNEVILLE OVER AN OFFICIALLY TIMED (FIA) COURSE AT SPEEDS SUBSTANTIALLY ABOVE THOSE OF: a. CAMPBELL 403 mph (FIA RECORD), b. THOMPSON - 406 mph (ONE WAY, UNOFFICIAL), & c. BREEDLOVE - 407 mph (FIM RECORD), 3 WHEELED JET.

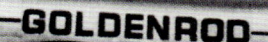

ON AUGUST 17, 1964 WORK WAS ACTUALLY STARTED ON "GOLDENROD" A RIGOROUS SCHEDULE WAS MAINTAINED. ONE YEAR & ONE WEEK LATER, ON AUGUST 24, 1965, THE CAR WAS COMPLETED & PREPARED FOR RECORD ATTEMPTS.

COSTS TO COMPLETE

CHASSIS & BODY
WIND TUNNEL TESTS	750.
MOD. & REPAIR-BODY	4,000.
UPHOLSTERING	75.
PAINT & SIGNS	150.
DECELERATION SYSTEM	300.
TIRES	600.
WHEELS	225.
MISC. MATERIAL	850.
OUTSIDE LABOR	1,835.
TOTAL	**8,785.**

ENGINE DEVP. CLASS B (3)
DYNOMOMETER	1,500.
LOW END & HEAD WORK	1,500.
MAGNAFLUX-X-RAY	700.
SHOT PEENING	125.
PISTONS	600.
BLOWERS	525.
CAMS & KITS	600.
MAGNETOS	165.

[FUEL INJECTORS etc.]
FUEL INJECTORS	275.
WRIST PINS	105.
MISC. PARTS	300.
TOTAL	**6,395.**

ENGINE DEVP. CLASS C (2)
DYNAMOMETER	500.
MAGNAFLUX-X-RAY	300.
SHOT PEENING	75.
SPARE ENGINE PARTS	450.
TOTAL	**1,325.**

SUPPORT EQUIP.
FIRE EXTINGUISHERS	250.
DRIVER FIRE SUIT	195.
TENT	50.
TRAILER IMPROVMTS	200.
TOTAL	**695.**

U.S.A.C. RECORD RUNS
TRANSPORTATION-INS.	650.
CREW WAGES	1,350.
U.S.A.C. TIMING	5,000.
INSURANCE/PATROL	260.
AMBALANCE	400.
FUEL & OIL	580.
RENT-MOTEL & SHOP	370.
RENTAL 1½ TON TRUCK	500.
GAS & OIL	350.
BOND-BONN. ASSOC.	500.
TOTAL	**9,960.**

OVERHEAD
WAGES	12,000.
UTILITIES	1,100.
SHOP RENT	250.
TOTAL	**13,350**

GRAND TOTAL $40,610.00

PLUS - 4 NEW 413 OR 426 ENGINES - LESS EXTERNAL ACCESSORIES

The Summers Brothers prepared a presentation book to show perspective sponsors some of their history and accomplishments and reinforce why they deserved sponsorship. Tiffany Summers kindly provided these samples that show early entries and later entries from after the record was set. The estimated costs are an eye-opener even for 1965. It is interesting to note that they cite Breedlove's early thrust record as one of their goals and they exceeded it even though the jets soon went much faster.

GOLDENROD

"Bob Summers, designer, driver, and co-builder of the sleek Goldenrod streamliner checks the scale model against the actual 32-foot-long car as it is under construction. The four-engined vehicle is expected to hit 450 mph, with 500 mph a reasonable goal." - *Wayne Thoms*

better part of the next year to generate interest in the attempt. Friends chipped in to help as best they could and Bob's friend Ray Brock, editor of *Hot Rod Magazine*, bought him a suit to wear when approaching major corporations for sponsorship. They took a cue from Craig Breedlove and commissioned a batch of professional presentation kits with artist's renderings and flip charts detailing the car's construction and high-performance potential. Bob criss-crossed the country in pursuit of additional financing, but none was forthcoming.

The major sponsors he approached all indicated that they would join in if everyone else did, but no one was willing to go first. Finally, George Hurst of the Hurst Corporation stepped forward and offered to back them. Hurst had shrewdly recognized the enormous public relations potential for his high-performance shifter company should they succeed. His endorsement prompted the welcome addition of Mobil Oil, Firestone Tire & Rubber, Champion Spark Plugs and the Chrysler Corporation, all critical resources that brought access to purpose-built high-speed tires, powerful new Hemi engines and a crucial association with Lockheed aerodynamicist Walter Korff. The brothers also received $100,000 from Chrysler for the project. While this sounds substantial for 1965, it was a mere pittance compared to the millions poured into Donald Campbell's turbine-powered Bluebird.

Bob and Crew Chief Jim Crosby labored around the clock building the car while Bill managed the equally challenging tasks of locating and acquiring all the necessary parts and materials. Their combined efforts delivered a stunning engineering masterpiece in only nine months. The car was constructed within the weathered walls of an old run-down garage behind a fruit stand on Mission Blvd. in Ontario, CA; hardly an auspicious beginning for a world record holder. From the outside, you would never suspect that a sophisticated land speed record car was secretly being constructed behind the decaying clapboard walls. Bill Summers enjoyed relating the story of the car's maiden voyage down Mission Blvd., escorted by a surprisingly supportive local sheriff. The engines were fired up, and the car was driven slowly for the first time. From there it was on to Riverside Raceway for faster shake-down runs on the long back straightaway. *Hot Rod Magazine's* Eric Rickman was on hand to record some amazing pictures of the initial testing activities. The testing revealed some minor flaws that were quickly remedied. A front driveshaft coupler exploded, carving a nice dent in the frame rail, but the integrity and teaming of the fuel-injected engines and complicated driveline system were verified.

ENGINE OVERVIEW

Summers' budgeting chart (page 14) shows that he initially considered 413/426 RB MaxWedge engines as an alternative to the Hemis. For the gasoline-fueled package, and even in normally-aspirated methanol-fueled trim, the wedge engines could have delivered comparable power with less weight and better packaging in the engine bay, especially the left side driveline clearances. Chrysler participation likely hinged on the use of the newly introduced Race Hemi engines.

The Goldenrod's engines were hand-built racing versions of the new 1964 426-cubic-inch Chrysler Hemi V8. Chrysler was just releasing Race Hemi versions for NASCAR and drag racing applications and the Chrysler engine lab, under the direction of Pete Dawson, modified four of them to suit the unique power requirements of high-speed racing at Bonneville. Two backup engines were also prepared for a total of six. The record-setting fuel-injected engines burned alcohol fuel via custom-fabricated Hilborn cross-ram fuel injection manifolds. Camshafts were provided by Ed Iskenderian. Chrysler engineers selected Isky 550 Super Le Gerra flat tappet cams to optimize power and provide strong mid-range performance to accelerate the car. The engines were mounted inline and back-to-back in pairs, minimizing the car's frontal area and allowing the paired engines to provide torque cancellation because one engine in each pair counteracted its mate.

Each engine's valvetrain was upgraded with a combination of factory and Isky high-performance components. Factory rocker arms, lifters, pushrods and retainers were coupled with Isky valve springs for the record application. The engines and the chassis were coupled together in a very rigid structure with eight

Chrysler backed the Summers Brothers with a total of six new 426-cubic-inch Race Hemi engines suitably modified for salt flats duty with Isky cams, Hilborn fuel injection, dry sump oiling and Prestolite ignition systems.

GOLDENROD

George Hurst (center) became the prime mover of the Goldenrod project when he stepped up with the initial financing to get things rolling. Hurst's confidence was enough to engage the valuable participation of Mobil Oil, Firestone Tire & Rubber Co., Champion Spark Plugs and the Chrysler Corporation.

aluminum bulkheads; a critical requirement due to the car's considerable weight and 32-foot length. Engine development and testing was done in the Chrysler engine lab by the race group engineers and technicians. Three stock oil pumps were modified and stacked on each engine to form the scavenge and pressure sides of a dedicated dry sump lubrication system fabricated in the lab by Pat Brady and Joe Trybus. They built low-profile oil pans that enabled the four engines to be mounted lower in the chassis to reduce the car's height to achieve a sleeker aerodynamic profile.

Each Hemi engine was equipped with its own front-mounted alcohol fuel pump, a Hilborn #150 mechanical unit driven off the camshaft via custom-machined aluminum timing covers. Eight mechanical injectors and low-ram inlet tubes were housed in sealed air boxes fed by a central inlet plenum directly under each external air scoop. Each air scoop fed air to a pair of engines. Directional vanes in each centralized plenum routed incoming air to the ram-tubes inside a sealed air box above each engine. Offset scoops kept them aerodynamically clean and provided a clear line of sight. The center engines are fed from a common saddle-bag-style fuel tank sandwiched between them while the front and rear engines each had their own individual tanks mounted inside the frame rails. All fuel tanks were sealed with

Firestone-designed rubber fuel bladders. Each engine also had its own 18-quart dry sump oil tank tightly packaged within the frame rails. Engine coolant stored in the nose coolant tank was circulated via surplus electrically driven aircraft pumps obtained at G&J Aircraft Salvage in Ontario, CA. Coolant was routed down the inside of the right frame rail and directed to each engine via appropriately located bungs and hoses. It was then returned to the tank through the left frame rail. Two of the battery-driven pumps were used to obtain the desired flow rates. Each pump served as a backup to the other; hence coolant would always continue to flow unless both pumps were to fail simultaneously.

Gary Hooker of Hooker Headers personally fabricated the beautiful low-slung side exhaust headers to match the Hemi's anticipated engine speeds and exhaust scavenging requirements according to Chrysler calculations. Hooker had to build the headers in Willie Sutton's North Hollywood shop as he was required to build them at the same time that Sutton was fabricating the body.

The Chrysler dual-point distributors, boosted by Prestolite ignition amplifiers, provided the car's ignition source and Champion spark plugs

Chrysler-built Race Hemi engines arrived in drag racing trim and were subsequently modified for the unique LSR application. Chrysler-designed and Hilborn-manufactured fuel injection systems were substituted, and the engines were retested at Keith Black Racing Engines. The best four out of six engines were selected for the land speed record attempts.

GOLDENROD

delivered the spark to the cylinders. Paired engines were coupled via crankshaft-driven spuds that engaged a notch on the hub of the transfer case mounted between them. Stock flywheels on each crankshaft held the engine drive spuds. Schiefer eleven-inch racing clutches provided solid engagement. When coupled, the transfer cases directed torque to the driveshaft system which ran the entire length of the car on the left.

Pete Dawson recalled the engines averaging about 575-585 horsepower on gasoline, and that figure is confirmed by engineer Steve Baker who supervised the dyno testing. That output would almost certainly have been diminished by the local atmospheric conditions (4,200 feet base altitude plus ambient air density from weather conditions) and parasitic losses in the complicated driveline. Additionally, the engines were dyno tested on gasoline and the record runs were made with methanol. Calibration issues caused some concern initially, but they were worked out. Official records for November 12, 1965, indicate cloudy overcast conditions with temperature ranging from 43 to 51 degrees over the course of the runs. At standard conditions (60 degrees with dry air) Bonneville's 4,200-foot altitude would absorb roughly four percent power; in this case perhaps only three percent with reduced temperature and moderate humidity.

Steve Baker recommends using 575 horsepower as a baseline since that is consistent with the original testing. Factoring in the three percent loss for altitude and weather yields a 23 horsepower loss which might be roughly mitigated by the alcohol fuel. If we accept that and go with 575 horsepower, we derive a total of 2,300 horsepower. The rotating mass and frictional complication of the drive system may have accounted for an estimated 200- to 300-horsepower loss. So Goldenrod most likely achieved the record with roughly 2,000 or less horsepower instead of the often-quoted 2,400 horsepower based on the 600 horsepower assumption, which Baker confirms they never achieved on the dyno.

It has been speculated that since the engines were originally tested with extra-deep wet sump dyno oil pans, they may have gained an additional 10- to 12-horsepower each once fitted with dry sump lubrication systems. According to Baker, the difference was almost imperceptible. The dry sump systems provided much needed clearance, and they were only a few horsepower shy of the extra-deep wet sump dyno pans. The primary attraction of the dry sump system was the ability to lower the engines in the chassis to achieve a reduced aerodynamic signature.

Local tuning factors, mixture calibration issues, and possible misfires may also have affected the car's final performance. Engine expert and former 200 MPH Club President Art Chrisman told me that one of the engines failed to fire because of an undiscovered loose coil connection. That would have contributed significant drag on the system as that engine would have had to have been motored by the other three engines.

The record was set with large tall-mouth scoops fabricated on site as Chrysler engineers felt the engines were starving for air at lower speed. The larger openings on these scoops were thought necessary to pass enough air to the engines at lower speeds. The calibration issues on gasoline proved formidable, so they switched to methanol which is easier to tune and also offers an unspecified power increase. The record was accomplished with Mobil-supplied methanol. After optimum calibrations were determined, they reinstalled the high-speed aerodynamic scoops designed and built by Bob Summers and racer friend Bob Herda. These scoops were on the car the next day when it achieved a significantly higher speed of 425.99 mph. According to Crew Chief Crosby,

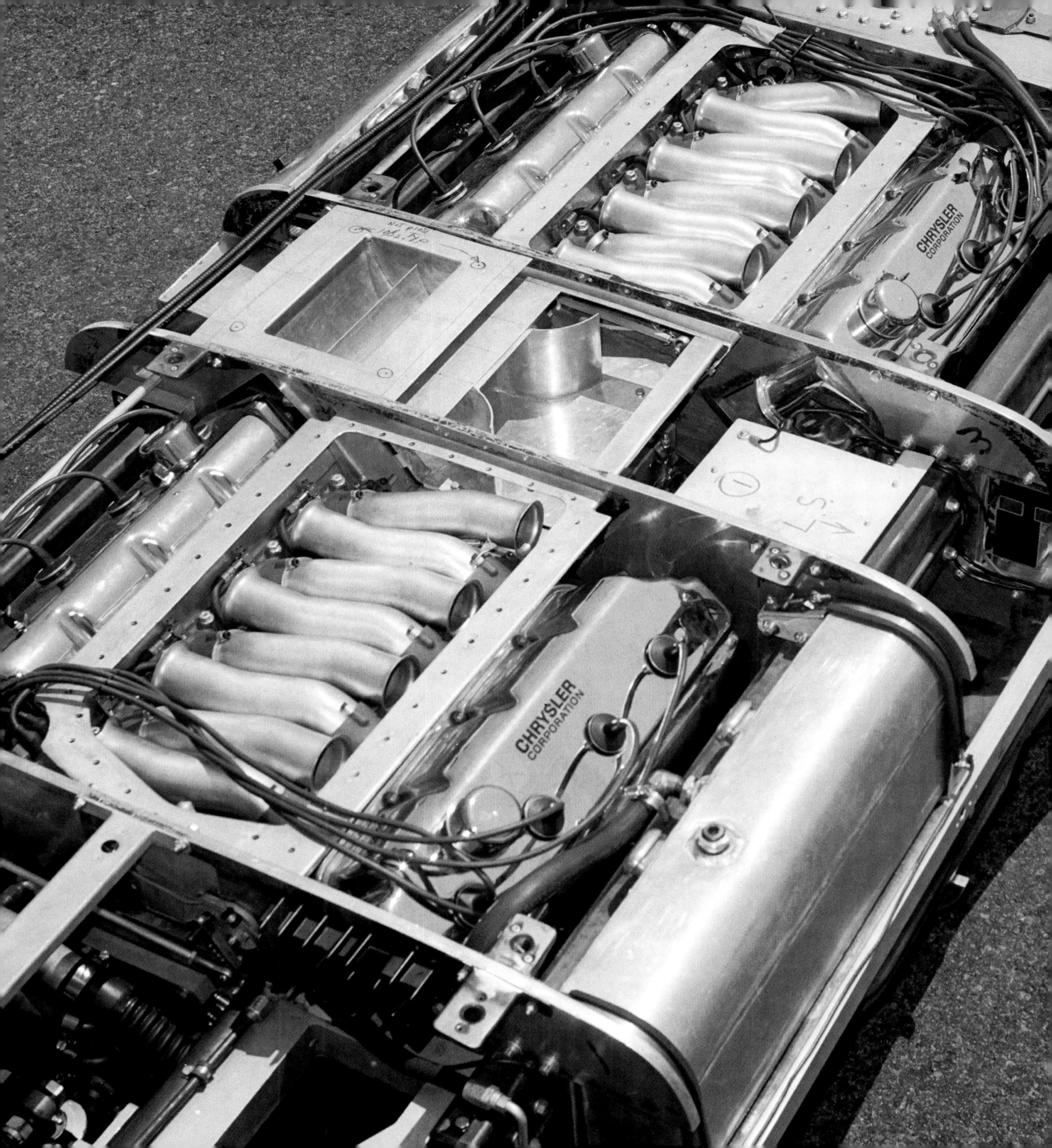

GOLDENROD

the high speed scoops delivered a positive air box pressure of 4-5 psi. Chrysler driveline engineer George Wallace's calculations indicated that the car should have achieved higher speeds and that is reinforced by the 425-mph one-way pass recorded with the high-speed air scoops the day after the record runs. It also illuminates the fickle nature of land speed record racing and how so many independent factors combine to affect performance on any given day; one of many reasons why breaking the unlimited land speed record is one of the most difficult challenges in all of motorsports.

Goldenrod ran in poor weather on damp salt with a short track. At 8,435 pounds plus an additional 800+ pounds of aerodynamic loading, the Goldenrod left marks in the soft damp track. It was designed for 500 mph, and some knowledgeable authorities still believe it was capable of that performance if afforded available track length and development time. Given more time and adequate funding, Bob Summers would most certainly have been able to acquire greater familiarity with the car's characteristics, enabling him to push it closer to their ultimate goal. Nonetheless, a new land speed record was ultimately achieved and it withstood a lengthy test of time from multiple challengers.

Forty-five years later the Goldenrod's official FIA record for an unblown wheel-driven car was eclipsed by Charles Nearburg's Spirit of Rett, which ran 414.316 mph with a single normally-aspirated big block Chevy engine built by Reher-Morrison Racing Engines of Arlington, TX. But nearly half a century earlier, a small group of persistent young hot rodders and the always formidable Chrysler Hemi brought the world's land speed record back to American shores making the Goldenrod a timeless icon of land speed racing history.

DRIVELINE OVERVIEW

All four of Goldenrod's wheels were driven via a unique combination of 1:1 ratio power transfer cases and a multi-coupled driveshaft arrangement that ran down the left side of the car (see illustration below). The transfer cases fitted between each pair of engines transferred power out to the driveshaft assembly. At the front and rear of the car, another pair of transfer cases routed power back to the centerline where it was coupled to the front and rear transmissions. The front and rear driveshafts were coupled together to ensure that front- and rear-wheel speeds were equal. Both the trans-

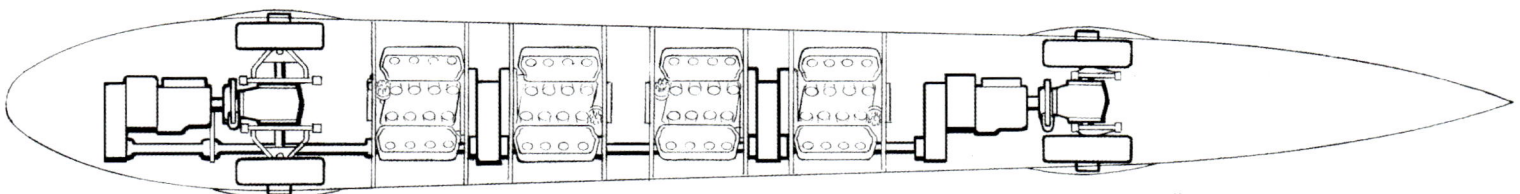

The front and rear gearboxes are driven by a common driveline along the left side of the engine bays. Engines are paired via crankshaft drive spuds and four-geared transfer cases that send power outboard to the driveshafts. Additional three-gear transfer cases at the front and extreme rear send power back to the centerline for each transmission to drive the gearboxes, thus ensuring equal wheel speed at all four wheels. Note that engines 1 and 3 face forward. Engines 2 and 4 face rearward. All engines ran in standard rotation with the two rear-facing engines providing torque cancellation because they were, in effect, turning the opposite direction. The transfer cases between each pair of engines incorporated an extra idler gear to provide the correct rotation to the driveline.

missions were heavy-duty Dana Spicer truck 5-speeds laid over on their sides to help reduce the car's height and thus its aerodynamic cross-section. Low gear was not utilized. The transmissions were coupled to Hays clutch assemblies transferring power directly to the center sections. Great care was taken to ensure that both transmissions shifted in unison. The aluminum center sections were specially cast Summers-designed housings with 1:1 ratio locked ring and pinion gears that spun free-floating axles connected to beefy Dana truck hub assemblies. The magnesium alloy wheels were Hurst-designed 16 x 6-inch units cast by Harvey Aluminum and precision machined by Jerry Swenson. Firestone designed the 24-inch tires for the car's anticipated speeds. The Summers Brothers' new record verified the integrity of the tires which endured rotational speeds approaching 6,000 rpm.

BODY OVERVIEW

Goldenrod's sleek wind-cheating body was designed by noted Lockheed aerodynamicist Walter Korff in close concert with Bob Summers. Korff's aviation background found him uniquely qualified to address the aerodynamic challenges of land speed racing. He applied his considerable expertise to achieving the lowest possible drag coefficient, negative lift, and the best possible high-speed stability without resorting to the use of external wings, fins, spoilers and/or ballast to mar the perfect shape of the body. Adding downforce with the body alone was a priority. Wind tunnel testing was conducted using a six-foot model in the Graduate Aeronautical Laboratory California Institute of Technology wind tunnel, or GALCIT, as it was technically referred to.

One of the transfer cases between the paired engines with the driveshaft passing through the aluminum bulkhead inboard of the headers.

Goldenrod's 8.53-square-foot frontal area and final drag coefficient of 0.1165 has yet to be surpassed. Once Korff put his stamp of approval on the shape, the all-aluminum body was hand-formed by noted metal worker Willie Sutton in his North Hollywood shop. A split upper and lower design with panels separating at the beltline made this possible. Upper panels could be quickly removed to gain access to the car's systems for tuning and service. Access doors were also provided for service components. California Metal Shaping's Don Borth also performed some metal finishing work for final body alterations.

Goldenrod Wind Tunnel Model

Wind tunnel model with tentative paint concept.

GOLDENROD

**Summers Brothers Press Release
Illustration by C.O. LaTourette - 1965**

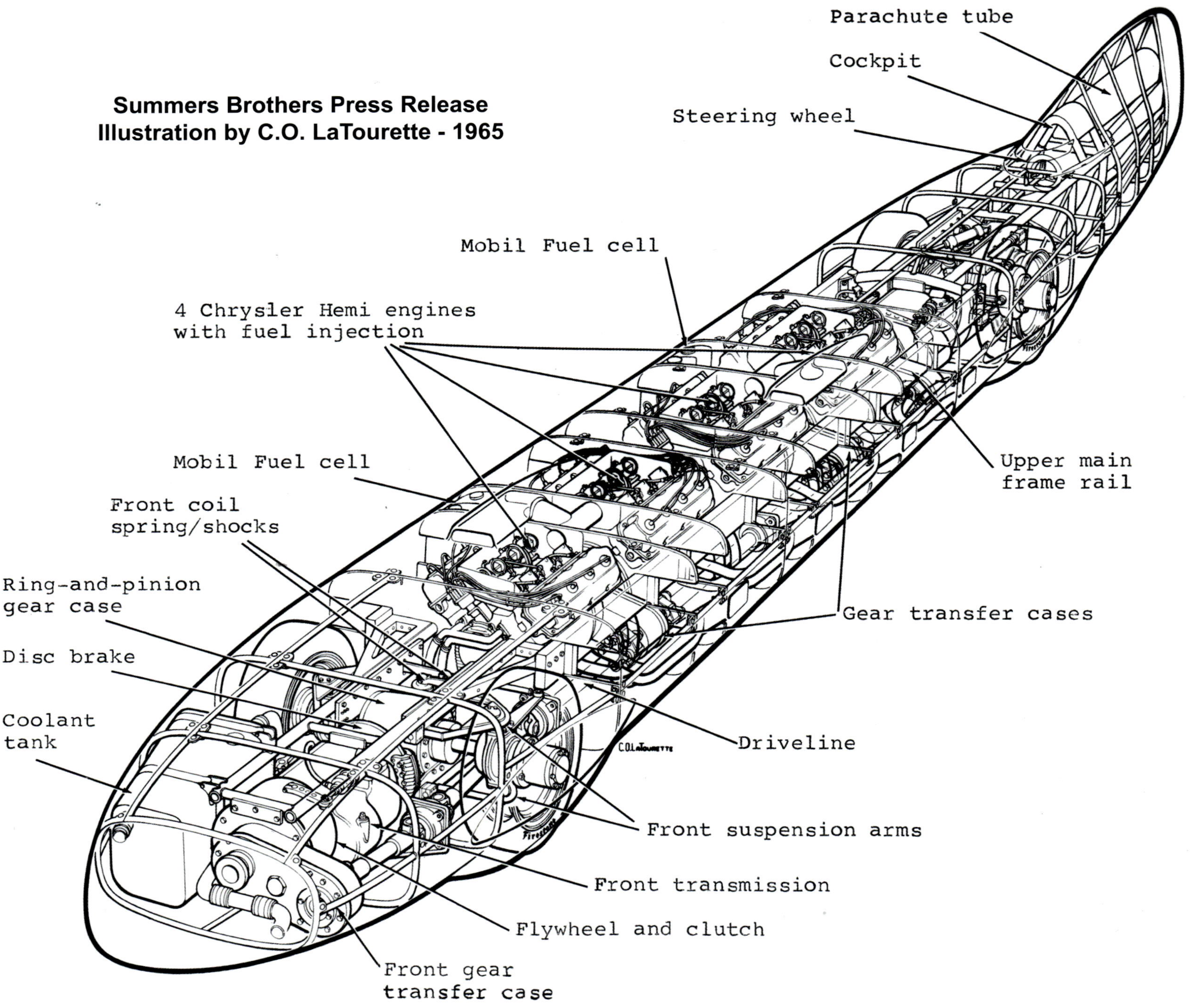

- Parachute tube
- Cockpit
- Steering wheel
- Mobil Fuel cell
- 4 Chrysler Hemi engines with fuel injection
- Upper main frame rail
- Mobil Fuel cell
- Front coil spring/shocks
- Ring-and-pinion gear case
- Gear transfer cases
- Disc brake
- Coolant tank
- Driveline
- Front suspension arms
- Front transmission
- Flywheel and clutch
- Front gear transfer case

GOLDENROD SPECIFICATIONS

ENGINES:
Four Chrysler Race Hemi V8s mounted inline and coupled in pairs back-to-back with the front pair driving the front wheels and the rear pair driving the back wheels via a common driveshaft arrangement to maintain equal wheel speed. All engines were standard rotation with torque cancellation provided by the unique back-to-back configuration.

BORE AND STROKE:
4.25 x 3.75

DISPLACEMENT:
426 cubic inches each

HORSEPOWER:
585-600 HP on methanol

TRANSMISSIONS:
Two heavy-duty 5-speed Dana Spicer truck transmissions utilizing only the top four gears

RATIOS:
2nd — 2.6:1   4th — 1.19:1
3rd — 1.5:1   5th — 1:1

SHIFTER:
Synchronized shifting via special Hurst-designed custom shifter

CLUTCHES:
Two Schiefer dual-disc, hydraulically activated

RING AND PINION RATIOS:
1:1, locked rear ends
Final Drive Ratio: Can vary from 0.95 to 1.05

STEERING:
Chrysler hydraulically activated, 10 degree limit

SUSPENSION:
4-wheel independent with upper & lower control arms, Monroe coilover shocks

LENGTH AND WIDTH:
32' 9½" w/tail cone x 48" wide
28" tall at hoodline

HEIGHT:
42" to top of tail fin
28" to hood surface

GROUND CLEARANCE: 5"

AERO SPECS:
Frontal Area: 8.53 sq. ft.
Coefficient of Drag: 0.1165

FRAME:
Lower Rails: 2" x .125" wall, mild steel
Upper Rails: 2" x 6" x .183" rectangular, mild steel
Bulkheads: Eight .500" 7075-T6 aluminum plates

BODY:
Harvey 303 aluminum alloy, .064" thick

WHEELS:
Aluminum, Hurst-designed
Forged by Harvey Aluminum
16" x 6.5" width with demountable rim

TIRES:
6.50" x 16" Firestone tubeless nylon
Special low-profile treadless design
Contact Area: 4"
Static Diameter: 23"
Inflation: 150 psi
Design Speed: 600 mph

BRAKING SYSTEM:
Airheart single-piston calipers, front & rear pinions
Gear coupler flanges for use below 100 mph
Deist parachutes for high speeds
First Stage: 8' pilot chute for high speeds
Second Stage: 20' chute for below 250 mph
Third Stage: 8' emergency chute
Automatic systems with manual override

SAFETY EQUIPMENT:
Deist 5-point safety harness
Summers head restraints
Cockpit side & top armor plating

TOTAL WEIGHT:
8,435 lbs. with driver

GOLDENROD

Sherman Summers with his two sons, Robert and William. Summers was a hard-working man who instilled good values in his boys. Their later achievements are fitting testament to a good upbringing.

The Summers Brothers

The Summers Brothers sprang from a quite humble wartime childhood, not unlike most youngsters growing up in the 1940s. In the late 1930s, an enterprising Nebraska salesman named Sherman Summers pulled up stakes and moved to Washington with his wife Mary in search of greener pastures. When that didn't exactly work out, he moved on to Ontario, CA, where he achieved a newfound measure of stability and success when he opened a Union Oil service station.

Sherman and Mary raised three children: Susan, William, and Robert. No one back then could have predicted that the two brothers, Bill and Bob, would go on to achieve worldwide acclaim and legendary hot rodding status as the American Speed Kings. Perhaps their father's service station provided the early inspiration that eventually catapulted them to center stage in the land speed racing arena.

The boys began souping up old cars in high school and racing them regularly on the local dry lakes. After high school, Bill Summers briefly worked at a Ford dealership before taking a job as a short-haul truck driver, and Bob worked as a welder. In 1953, they acquired a budding attraction to the Bonneville Salt Flats through a close hot rodding buddy, Dawson Hadley. You might say the hook set deep and they quickly determined to make the salt flats their primary racing venue.

Bill bought an old 1936 Ford coupe and picked up an early Chrysler Hemi to power the new project. A painfully slow progression of used parts were used to build it up to race at Bonneville in 1954. That first trip was an eye-opening experience. They had no money, slept in the dirt and nearly starved, but somehow an unforgettable adventure unfolded. The cobbled-together coupe ran a disappointing 136 mph and

GOLDENROD

Bob "Butch" Summers

Bill Summers

Sherman Summers' Union Oil service station in Ontario, CA, provided a stable family life for the boys and their sister and served as incubator for their automotive endeavors that surfaced early in high school.

was not at all competitive, but it served to cement their attraction to the salt and the desire to break records.

Bob Summers died of a heart attack in 1992, still holding the Goldenrod's world record. Bill passed away in 2011 at the age of 75, with the record still intact. The Summers Brothers' legacy of technical innovation was repeatedly challenged, yet despite numerous near misses, it remained unbroken for nearly 45 years. Like Malcolm and Donald Campbell's Bluebirds, Henry Segrave's Golden Arrow, Eyston's Thunderbolt and John Cobb's Railton Special, the Goldenrod established a new level of sophistication for its time. Unlike others, the Goldenrod was minimally sponsored and constructed by amateur hot rodders in a run-down shack. Despite their amateur status, the Summers Brothers assumed their rightful place alongside those legendary pioneers of speed, firmly upholding their credibility with what has since become the longest standing, and for many, the most admired land speed record in history.

While Bob Summers receives most of the attention for being the designer, fabricator, and driver of the cars, no one can discount Bill's vital contributions to their efforts. They started with Bill's coupe after all, with Bill doing the driving. From the very beginning,

Bill's 1936 Ford time machine (left). It was rough, but relatively fast with hopped up early Hemi power. It was their first salt flats car and most certainly did not foretell the remarkable story to follow a decade later. At the 1954 Nationals, the Summers Brothers campaigned a 331ci Hemi-powered '32 Ford Coupe that ran 120 mph. These poor quality original photos are the only existing shots of the Summers' first racing machines.

Bill exhibited a keener knack for making contacts and getting things done in terms of securing parts and supplies and making sure nothing slowed them down. Bob gravitated toward the welding and fabrication side, and with good drafting skills, he also became the default designer.

Each brother settled into his most comfortable niche, and together they built a formidable racing team and a fledgling performance business at the same time. Their amazing evolution has all the earmarks of the great American success story; humble beginnings, toil and struggle, near poverty and ultimate triumph and heroics as world record holders. It would be decades later before people actually realized the true enormity of their stunning achievement. Despite the essential backing of solid American companies, the Goldenrod still was built in an old shed and campaigned on a relatively shoestring budget. You can't put a definitive value on all the long hours and enormous mental and physical effort expended by both of the Summers Brothers, James Crosby, numerous friends and all of the associated hot rodders, sponsors, and engineers who contributed to the effort.

Bob Summers served weekends in the U.S. Naval Air Reserve as a sonar operator on an anti-submarine warfare helicopter. Brother Bill served two stints in the U.S. Army, having been recalled once after his initial discharge.

THE ROADSTER YEARS

Innovation was a consistent hallmark of the Summers' thinking and their approach to racing and record breaking on the salt always featured new and creative ways of attacking the record. In 1955 they assembled a budget-based 1929 Ford roadster on '32 rails with their long-favored Chrysler Hemi engine. It ran 178 mph and won the C/Roadster class with Bill driving. They were completely stoked, but still had no idea how far their racing ambition might take them.

Ever the innovators, they built a new race car; a D/Modified mid-engine roadster with a Model T body. The Hemi (a Desoto) was again tapped for power, but this time they mounted it amidships. Bob took over driving and ran 196 mph on alcohol in 1957. Two years later, he got the car up to 240 mph and then survived a 225 mph flip that proved less damaging than it appeared. They pieced the car back together overnight and still set a new record at 225 mph.

It is truly remarkable how, in a relatively few short years, the brothers progressed from local hot rodders to dry lakes racers and Bonneville record holders with a small, but extraordinary variety of vehicles that showcased their talents and foretold much bigger things to come.

The success of the roadsters whet their appetite for speed and records and the Summers soon evolved a unique and broadly innovative front-wheel-drive racer to suit their speedy ambitions.

Halibrand quick-change rear end with heavy duty half-shafts and full suspension displays the Summers' early understanding of putting power down on the salt.

The Summers Brothers' engine of choice for all their cars was the V8 Chrysler Hemi.

Summers cars were always Hemi-powered. The original Hemi they purchased and modified to run in Bill's '36 Ford was repeatedly rebuilt and supercharged for use in the boys' roadsters and the Pollywog. A lot of innovative thinking went into their cars long before they ever conceived the Goldenrod.

The Summers Brothers' rear-engine roadsters were competitive from the get-go. Bill Summers set the C/Roadster record at 174.133 mph in 1955.

Summers Brothers Racing Records

Date	Entry	Class	Speed	Place	Record	Course
6/27/54	Summers/Rhienicker	A/Coupe	116.50	2nd		El Mirage
10/10/54	Summers Brothers	GOB/Coupe	120.28	1st		El Mirage
1954	Summers Brothers	C/Coupe	123.07	10th		Bonneville
8/20/55	Summers Brothers	C/Roadster	178.21	1st	174.133	Bonneville
9/18/55	Summers Brothers	C/Roadster	162.60	1st	162.60	El Mirage
6/3/56	Summers Brothers	C/Roadster	167.83	1st	167.83	El Mirage
1956	Summers Brothers	C&D/MR	213.80	1st/1st		Bonneville
8/20/56	Summers Brothers	C&D/MR	213.14	1st/1st		Bonneville
9/16/56	Summers Brothers	GOC/Coupe	99.14	4th		El Mirage
10/14/56	Summers Brothers	GOC/Coupe	108.79	1st	108.79	El Mirage
1956-57	Summers Brothers	A/M Coupe	140.89	1st	10.17 ET	Colton Drags
1957	Summers Brothers	D/MR	196.57	1st		Bonneville
8/20/57	Summers Brothers	E/MR	195.86	1st		Bonneville
5/18/58	Summers Brothers	F/R	185.56	1st		El Mirage
5/25/58	Summers Brothers	X/MR	184.80	1st		El Mirage
6/15/58	Summers Brothers	F/R	128.28	4th		El Mirage
7/13/58	Summers Brothers	GOF/Coupe	107.27	6th		El Mirage
8/20/58	Summers Brothers	E/MR	227.12	1st	221.062	Bonneville
9/21/58	Summers Brothers	F/R	213.27	1st	213.27	El Mirage
9/28/58	Summers Brothers	X/R	204.08	1st		El Mirage
10/19/58	Summers Brothers	F/R	215.31	1st	215.31	El Mirage
1958	Summers Brothers	B/MR	227.71	1st	221.09	Bonneville
1959	Summers Brothers	B/MR	240.38	1st	225.37	Bonneville
5/3/59	Summers Brothers	X/R	121.13	3rd		El Mirage
8/20/59	Summers Brothers	B/MR	240.71	1st	225.078	Bonneville
10/25/59	Summers Brothers	X/R	192.30	1st		El Mirage
8/20/60	Brissette/Summers	A/L	264.70	1st	251.07	Bonneville
10/30/60	Brissette/Summers	A/L	227.27	1st	227.27	El Mirage
8/20/61	Summers Brothers	C/S	302.317	1st		Bonneville
8/20/62	Summers Brothers	C/S	322.79	1st		Bonneville
9/23/63	Summers Brothers	C/S	316.37	1st	308.941	Bonneville
11/12/65	Summers Brothers	U/S	409.277	Land Speed Record		Bonneville

Legend: R = Roadster | M = Modified | X = Experimental | L = Lakester | S = Streamliner | U = Unlimited | GO = Gas Overhead (Russetta Timing Assoc.)

THE POLLYWOG

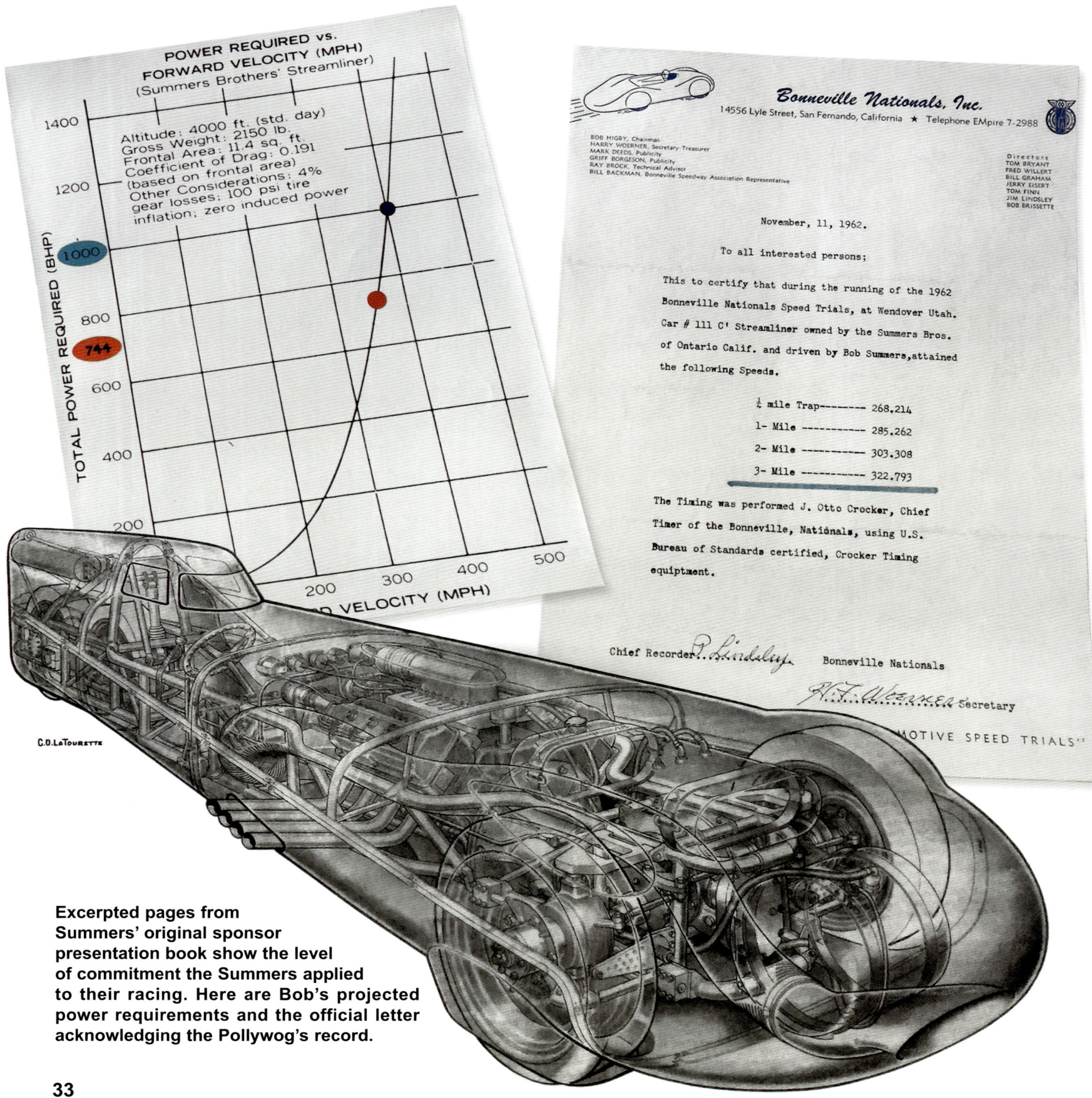

Excerpted pages from Summers' original sponsor presentation book show the level of commitment the Summers applied to their racing. Here are Bob's projected power requirements and the official letter acknowledging the Pollywog's record.

33

As these period photos depict, all of the Summers Brothers' cars were built in cramped garage conditions. This was low-buck racing fueled by pure passion. Note the crude but effective two-wheeled trailer with bald tires. At the upper right, Bob works on the front of the car while land speed legend Ermie Immerso checks out the engine layout.

With their Summers Brothers axle company successful and growing, Bob decided to elevate their racing efforts by designing an all new and innovative streamliner to challenge FIA world records as well as SCTA class records. Teardrop-shaped and tapering sharply to the rear, the new "Pollywog" featured front-wheel drive, tandem rear wheels and the tried and trusty Hemi engine that had powered all of their cars thus far. The Pollywog proved its mettle early on by running over 302 mph right out of the box in 1961. In 1962, Bob threaded the timers with a peak speed of 322.79 mph hour and then established a C-class speed record of 308.941 mph in late 1963. The Summers Brothers' unconventional approach made the Pollywog the fastest piston-powered car and strongly foreshadowed the subsequent design and construction of the forthcoming Goldenrod. The Pollywog was later sold to landspeed racer Tim Rochlitzer who intended to revive it for competition. It was modifed and the body discarded. The project ultimately languished and was sold off after Tim's untimely passing.

It never became a World Land Speed Record contender as it ran afoul of an FIA regulation that required all four wheels to have their own individual track. The unusual tandem rear wheel arrangement meant that they would have to

GOLDENROD

The Pollywog was a clear nod to the follow-on land speed record Goldenrod. Its teardrop shape, front-wheel drive and innovative rear track all contributed to a 322.79 mph top speed in the C/S Streamliner class.

Pollywog's unique front-wheel-drive setup bucked the trend and unknowingly provided some key design features that were subsequently incorporated into the final design of the Goldenrod.

modify the car or confine their ambitious efforts to challenging more SCTA records at Bonneville.

Still, the Pollywog provided invaluable design experience with high-speed cars, and it was an exercise in budgeting as well. Fabricator Willie Sutton's grandson confirmed to us that a custom Sutton-built body ran about $3,000-$3,500 back in the day. No one knows what he charged the Summers Brothers for the Goldenrod, but the extra-large car involved a tremendous amount of intricate fabrication that may likely have run twice that amount or more. When compared to their relatively inexpensive roadster efforts, and even the Pollywog, the Goldenrod was off-the-scale expensive and labor intensive. It did, however, deliver the goods and made the Summers name a legend in the world racing community.

Bob Summers and Jim Crosby were the primary fabricators of Goldenrod. It was a remarkable feat of engineering for a pair of talented young men with limited funds and facilities.

Building a Record Holder

With the notable exception of Walter Korff's aerodynamic contributions, the Goldenrod came almost entirely out of Bob Summers' head. It represents an unprecedented achievement in land speed racing because it was designed, built, and driven by an extraordinary young hot rodder to set a World Land Speed Record.

Until you explore deep inside the Goldenrod and see the extraordinary sophistication and attention to detail in its design, you can't fully appreciate the genius that resided within Bob Summers. Within the sleek shell specified by aerodynamicist Walter Korff, Summers packaged an amazing array of high performance technology and hot rodding ingenuity. The plan had evolved in Summers' mind for a long time, and he refined it even as construction began. The basic layout grew out of a conversation with his friend Tony Campana, who suggested that an inline configuration offered a much smaller frontal area while still accommodating up to four engines and the necessary driveline components. Bob Summers and his co-builder Jim Crosby further determined that the car's driver should be positioned at the extreme rear in a separate caged structure with the parachutes to provide the best protection in the event of a crash.

Rear axle and hub assembly looking forward toward the rear transmission. The rear portion of the car has yet to be fabricated in this view.

GOLDENROD

The rear drive assembly consists of the rear gear case and coupler, transmission and clutch can, and the rear transfer case for the driveline. The aluminum Spicer transmission was laid over on its side and securely mounted to the upper and lower frame rails.

This configuration solved a multitude of aerodynamic requirements and maintained Korff's initial design shape. It also required very careful packaging to fit the necessary performance elements into Korff's pre-defined space. The transmissions, clutches and center section assemblies also fit inline and required transfer mechanisms to transmit engine torque outboard to a lengthy driveline system along the lower left side of the car. A 1:1 ratio transfer case between each pair of engines fed torque to the driveshafts. At the front and rear, another set of transfer cases connects to the clutches and transmissions. The entire system is tied together in one assembly to ensure equal wheel speed at both the front and rear wheels.

The drive system passes through the eight aluminum bulkheads along the lower left side of the car next to the engine blocks. The driveshafts are relatively short to prevent whipping, and they are anchored with bearing blocks at the front and rear to provide further stability and smooth operation. The inner gear on each transfer case connects to a hub with a milled slot that accepts a drive spud attached to the rear flange of each crankshaft. It forms a solid direct drive system capable of transmitting all the torque supplied by the powerful Chrysler engines.

This driveline arrangement was remarkably innovative and yet it still involved considerable parasitic loss due to the complicated geometry and heavy-duty makeup of all the components. But it was the best way to accomplish the task within the confined space dictated by Korff's aerodynamic design requirements.

When restoration was completed, it was quite surprising how little effort it took to turn the entire drive train by hand. One has to marvel at the extraordinary ingenuity of this engineering effort and the undeniable fact that it performed almost flawlessly under pressure. Such was the genius of Bob Summers.

Opposite: Front suspension detail shows upper and lower tubular A-arms and independent drive hub assembly. The center section is rigidly mounted at the top and bottom with heavy aluminum plates attached to the frame rails. The number one engine is conventionally mounted facing forward. The second engine backs up to it with a power transfer case in between them. Both engines are standard rotation. They achieve torque cancellation by virtue of facing in opposite directions.

Next Page: Transfer cases between the paired engines incorporated an extra gear to merge the opposed rotations for transfer to the driveline. The transfer cases and short bellhousings were all fabricated in-house. Mockup bulkhead to the right shows how the cylinder head and valve cover interfere with the bulkhead. Revised bulkheads received proper cutouts and/or milled depressions to accommodate these fitment problems.

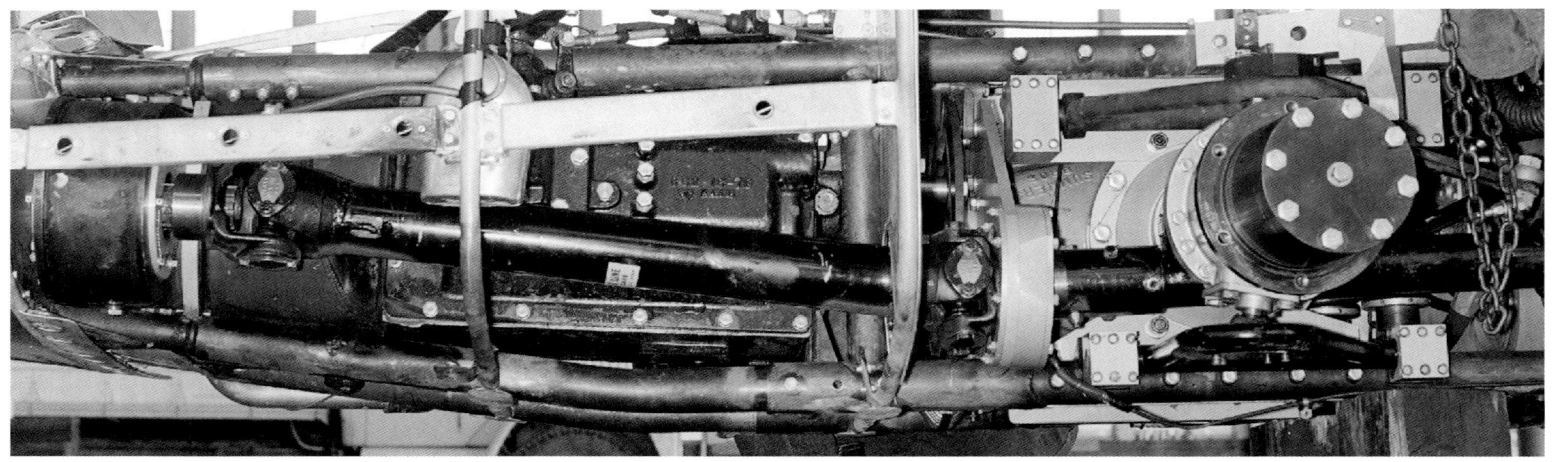

41

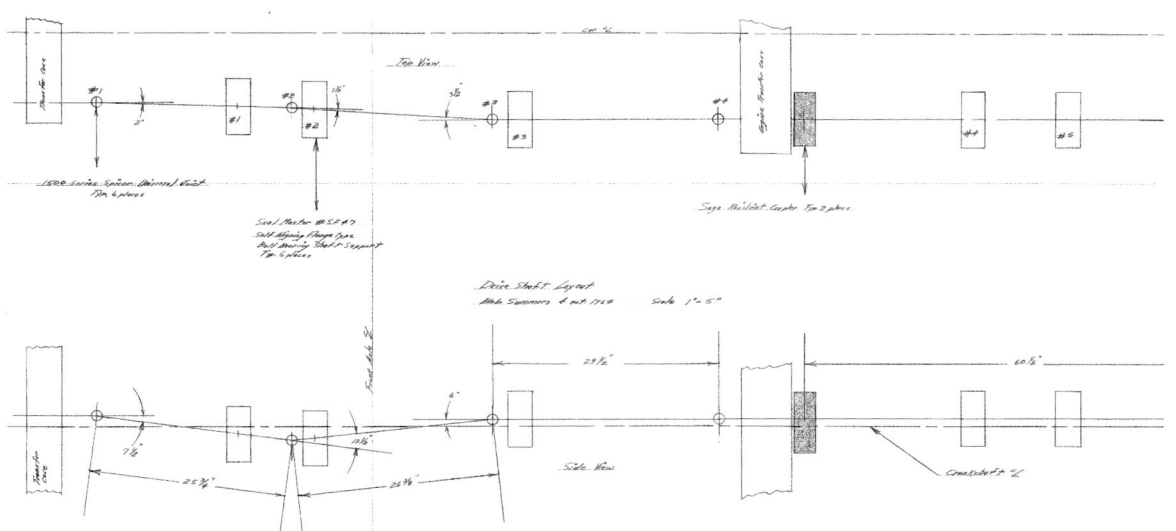

Driveline angles and components list by Bob Summers.

NOTE: Front driveshaft was angled upward to accommodate the nose design that Walter Korff deemed necessary for optimum aerodynamic efficiency.

GOLDENROD

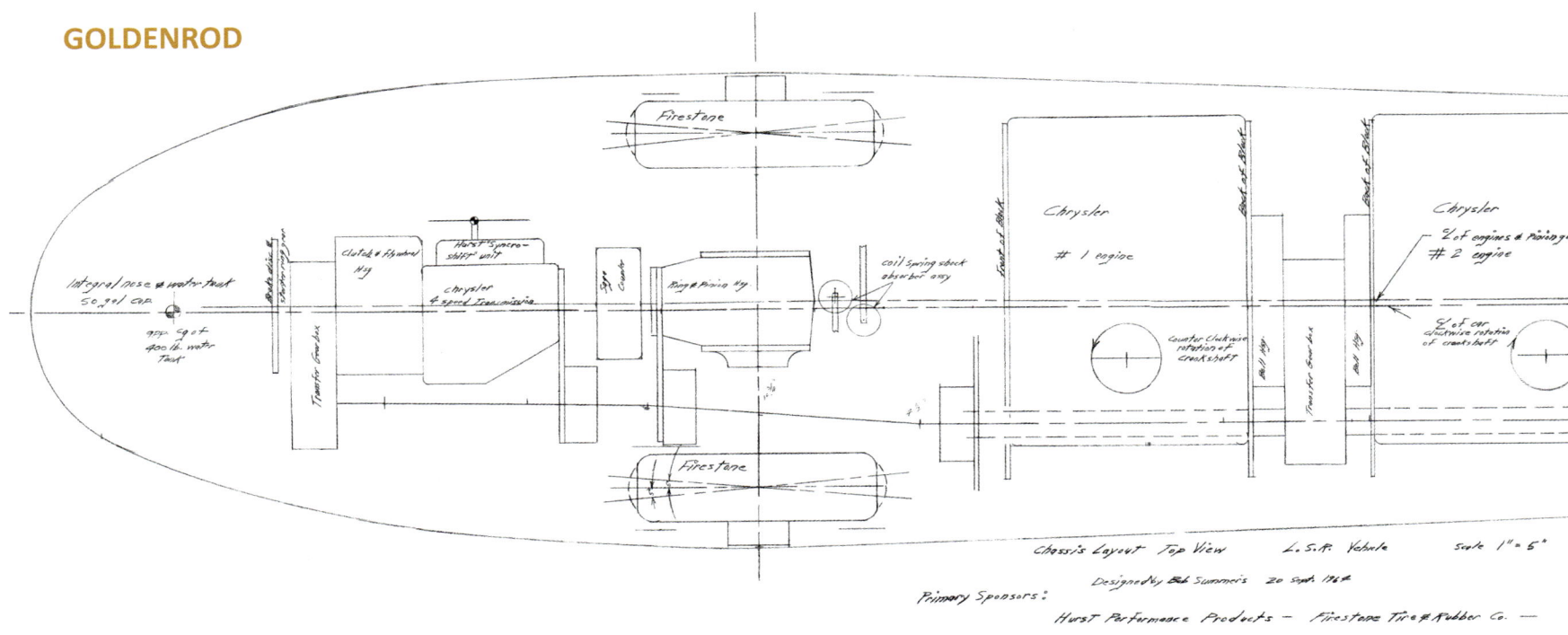

Original blueprint drawn by Bob Summers

Rolling the aluminum Spicer transmission over on its side accommodated the car's low cowl height which Korff insisted could not be compromised. This drive assembly alone is almost six feet long.

GOLDENROD

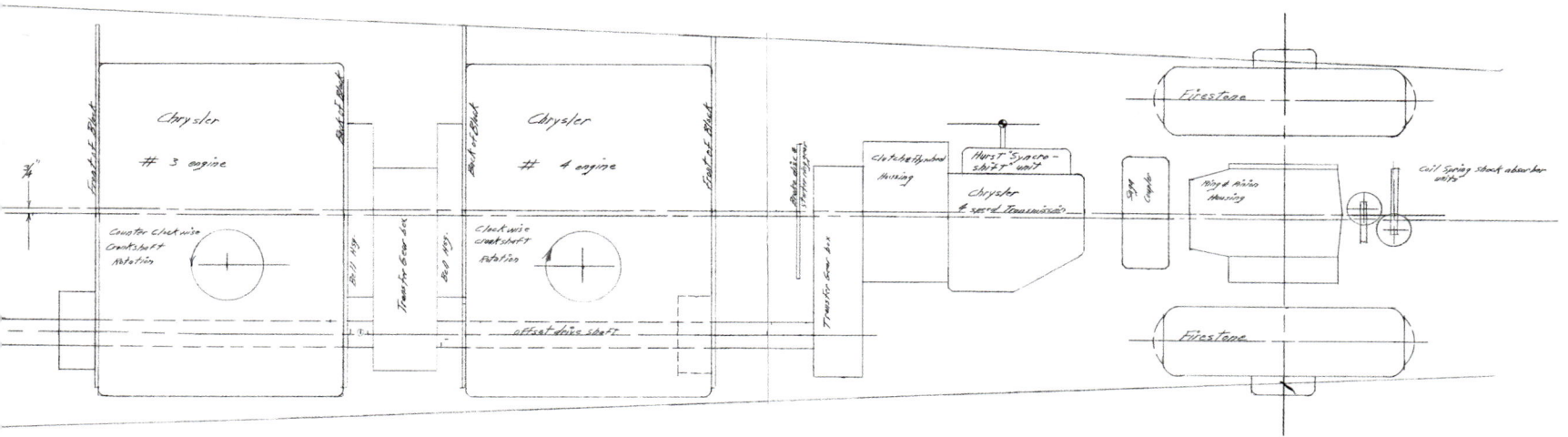

Owned by Summers Bros.
— Chrysler Corp.

"The crankshaft rotation notes on this design drawing show the #1 and #3 engines installed nose forward and the #2 and #4 engines installed nose aft. This produces a counter-rotating set of four engines using all standard hardware, no reverse camshafts, no inverted thrust on the intermediate shafts, no reverse rotation ignitions, no reverse rotation oil pumps, and no mirror image crankshafts. This is especially advantageous with four installed engines and two spares to keep all of the hardware common for servicing at the track." - *Tom Burkland, WLSR Record Holder*

Looking forward from the rear axle assembly you can see the rear transmission, clutch can, transfer case and the timing cover on the rear engine. The drive coupler shown here is temporary. The flexible coupler was not yet built.

44

GOLDENROD

FRONT UPPER CONTROL ARM DETAIL

"Front suspension detail shows pillow block mounts for the upper and lower control arms and plate assemblies to attach them to the frame. Summers' drawing indicates the steering arm on the upper assembly, mounting plate to the upper frame rail and relative position of the hub, tire, and wheel. The large offset of the tread center plane inboard of the hubs may have contributed increased wheel bearing loads and component failures during the runs at Bonneville." - *Tom Burkland*

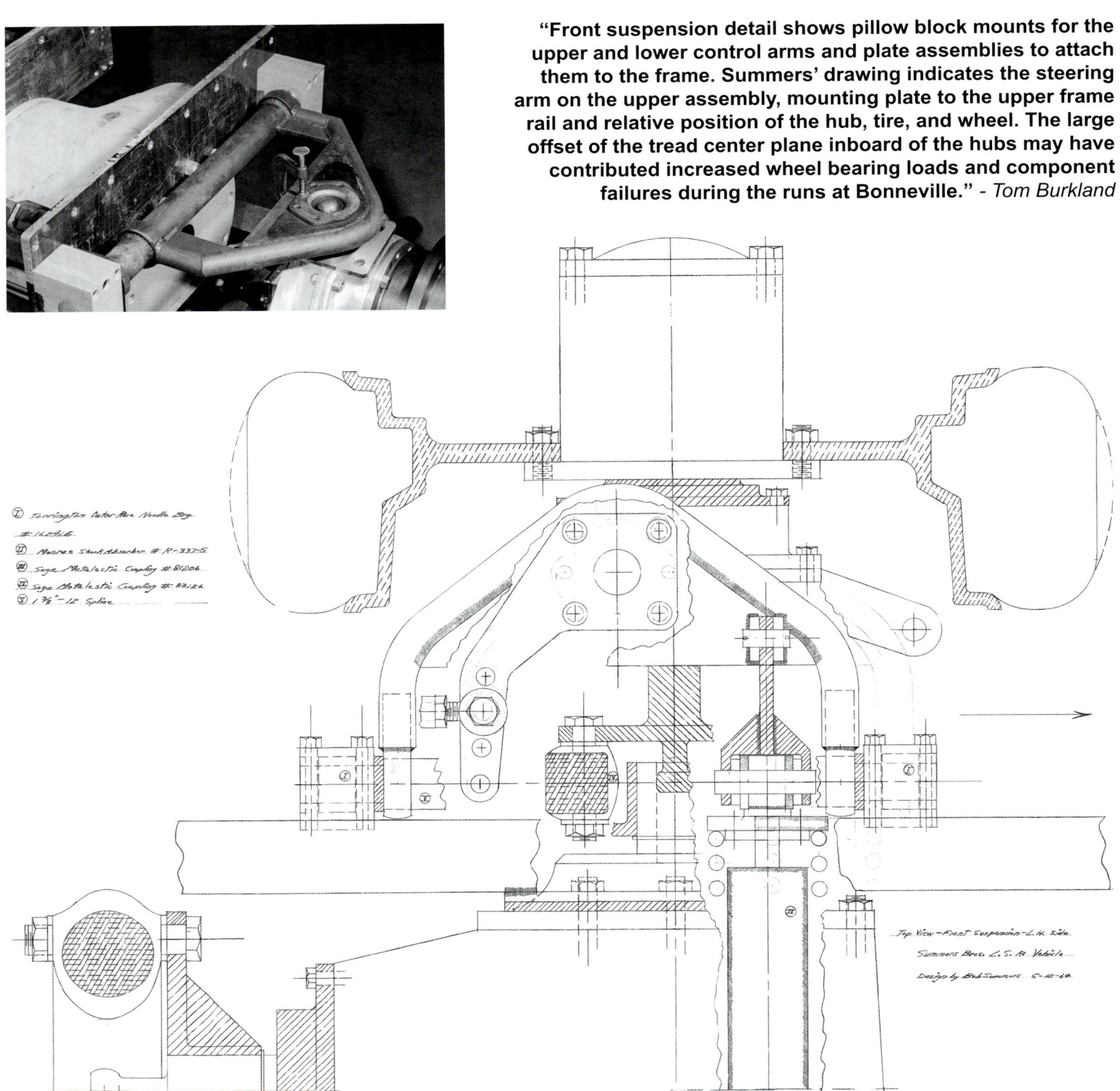

REAR UPPER CONTROL ARM DETAIL

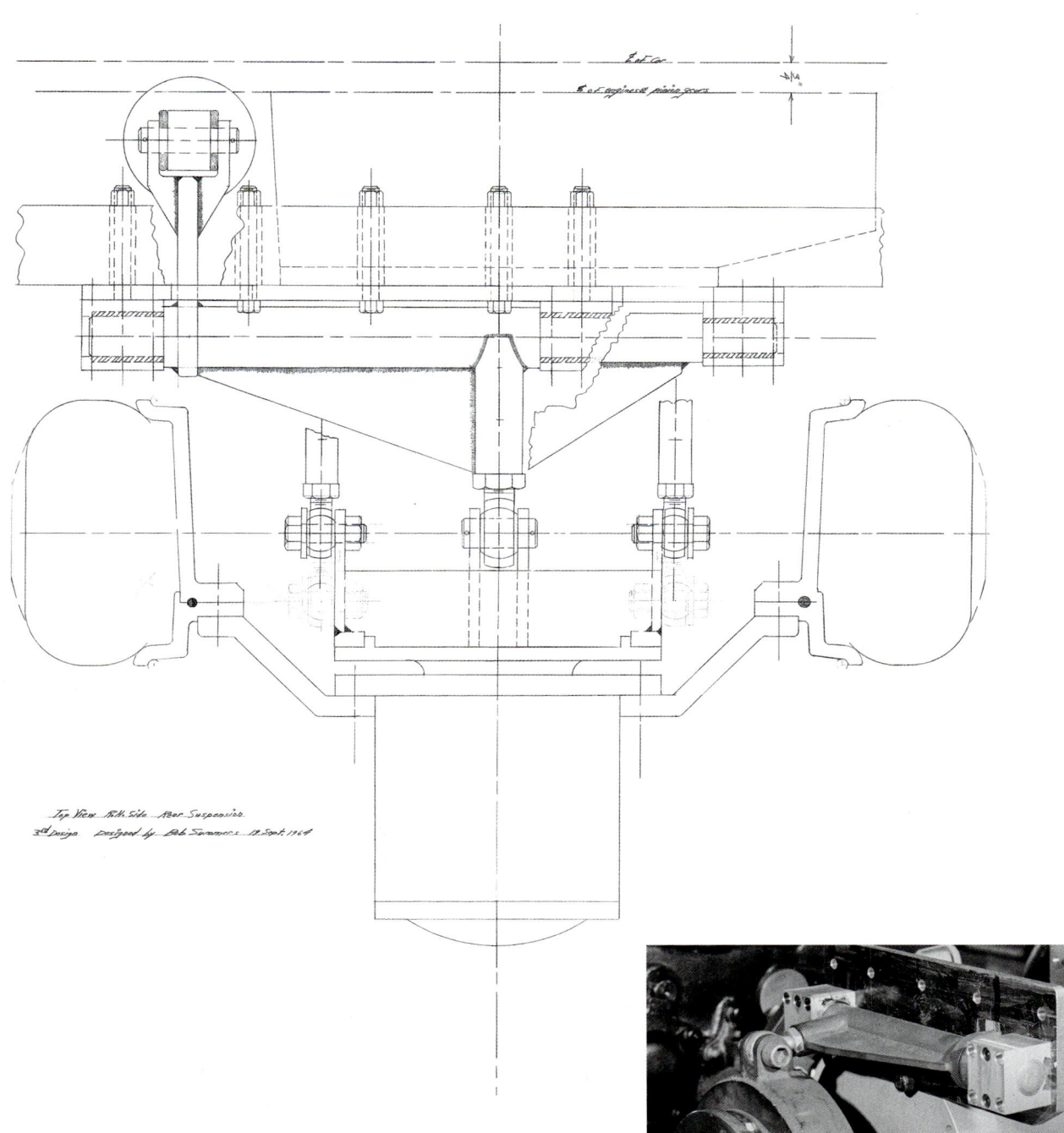

Rear suspension detail shows the pillow block mounts for the 3-point upper control arms and the adjustable front and rear lower rod assemblies. The pillow blocks mount to plates attached to the frame rails and the rear end housing as shown in the photo.

FRONT SUSPENSION

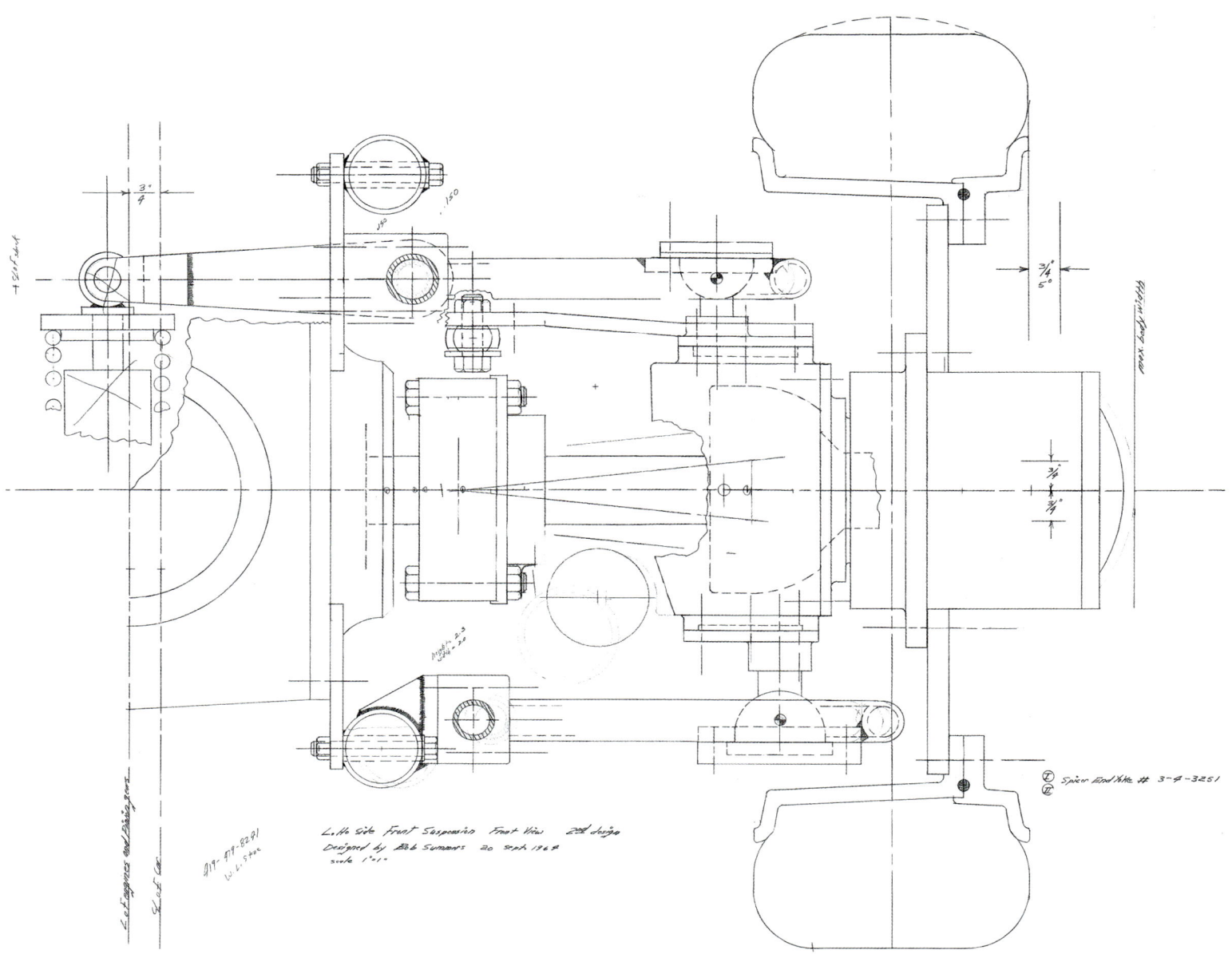

"Summers' blueprint shows the inboard mounted coil-overs and inner CV joint. The giant splined exterior six-ball CV joints used at the end of each axle shaft, eight total in the car, are DANA Spicer components designed to drive the rolls in steel mills. Interestingly enough, the Burkland 411 streamliner uses these same parts as steering joints inside the front hubs. Twenty-five years later they were still the only industrial grade hardware that would handle the torque and shaft speed for this application. Scrub radius is about two full inches positive, resulting in rather large steering torques when running under power, and opposite torque steer under trailing throttle. This was apparently not a major issue as Bob was always very complimentary of the handling and stability of the car, and he was the only one to ever drive it under power." - *Tom Burkland*

Detailed view of the right front upper control arm and attachment plates for the center section. An adjustable connecting tube to the left front hub assembly provided adjustment for toe-in (not shown here). A bar off the rear of the control arm passed through the mounting plate and attached to the top of the inboard shock assemblies. You can see the forked mounting bar behind the plate at the lower left center of the photo.

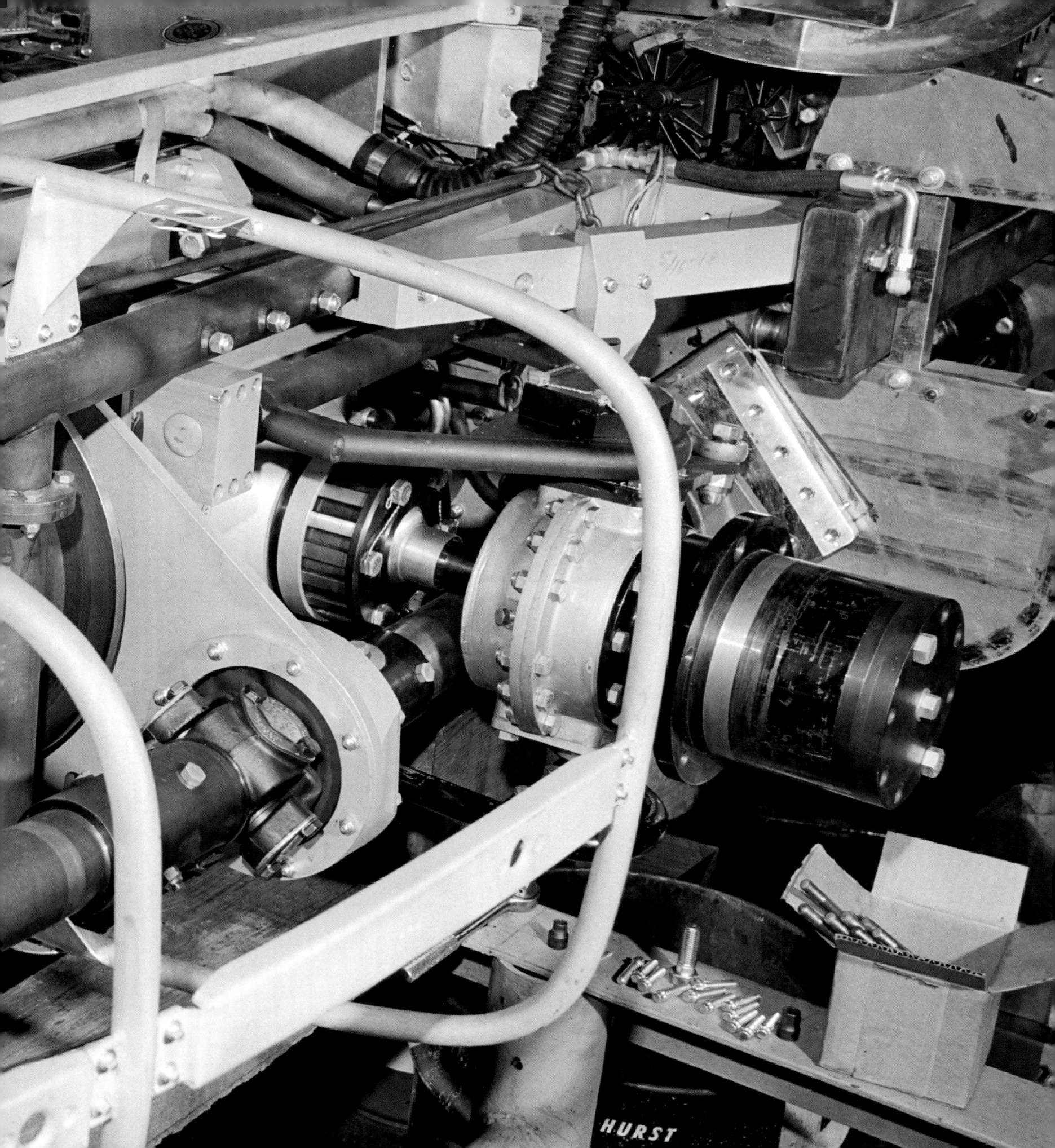

Top: Battery box for the 24V aircraft surplus coolant pumps from G&J Salvage in Ontario, CA, fits snugly between the pumps, transmission and the clutch housing. The batteries are 24V aircraft batteries. The nose coolant tank holds 30 gallons and provides about 250 lbs. of forward ballast to support proper balance and CG position. Bottom: Front drive assembly with stationary bearing housing adjacent to the front tire and vibration damper attached to the front U-joint at the rear of the front transfer case. Opposite page: Detail of front suspension mounts and triangular upper brace designed to narrow the front frame for tire and steering clearance.

GOLDENROD

At the upper right, a hydraulic accumulator (probably nitrogen charged) is bolted to the frame rail (see Pg. 134 top). It is also visible in other period photos. Summers used it to provide volume compensation for the steering actuator (lower left) at full range. It was definitely run at the salt (Pg. 143 top), but at some point, he removed it as steering deflections were small enough not to require it and it decreased steering feel in the cockpit. This component is lost to time, but you can see the empty bracket holes in the frame rail and how it was re-plumbed in Chapter 8 (Pg. 257 top).

Note the clever reversal of the upper frame rail (right side) to accomplish the narrowing necessary to accommodate Korff's tapered body design. This photo also shows how the master throttle rod used individual bellcranks to transition to the throttle linkage in each air box and how the opening in the bulkhead was necessary to accommodate this hardware. You can see the cross-connections for the coolant lines emerging from the block, the Hilborn fuel pump and the pressure lines. This view also confirms the use of factory dual point distributors.

Jim Crosby - Crew Chief
1937 - 2017

Crew Chief of the Goldenrod, Jim Crosby, was Bob Summers' best friend and a fundamental asset to the car's construction. He worked alongside Summers throughout the construction of the car and the subsequent trips to Bonneville seeking the record. Among the unsung heroes of the Summers Brothers' monumental achievement, Crosby never received the credit he quite rightfully deserved for his tireless contribution and perseverance in making the Goldenrod a success. Crosby's crew chief title and responsibilities reflect the high level of trust he had earned in Bob Summers' eyes and the degree of confidence he placed in Crosby's car preparation so that he could simply disconnect and drive the car.

It was certainly gratifying for Crosby (second from the right in the photo below) to see the Goldenrod resurrected and restored to its former glory and to be there for its unveiling. Resoration partner Mike Cook reminded me that Crosby initially had been skeptical about our restoration efforts, but after visiting the shop, he warmed up to it considerably and offered valuable comments and insights. He said we asked all the right questions and that's when he was satisfied that the car was going to be done right. Jim Crosby left us in January 2017, but he also left an undeniable legacy to the land speed racing community. Our thanks to his wife Lorna and son James for allowing us to share these great photos.

Crosby Goldenrod Album - 1965

JUL 1965

JUN 1965

JUN 1965

JUN 1965

Crosby Goldenrod Album - 1965

JUN 1965

JUN 1965

JUL 1965

JUN 1965

Crosby Goldenrod Album - 1965

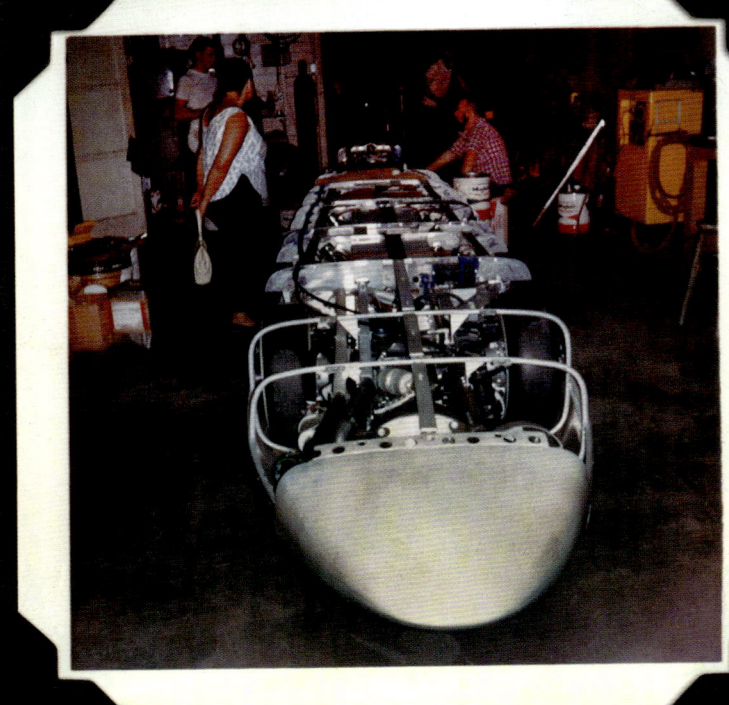

Crosby Goldenrod Album - 1965

Crosby Goldenrod Album - 1965

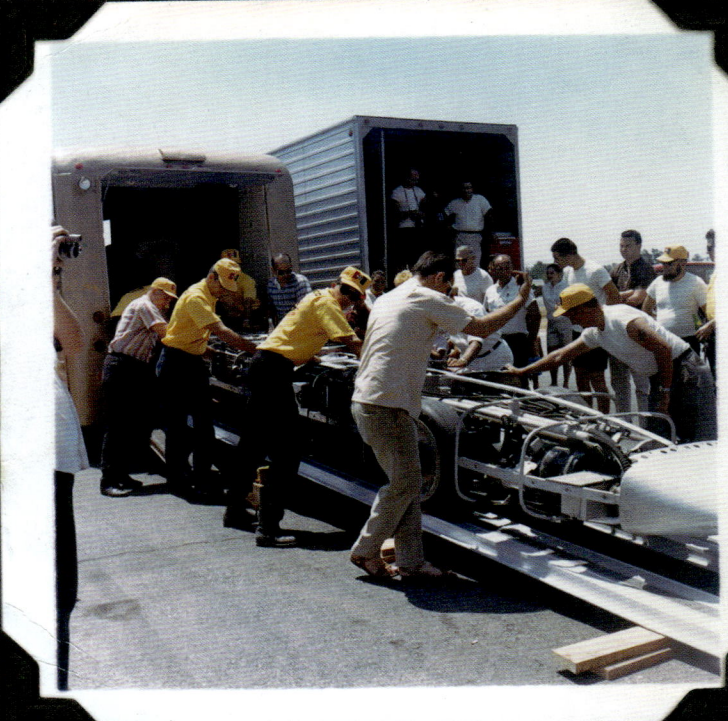

Crosby Goldenrod Album - 1965

GOLDENROD

AERODYNAMICS

"It's the longest, narrowest, lowest package of piston horsepower in the history of the land speed record."
- Wayne Thoms

GOLDENROD

Setting speed records aided by aerodynamic efficiency was intuitively recognized by the earliest pioneers of speed record setting. The Belgian electric car manufacturer Camille Jenatzy fashioned a torpedo-like body for his electric car to gain an aero advantage over his arch rival Count Gaston de Chasseloup Laubat, a Frenchman who in 1898 had set the first officially recorded land speed record at 39.23 mph driving a Jeantard electric vehicle. The two early racers exchanged records multiple times in a popular duel of speed with the Count finally gaining the upper hand with a speed of 57.59 mph. Determined not to be outdone, Jenatzy contrived a specially modified new vehicle to challenge the record. It was to become the first vehicle specifically built to challenge the land speed record.

Jenatzy christened it "La Jamais Contente" which translates to "Never Satisfied." It was a radical departure from his previous production vehicle. The all new torpedo-shaped car was purposely streamlined to minimize drag.

The Goldenrod pioneered the long, narrow, aerodynamic inline configuration that has become the standard in land speed racing.

Jenatzy also recognized the value of minimizing weight as he constructed the body from the new lightweight alloy partinium. This first attempt at streamlining was likely minimally effective as the streamlined body sat atop a fully exposed automotive chassis with the driver positioned upright in the open airstream. Still, it foretold what would quickly become one of the most important components of all successful speed record attempts.

Camille Jenatzy's torpedo-shaped La Jamais Contente "Never Satisfied" effectively became the first land speed record streamliner in 1899. It was the first vehicle to exceed 100 kph, raising the land speed record to 65.79 mph utilizing electric power and rudimentary aerodynamics.

The Summers Brothers recognized from the outset that they needed competent aerodynamic advice. While the fast and successful Pollywog had adhered to basic aerodynamic principles with its teardrop shape, minimal frontal area, and tapered body, they clearly recognized the challenges facing a new vehicle designed to be as much as 200 mph faster. Accordingly, they sought the assistance of the highly regarded Lockheed aerodynamicist Walter Korff. By the mid-sixties aerodynamics was a well-advanced science and Korff's mastery of it is evident everywhere in Goldenrod's design. A recent appointee to the Society of Automotive Engineers' Aerodynamics Board, Korff eagerly took to the challenge. In a technical article he later penned for *Sports Car Graphic* magazine, Korff wrote that he worked directly with Bob Summers on the preliminary design to identify the essential requirements and characteristics necessary to the task. Korff generated the initial performance calculations, designed a wind tunnel model and supervised the testing in the nearby Cal Tech wind tunnel. When the design progressed, Korff performed

 **GOLDENROD**

GOLDENROD

The Goldenrod is almost the optimum aerodynamic shape; essentially an elongated teardrop with a 3-1/2 degree taper that was dictated largely by the width of the big Hemi engines. Designer Korff used every trick in the book to make it slick, including shaping the cockpit and the vertical wedge tail to function as an integrated body fin for maximum directional stability.

the full scale layout of the final body shape with aerodynamics ruling the design process and fully influencing the final construction of the chassis and formidable powertrain components.

Korff and Summers agreed that the car's aerodynamic signature could not be compromised; hence all of the design decisions were framed within the essential requirements of stability, control, traction, and speed. With Korff specifying the overall shell, Summers worked to design the frame, suspension, and powertrain to fit within Korff's uncompromised envelope. This included the chassis and suspension, engines and drivetrain, wheels and tires, and tight packaging of fluid tanks, power sources and control mechanisms.

Korff sought to achieve the smallest frontal area possible and completely agreed with the suggestion from Summers' friend Tony Capanna to mount the four Hemi engines in line with each other to minimize the overall cross-section. With four relatively heavy engines, transfer cases and the equally heavy truck transmissions plus the cockpit, the vehicle's length grew to 32 feet and necessitated an innovative approach to packaging the internal components. Summers solved the primary concern of torsional stiffness and bending loads by making the engines an integral part of the chassis held together with a pair of beefy 2 x 6-inch longitudinal rectangular upper rails and eight aluminum bulkheads framing each of the engine bays and transmissions. Two-inch round tubing rails under the engines tied the lower end together at each bulkhead, eliminating the need for any diagonal bracing members in the frame. This innovative design

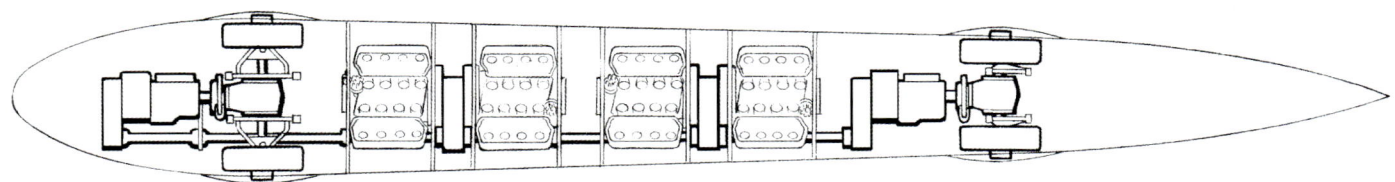

The inline engine configuration was a radical departure from contemporary thinking, which ultimately proved to be aerodynamically superior to any approach then or since.

FUNDAMENTALS OF AERODYNAMIC DRAG

The commonly referenced C_d or coefficient of drag is a dimensionless quantity used to reference drag or resistance to movement of an object through a fluid such as air. The primary contributors to drag are skin friction and form drag. Roughly translated, skin friction refers to the area of the car's surface in contact with the air (fluid) while form drag references the pressure resistance created by the actual shape of the vehicle. The primary equation for aerodynamic drag references the following components:

AERODYNAMIC DRAG

$Drag_{force} = C_d A (\rho/2) V^2$ (units of force)

C_d = Non-Dimensional Drag Coefficient

A = Frontal Area (units of length^2)

ρ = Ambient Air Density (units of mass/volume)

V = Velocity (units of distance/time)

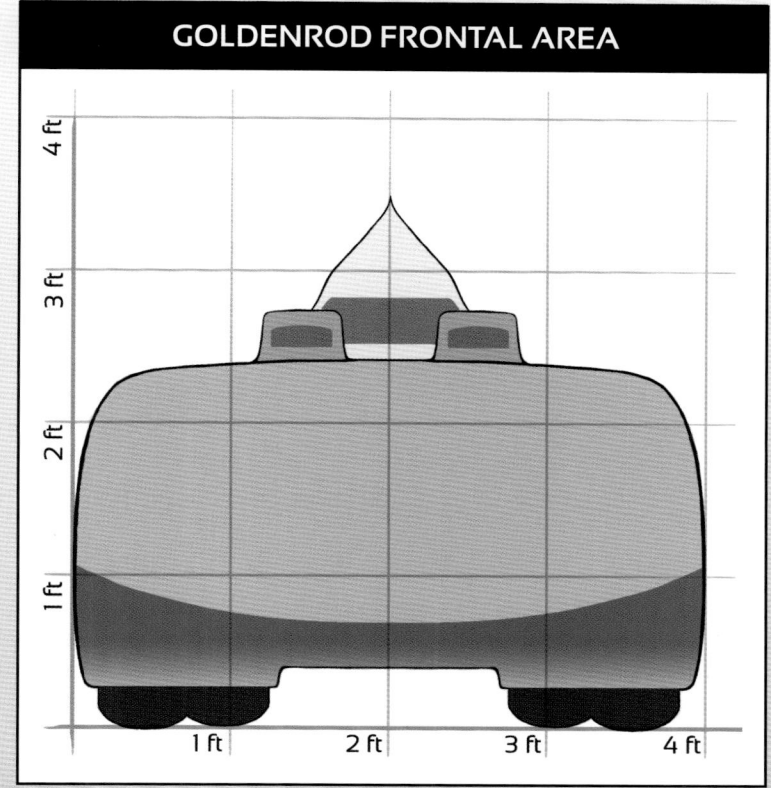

GOLDENROD FRONTAL AREA

Note that being a non-dimensional multiplier, C_d affects the rest of the equation proportionately. A higher or lower C_d changes the drag force. The coefficient of drag has become synonymous with the overall concept of drag. A lower C_d implies less drag and greater aerodynamic efficiency.

POWER TO OVERCOME DRAG

Power (t) = Force x Velocity

Power = Drag Force x Velocity

Power = $C_d A (\rho/2) V^2$ x V

Power = $C_d A (\rho/2) V^3$

As drag increases non-linearly with velocity, the power requirement rises as the cube of the velocity. Hence, we have the C_d multiplied by the vehicle frontal area, multiplied by air density divided by 2, multiplied by velocity cubed. The faster you go, the greater the aerodynamic resistance and the amount of power required to overcome it, assuming perfect traction at the tire/ground interface.

In his 1968 presentation at the AIAA Symposium on The Aerodynamics of Sports Cars & Competition Vehicles, designer Walter Korff subsequently cited three primary aerodynamic achievements related to the final aerodynamic design of the Goldenrod land speed car.

1. **The lowest drag coefficient of any four wheel surface vehicle. C_d = 0.1165.**

2. **Aerodynamic down load (negative lift) by the shape of its basic body alone.**

3. **High-speed stability without the addition of horizontal or vertical fins, spoilers or weight (ballast).**

AIAA - American Institute of Aeronautics and Astronautics

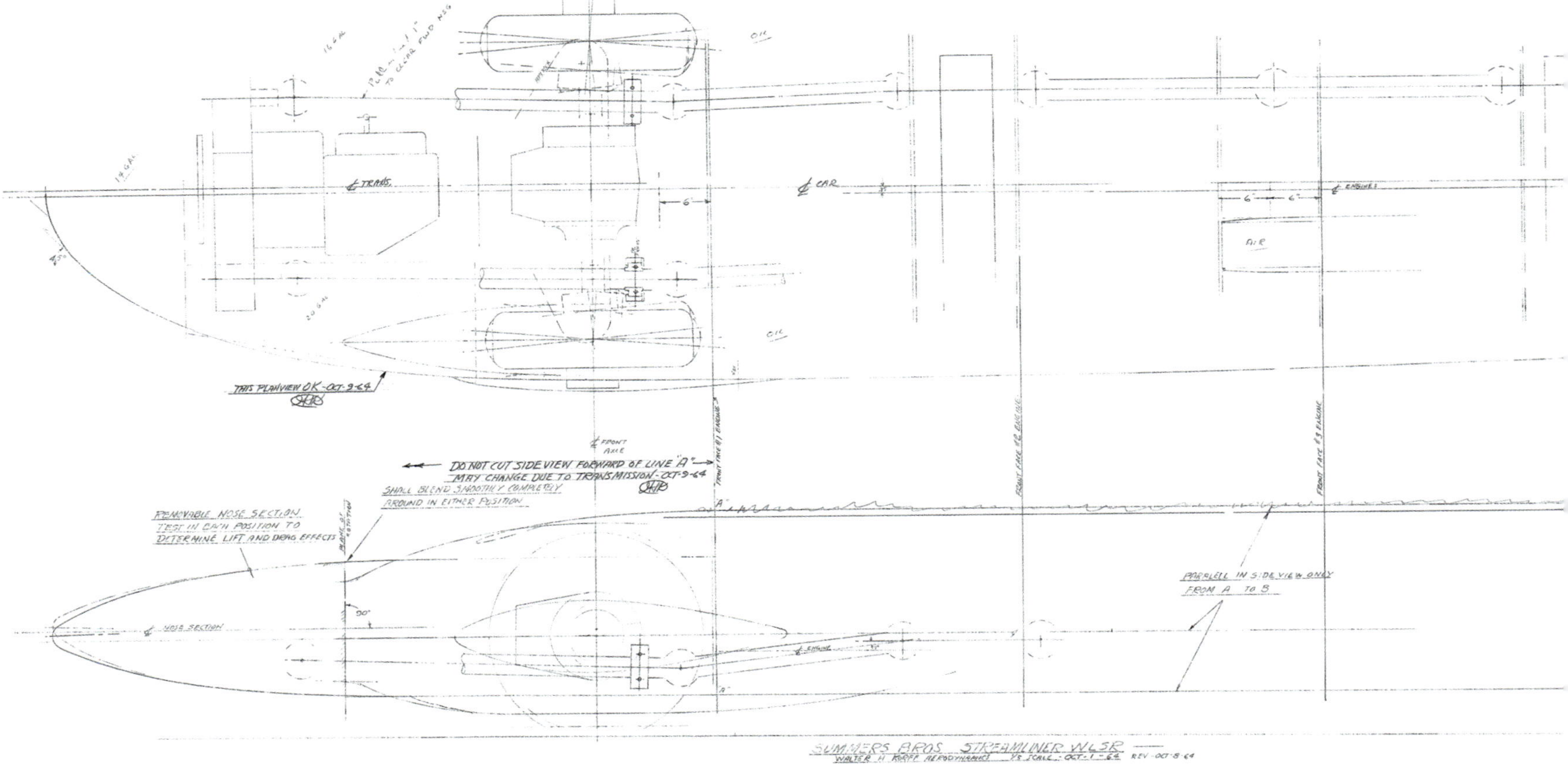

GOLDENROD

The fiberglass tail cone completed the aerodynamic taper specified by Korff. It was blown off with an explosive charge so the parachutes could be activated. Fortunately, collector Stuart Thompson was able to return the only remaining copy.

offered plenty of room at the lower sides and bottom of the car for easy packaging of the exhaust headers and driveshaft assemblies.

Aerodynamics dictated every facet of the design. To achieve minimal frontal area and minimize aerodynamic lift, Korff required a near-symmetrical shape to the nose in side view and the nose also had to taper inward in plan view. To accommodate this, Summers tilted the front transmission upward so aerodynamic efficiency would not be compromised. At the rear he narrowed the gearbox and control mechanisms to remain within Korff's defined contour in plan view. Routing the driveline around and under the left front suspension arms presented a formidable engineering challenge that Summers and Korff tackled together.

Korff stated that optimizing the U-joint angles, minimizing torsional vibration, bearing supports

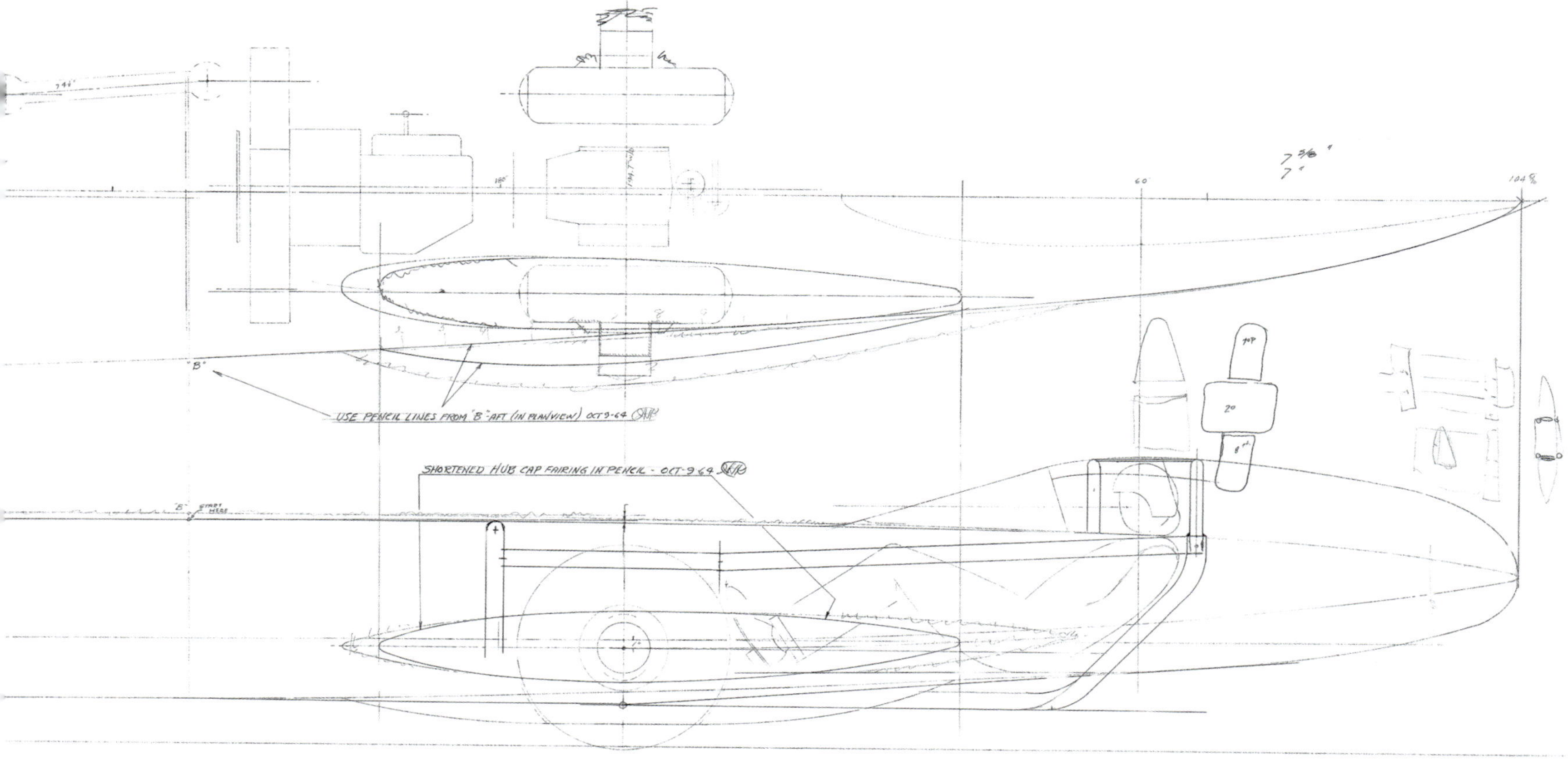

GOLDENROD

Bob Summers: builder, driver, world record holder. A very intense and determined young man, uncompromised by ego and talented beyond his years.

68

GOLDENROD

Designer Walter H. Korff and Summers discussing the car's handling and stability characteristics. The car met all their objectives, and Bob Summers was clearly pleased with its performance. This is a scan of a period photo.

and critical shaft lengths dictated by high engine speeds caused considerable evaluation and design revisions. With the engines mounted inline there was further concern about high engine torque upsetting the stance under power. This could cause unwanted non-symmetrical handling problems with excessive suspension and tire loading to one side of the vehicle. Summers solved this problem by mounting the engines back-to-back in normal rotation, allowing them to generate torque cancellation due to their reversed positions. This was supported by gearbox transfer cases with an uneven number of gears for each engine. Inside the transfer case, one engine turned three gears and the opposite engine turned four gears. Together, they transferred torque to the driveline in the correct rotation. Independent rear suspension further aided the design by ensuring that the car would not perform any errant maneuvers when applying power or coming off the throttle at very high speed.

The tapered design at the rear required a very narrow track (only 24 inches) fit within the highly tapered rear body. A vertical wedge shape offered the best approach. It required gradual tapering from the nose to tail to prevent airflow separation along the sides. Note in the photos that the body transitions from its flat shape to a tapered vertical wedge with tail cone. Summers' seating position set his eye level one inch above the long flat upper body surface. Offset air scoops were incorporated so he could see between them.

Bob and Bill Summers cleaning up the one-fifth scale test model of the Goldenrod on the balance platform to run aero tests in the Caltech ten-foot-diameter wind tunnel.

The wedge behind the driver housed the parachute canisters with no compromise in aerodynamic efficiency although it was raised from the original design to accommodate the chutes. The cockpit area and tapered rear wedge served as a minimum drag directional fin. The vertical wedge served to eliminate airflow curl exiting the rear of the car so that the air would separate smoothly at the tail. Tapered wheel covers were also designed to minimize airflow interference, and the header exits were shaped so the exhaust could contribute a small amount of thrust while also increasing boundary layer air speed along the side of the car.

Airflow under the car was critically examined as it is typically turbulent and erratic. Korff and Summers agreed on a slight rake angle toward the nose to help balance the growth of boundary layer air beneath the car. Korff calculated the optimum rake angle but found that it would expose part of the rear ring and pinion housing and lower rear suspension. He settled on a lesser angle to avoid the drag penalty of exposing these components. He also determined that the fairings around each tire opening would cause a venturi effect or airspeed increase between them if they were all symmetrical. To compensate, the forward portion of each fairing was angled inward slightly so the fairings would tend to direct air outward, reducing pressure under the car.

Design considerations intended to minimize cross-section and drag also had to work in concert with the effects of center of gravity and

GOLDENROD

The wind tunnel model with pressure ports visible on the nose and sides. The model did not incorporate the vertical wedge shape at the rear, but it was simulated during testing. Scoop shape and locations were also altered after testing. The model was later repainted gold for display and now resides in The Henry Ford museum motorsports collection.

center of aerodynamic pressure to ensure optimum directional stability. As speed increases, aerodynamic forces multiply by the square while traction begins to fade. If the center of gravity is biased to the rear more fin is required to remain stable. Korff sought to balance these forces with a center of gravity about 12 inches forward of the midpoint of the wheelbase. The dynamic thrust lines from the tire/ground contact patch slope forward according to the predicted coefficient of traction. He calculated the balance for equal weight and traction at all four wheels at projected speed. These calculations were made in the days when slide rules were still the norm and without the aid of computer simulations. Korff's reasoning was brilliant and Summers' design skills proved the perfect complement.

From his vast aviation experience, Korff also knew that air movement within the body itself was a source of high drag. Accordingly, he closed off all the wheel housing openings to reduce turbulence and specified that the body be smooth and tight with no leaks. With this in mind Summers penned drawings of every component and Korff provided detailed specifications for a 1/5-scale wind tunnel model that was tested in the ten-foot-diameter tunnel at Caltech in Pasadena, CA. Korff worked closely with William Bettes, director of Caltech wind tunnel activities.

Program objectives sought to examine the effects of ground clearance on drag by varying the height of the model above the ground plate. Pitch angles were evaluated to determine the angle of no lift and to quantify pitching moments. Two nose configurations were evaluated, one symmetrical and one slightly drooped. The test regimen determined the drag, lift and pitching moments for each nose along with yaw angles up to 15 degrees in one degree increments.

GOLDENROD

Here's a great shot of the original wind tunnel model displayed on top of the car with a high-speed aero scoop and the large-mouth record scoops. Bill Summers later painted and autographed each record scoop. They originally ran in bare, unpainted metal which is why they appear white in the record run photo in Chapter 6. The original wind tunnel model, built by Bill, and the record scoops were recovered from Stuart Thompson, a land speed record memorabilia collector in the UK. Thompson purchased them from Summers, and curator Bob Casey negotiated their return for display with the car at The Henry Ford museum.

These tests were conducted without fins as projected in Summers' initial drawings and with the addition of more upper fin and an upper and lower fin. It was subsequently determined that the space for the parachutes required the use of all the space behind the driver and a somewhat taller fin-like extension that departed from the design of the original model.

Extensive testing also quantified wind resistance and drag coefficients under all conditions of pitch, yaw and ground clearance. This revealed a pleasant surprise when they achieved the lowest drag coefficient ever recorded for a four-wheel-driven automotive vehicle at 0.1165. To the best of this author's knowledge, that still has not been surpassed some fifty years later. Visual tuft studies were also conducted and they were pleased to observe smooth uninterrupted flow without separation from nose to tail. More testing revealed that their pitch and yaw characteristics were satisfactory and that either nose could have been used with only a minor change in the rake angle. The drooped nose reduced front driveline angularity and presented less pitching moment with more overall stability.

Ground clearance was found to be satisfactory, and the angle of no lift was within one-quarter degree of Korff's previously calculated values. From this they decided to add a mild amount of down load via a slight change in rake angle. This was deemed desirable for optimum stability, and it does not affect acceleration nearly as much as adding vehicle weight. The final chassis design came in about ten percent longer in wheelbase and overhang than the original model due to accommodations made for the tight packaging of all the necessary driveline and supporting components. Korff ran new calculations that were incorporated into the final body lofting lines with minimal body changes.

GOLDENROD

The wheel fairings were designed to cover most of the tire and clear the ground by approximately two inches.

Here you can just make out the toe-in Korff added to the fairings to prevent choking airflow between the wheels.

At the outset, Korff and Summers defined a dozen important characteristics which they considered vital to the Goldenrod's potential for success:

1. Independent suspension on all four wheels was desired to improve traction, however, maximum suspension travel was limited to minimize pitching changes.

2. All-wheel-drive was deemed essential to ensure maximum traction. Considerable effort was also applied to making the rear track as narrow as possible to maintain the optimum body shape and the required rear track width.

3. Korff also stressed the "slingshot" driver's position aft of the rear axle. They found it superior to a forward position because it provided a "gun sight" steering position and the opportunity to separate the driver from dangerous engine and transmission components. The cockpit was also armored with steel plate material to further protect the driver. This configuration also permits the cockpit structure to form an aerodynamic aid, supporting vehicle stability without a fin. The aft housing forms a vertical wedge shape around the parachute cannisters and helps to minimize any disturbance of aft body airflow.

4. A forward center of gravity was also specified with the CG located on a diagonal line sloping 45 degrees forward from the ground at the midpoint of the wheelbase. This position offers near equal weight to all four wheels for equal traction and reduces the need for fin area to support stability.

5. The inline arrangement of engines, transmissions and drivetrain elements as suggested by Tony Campana significantly reduces frontal area and aerodynamic drag.

6. Minimum front and rear track. The front tread is 36" with 5° of steering angle. The rear is 24". The narrow track caused the wheel hubs to protrude beyond the wheel rims and thus required the designing of aerodynamic wheel fairings.

GOLDENROD

7. Carburetors were discarded and replaced with dedicated mechanical fuel injection to lower the hood contour. Likewise, the engines were fitted with dry sump oiling and shallow oil pans to permit lowering the engines in the car for hood clearance and to lower the center of gravity for improved stability.

8. Air scoops on top of the hood to bleed air off the top of the body and aid in reducing lift while shortening the internal ducting and attending losses.

9. A tapered nose in plan view as well as side view to direct 50% of the air around the sides instead of over the car. This aided in reducing nose lift with the blended nose contour reaching maximum width just aft of the front wheels and slowly tapering to a vertical wedge at the rear. The exhaust headers were kept flush to the side body and directed rearward to promote jet thrust to help accelerate boundary layer air.

10. The underbody behind the front axle is molded to slightly rise with the rate of boundary layer buildup. This was designed in to alleviate the "choking" effect under the car and to provide some rake angle to aid in pitch control. Careful shaping of the nose and underbody resulted in a slight down loading at speed.

11. The underside wheel fairings were extended down as far as possible to reduce interference drag. Toe-in was incorporated to direct air outward and inhibit the "choking" effect between the wheels. The curved underbody accelerates air under the body. The wheel fairings further increase flow by inducing a venturi effect between the wheels which can become critical at speed, hence the toe-in feature to help minimize this effect. You can see these features in the two adjacent photos which clearly show the built-in toe-in applied to the front fairings.

12. It was deemed critical to achieve these results without the addition of horizontal or vertical fins or the addition of ballast weight.

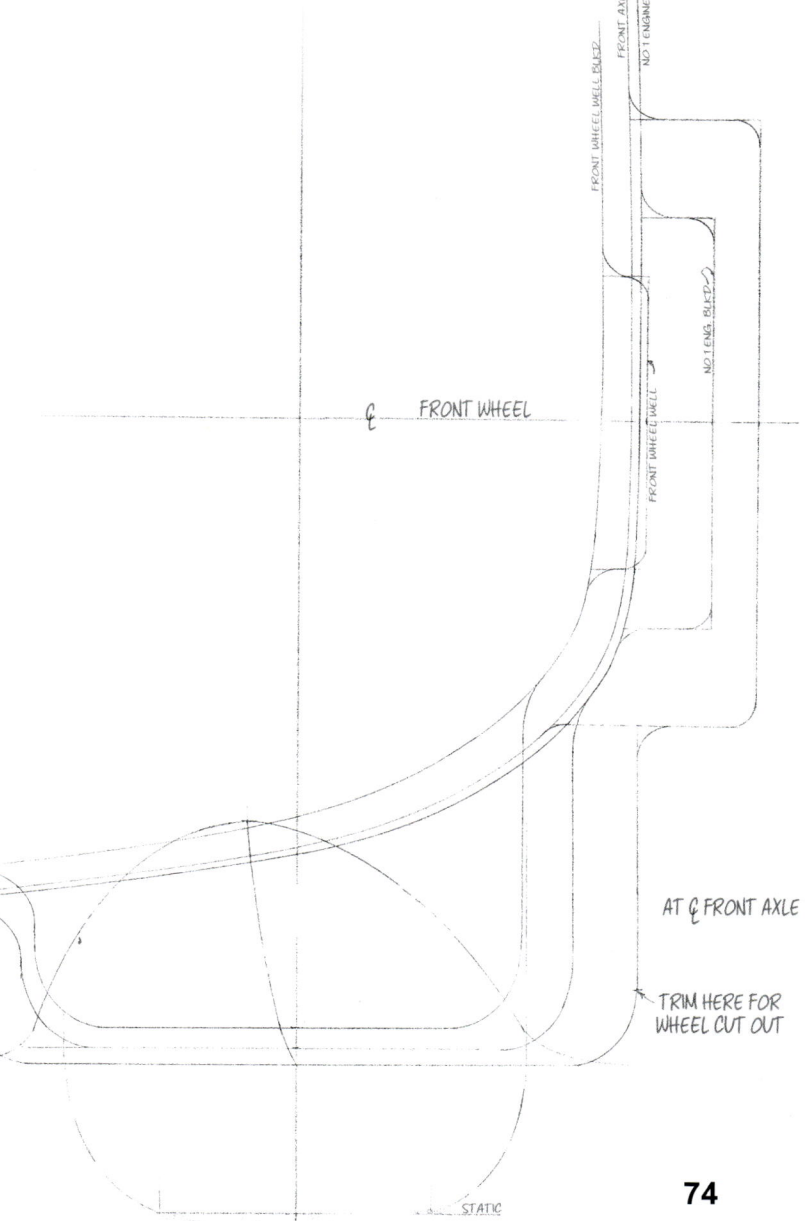

WHEEL HUB & LWR CUT OUT FILLETS - SECTIONS
SUMMERS BROS. WLSR CAR - FULL SIZE
W. KORFF - MARCH 9 '65

GOLDENROD

AERODYNAMICS: Inside the Goldenrod Wind Tunnel Program

Walter Korff kept voluminous notes and delivered several professional papers describing the Goldenrod project. The following commentary on essential Goldenrod design features is excerpted from Korff's original presentation to the American Institute of Aeronautics and Astronautics Symposium (AIAA) in Los Angeles in 1968. It details the entire test regimen and sheds clear light on the Goldenrod's superior aerodynamic qualities and the methods used to achieve them.

The Aerodynamic Design of the Goldenrod to Increase Stability, Traction and Speed

by Walter Korff, April 20th, 1968

Reprinted by permission of the American Institute of Aeronautics and Astronautics, Inc.

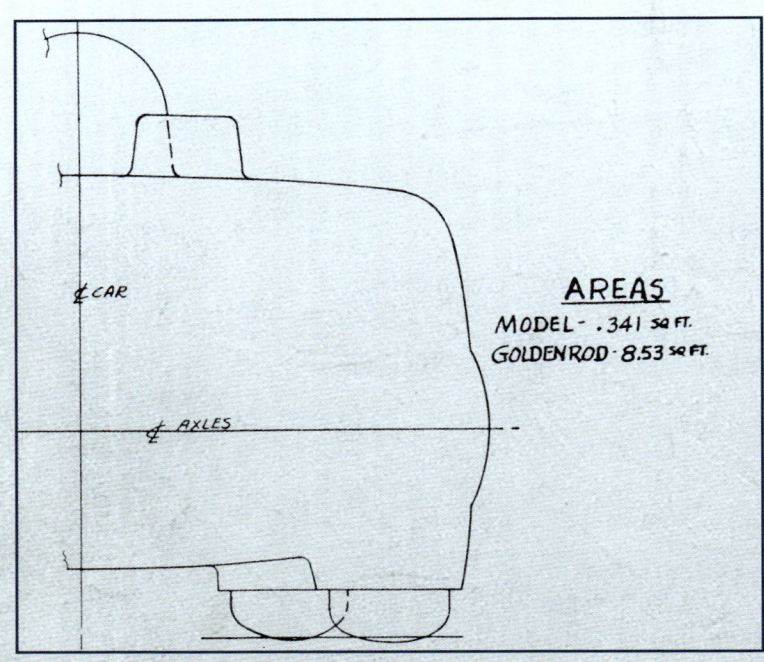

This drawing is one half of the cross-section of the car with a callout indicating the frontal area of the model and the full-size car.

PLANNING CONSIDERATIONS

The wind tunnel program had to be planned before initiation of model construction. Before describing the test program, a remark on the capabilities of such test programs and what the wind tunnel can provide is in order.

The wind tunnel does:

Measure forces and moments.

Provide a means for studying airflow paths on an object.

The wind tunnel will perform tasks 1 and 2 for any reasonable object mounted in its throat — at any angle of pitch, yaw or roll — properly streamlined or not.

GOLDENROD

The wind tunnel does not:

Decide what tests should be made.

Interpret its data.

Design objects or redesign them after a test.

> **Author's Note:** *In fluid mechanics, the Reynolds number (Re) is a non-dimensional number that gives a measure of the ratio of inertial forces to viscous forces for given flow conditions. The Reynolds number is an important parameter that describes whether or not flow conditions lead to laminar or turbulent flow. - JB*

In the final analysis the wind tunnel can be a very useful tool, but as with all tools, the end product varies with the skill and ingenuity of the end user.

In planning the Goldenrod wind tunnel program the following items were considered:

1. As large a model as possible to ensure a high Reynolds number, good detail in model construction and sufficient size to house the load recording mechanism with its strain gauges.

2. Ample length of ground plane ahead of and behind the model.

3. Sufficient tests to determine lift, drag and stability over the expected operating range.

4. Tests so arranged as to provide sufficient information for changes to the final design if required, without additional testing.

The program was thoroughly coordinated with Mr. William Bettes, Director, 10 Ft. Wind Tunnel at the California Institute of Technology, Pasadena, CA. Bill and his staff were most helpful. He obtained special equipment needed (on a loan basis), had the circular mounting plate modified to receive the model and assisted in the calculations.

GOLDENROD

MODEL INSTALLATION & INSTRUMENTATION

A one-fifth scale model size was chosen. This would house the strain gauge mechanism at the center of gravity location and was large enough to ensure good detail in model construction as well as yield reliable data. The electronic strain gauge is mounted on two struts bolted to the circular turntable. The turntable was rotated for directional stability tests. It is installed flush in the ground plane. The standard ground plane is ten feet long and is mounted 38 inches above the tunnel floor. A three-foot additional length was added, giving 13 feet overall for a model about six and a half feet long. The accompanying figure depicts half of the cross-sectional area of the car (page 75). Maximum cross-sectional area equals 49.1 square inches or .341 square feet. This corresponds to 8.53 square feet for the full-size car.

In comparing data, it is important to know how area is figured. In some cases, the maximum cross-section is figured alone. No allowance is made for any area ahead or behind that section that may protrude. For example, our maximum cross-section is at the front wheels. This alone is not as we figured it. We followed aircraft practice by adding the air inlets, the canopy, and the rear wheels even though they are located in smaller cross-sectional areas. The adjacent photos show the model mounted above the turntable. Air flowing along the ground plane builds up a boundary layer. If the model is located so its tires are above the ground plane by the thickness of this boundary layer, more accurate readings are obtained. In our case, 1/4-inch clearance for the model tires is about right. We also wanted to check pitch angles without providing variable adjustment of axle positions. We tilted the complete model by locating the front tires 3/4-inch above the ground plane in some tests and varying the rear tires 1/2-inch from this 3/4-inch mid or neutral position.

Raising the rear to $1\frac{1}{4}$-inch at the rear tires caused a rake angle (pitch) of $-.73°$. Lowering the rear at the tires to 1/4-inch caused a pitch angle of $+.73°$. A pitch angle change of $\pm.73°$ was chosen because this is close to the sum total of suspension and tire deflection variations.

Two nose shapes were tested; a symmetrical nose and one that drooped 1/2-inch at the front. Large differences in body design were not considered as we felt we were close to the desired configuration and wanted to study only small changes. The effects of Reynolds number and small spoilers were also investigated by the use of a series of transition strips and plates located on the nose.

TEST RESULTS & DISCUSSION

The following items were investigated in the wind tunnel test program:

1. The effect of pitch angle on lift (or down load) and pitching moments. Three angles of attack were tested; neutral, .73° up and .73° down.

   This range corresponded to full travel on the suspension with some tire deflection and with one axle at bump and the other at rebound.

2. The effect of nose shape on lift or aerodynamic downforce.

3. Altered ground clearance.

4. Two different tail configurations for directional stability evaluation.

5. Transition strips and spoilers of specified thickness in specified locations to determine if scale effect (Reynolds number) was above the critical range.

6. Tuft studies to learn of any possible critical flow separation, particularly on the surfaces adjacent to the exhaust headers, around wheel fairings and at the rear.

The test run schedule and force moment data sheets from the Goldenrod wind tunnel tests are reproduced on the following pages.

NOSE SHAPE

Test runs number 5, 6 and 7 used the droop nose and runs 11, 12 and 13 used the symmetrical nose. These six tests confirmed our beliefs regarding pitch and lift effects. By directing half or more of the air around the sides of the car instead of nearly all over the top, we minimized pitch effects as well as lift. We achieved a down load as we wanted for increased traction on the salt by nose and underbody design. As you can see, the difference in forces are not great. The long wheelbase and narrow nose and tail yield small differences in pitch forces, too. Tire loading and handling would not be seriously affected. Note too that run #3 with the tires at 1/4-inch clearance shows a C_D = .1165, just as run #5 where the tires cleared the ground plane by 3/4-inch. Although there are small differences in runs #11 and 14 with the symmetrical nose, it is evident that height above the ground is not critical for this design.

TRANSITION STRIPS & SPOILERS

Runs #8, 9 and 10 are similar to run 5 except for the addition of a transition strip at three different distances back from the nose. Runs #17 and 19 are similar to run 18 except for the addition of a spoiler. These tests are related to scale effect or Reynolds numbers. The validity of wind tunnel test data depends in part on scale effect. Slow air flow on a model that is too small does not yield

Small transition strips placed across the nose of the model allowed them to determine the effects of the Reynolds number on scaling.

sufficiently accurate data because the airstream does not flow as it really does on a full-size machine. The boundary layers in the two cases are not similar. It is possible to calculate the transition point on a surface where airflow ceases to be laminar and begins to build a boundary layer. It can also be determined how thick the boundary layer is at any point aft of the transition point. Runs #8, 9, 10, 17 and 19 were tests to determine if the scale or Reynolds number was large enough to provide valid data.

Bill Bettes calculated the strip sizes and locations for these tests. Note that runs #8, 9 and 10 used a thin strip only .007 thick laid across the nose at a distance back from the leading edge. No significant increase in drag occurs over run #5. In fact, run #9 shows a C_D = .1165, exactly the same as run #5. This means that the thickness of the strip is no greater than the boundary layer thickness and the airflow was not disturbed. Separation did not occur. In run #17, a spoiler strip .17" high and 2.4-inches wide was used. It was located .65" back from the leading

GOLDENROD

edge. The drag of the model was $C_D = .1237$. This is just slightly over the drag of run 18 with its $C_D = .1165$ and indicates the airflow has not been tripped to cause separation.

In run #19 a spoiler .40" high and 6" wide was used. It was located further back near the nose and main body joint just ahead of the front wheels. This is also just ahead of the maximum cross-sectional area. In this case, .40" high was enough to trip the airflow and cause separation. It also was located far enough back to prevent a return to smooth airflow very soon. The C_D for this case was .1736, an increase of .0571 or 49%. From this it is clear that a low drag auto body does not need large drag flaps to spoil the flow and increase drag. A small spoiler in the right place is very effective, as it is on sailplanes and modern jet airliners.

TUFT STUDIES

Tufted models are useful in studying airflow paths around the body and identifying areas of separated flow. The adjacent photo shows the tufts in place on the car and flowing practically straight back. These tufts are made of strands of thread taped in place with their upper and low portions free to bend and flow as directed by the wind.

If the air separates from the body contour, the threads whip about like a flag, and the threads fan out. If the flow is smooth, the threads lay tightly to the body surface and stay together. They will bend in the direction of air flow. The behavior of the threads shows what is happening at that point. As air flow progresses back to the rear, it becomes increasingly difficult to avoid separation because of the growth of the boundary layer and because the body surface tapers inward. Wheel fillets and fairings and the extreme aft body are critical areas. Flow around and behind the air inlets can be critical. Flow low on the body near the ground sometimes is a problem.

Tuft studies indicated smooth air paths with no separation. No additional filleting is required.

DIRECTIONAL STABILITY

Runs #4 and #18 investigated directional stability. Run #4 used the body as is with the minimum aft body vertical area. Run #18 used the model with additional fin area in the form of thin aluminum plates mounted in slots on the model above and below. Run #4 indicates in the last column of Table II (page 82), under yaw, a series of numbers, all with plus values and of increasing magnitude. This means that the model is directionally unstable because the plus value of the moment tends to rotate the model further. The values are small, so the instability is not great. Run #18 indicates under yaw, a series of numbers, all (except 1° and 2° yaw) a minus (negative) value and of increasing magnitude. This means that starting with 3° and going upward to higher angles the model is stable because the moment is great enough to tend to return the model to a nearly straight line. If the thin aluminum plates had been thicker and of streamlined cross-section, they would have been a little more sensitive to small changes of yaw angle, thus helping the 1° and 2° positions. Note that drag did not increase significantly up to 7° yaw.

AFTERBODY TAPER

How much taper of the sides is permissible without causing separation and the attendant increase in drag? This question is answered for this model in runs #4 and #18. The sides of the model are smoothly curved from parallel to the centerline of the front axle to a long, nearly straight tapering surface of $3\frac{1}{2}°$ to the centerline in plan view at the rear axle. We knew this $3\frac{1}{2}°$ angle could be exceeded if it were blended smoothly, but by how much? The yaw tests show

GOLDENROD

Tuft test with strips of yarn proved Korff's design was aerodynamically sound. The air remained attached to the body for the entire length of the car with no sign of turbulence. Extensive tests were conducted with the car at varying degrees of rake, pitch, and yaw.

no increase in drag up to nearly 7°, i.e., a 10½° taper. This compares favorably with the 10° recommended for the roof line by Dr. Kamm and Mr. Gondert in Reference 3. (*This refers to a streamlined sports car body previously designed by Korff - not shown*). The author's design had a taper of 9° on each side and did not experience separation. Possibly this could have been increased 1° more. This information may be of value for use on designs of future cars.

> **Author's Note:** *In the case of the Goldenrod, the necessary packaging of the wide Hemi engines prevented Korff from tapering the body further than the indicated 3½°. - JB*

How much variation between under plane and ground plane can be tolerated without an increase in drag? Ground effect makes this angle more sensitive than the taper angle of the sides, I believe. However, small angles like the .73° of runs #5, 6 and 7 and 11, 12 and 13 show virtually no change in drag coefficients. I would hesitate to alter this underbody angle any more than about 1° without supporting test data. The additional interference effects of the wheels, tread width, ground clearance, air inlets and/or outlets, exhaust pipes and suspension members can also have a definite influence on lift as well as drag and air flow separation on the underbody of any new design. Do not neglect or eliminate this portion of a test program.

GOLDENROD

GOLDENROD WIND TUNNEL TEST PROGRAM RUN SCHEDULE - TABLE I

Run No.	Configuration	Dynamic Pressure q	Remarks
1	Droop nose — Model shakedown and Reynolds No. checks	30	Front and rear wheels ¼ in. from ground plane
2	Droop nose — Model shakedown and Reynolds No. checks	40	Front and rear wheels ¼ in. from ground plane
3	Droop nose	50	Front and rear wheels ¼ in. from ground plane
4	Droop nose	50	Directional stability runs; rotate model through 1-15° increments
5	Droop nose	50	Raise model; front and rear wheels ¾ in. from ground plane
6	Droop nose	50	Nose up pitch; front wheels ¾ in. and rear wheels ¼ in. from ground plane
7	Droop nose	50	Nose down pitch; front wheels ¼ in. and rear wheels ¾ in. from ground plane
8	Droop nose w/transition strip 1-5/8 in. back	50	Wheels ¾ in. from ground plane; add transition strip 0.007 in. thick
9	Droop nose w/transition strip 0.333 in. back	50	Wheels ¾ in. from ground plane; add transition strip 0.007 in. thick
10	Droop nose w/two transition strips 0.333 in. and 19 in. back	50	Wheels ¾ in. from ground plane; add transition strip 0.007 in. thick
11	Symmetrical nose	50	Wheels ¾ in. from ground plane
12	Symmetrical nose	50	Nose down pitch; front wheels ¾ in. and rear wheels 1-¼ in. from ground plane
13	Symmetrical nose	50	Nose up pitch; front wheels ¾ in. and rear wheels ¼ in. from ground plane
14	Symmetrical nose	50	Neutral position w/both wheels ¼ in. from ground plane
15	Droop nose with tufts	50	Neutral position w/both wheels ¼ in. from ground plane
16	Droop nose with probe only	50	Visual low speed: same position as above
17	Droop nose with spoiler 0.17 in. high and 0.65 in. back	50	Neutral position w/both wheels ¼ in. from ground plane
18	Droop nose with tail fin upper and lower	50	Neutral position w/both wheels ¼ in. from ground plane
19	Droop nose with tail fin plus spoiler No.2 (0.40 in. high and 1 in. forward of main body)	50	Neutral position w/both wheels ¼ in. from ground plane
Notes:	Engine air inlets were faired with clay for smooth airflow over inlet upper surface. All model gaps, including strut entry points, were sealed to eliminate model internal airflow.		

GOLDENROD FORCE & MOMENT TEST DATA - TABLE II

Force and Moment Data in Coefficient Form
Stability Access Coefficients

		Degrees		Forces			Moments		
				Lift	Drag	Cross Wind	Pitch	Roll	Yaw
Run No.	q, psf	a_g	ψ_g	$C_L = C_{Ls}$	C_{Ds}	C_{Cs}	C_{ms} c.g.	C_{is} c.g.	C_{ns} c.g.
1	30	0	0	-0.2216	+0.1160	-0.0419	+0.0251	-0.0003	+0.0034
2	40	0	0	-0.2181	+0.1170	-0.0635	+0.0248	-0.0005	-0.0014
3	50	0	0	-0.2164	+0.1165	-0.0343	+0.0229	-0.0003	-0.0042
4	50	0	-1	-0.2247	+0.1165	+0.0963	+0.0235	+0.0006	+0.0120
			0	-0.2164	+0.1165	+0.0093	+0.0229	+0.0001	+0.0063
			+1	-0.2335	+0.1165	+0.0157	+0.0223	+0.0007	+0.0101
			+2	-0.2164	+0.1165	+0.0018	+0.0229	+0.0010	+0.0140
			+3	-0.2429	+0.1165	+0.0198	+0.0175	+0.0023	+0.0231
			+4	-0.2003	+0.1165	+0.0809	+0.0182	+0.0031	+0.0375
			+5	-0.1665	+0.1192	+0.1163	+0.0177	+0.0033	+0.0488
			+7	-0.1249	+0.1192	+0.1959	+0.0131	+0.0045	+0.0759
			+10	-0.0039	+0.1210	+0.2865	+0.0245	+0.0071	+0.1232
			+15	+0.0764	+0.1210	+0.5394	+0.1076	+0.0123	+0.1803
5	50	0	0	-0.1806	+0.1165	-0.0260	+0.0233	-0.0002	-0.0067
6	50	+.73	0	-0.2098	+0.1103	-0.0039	+0.0635	-0.0001	-0.0067
7	50	-.73	0	-0.1991	+0.1146	-0.0529	-0.0265	-0.0006	-0.0045
8	50	0	0	-0.1731	+0.1201	-0.0227	+0.0185	-0.0002	-0.0087
9	50	0	0	-0.1682	+0.1165	-0.0428	+0.0192	-0.0003	-0.0053
10	50	0	0	-0.1696	+0.1210	-0.0260	+0.0190	-0.0002	-0.0067
11	50	0	0	-0.1715	+0.1156	-0.0429	+0.0180	-0.0003	-0.0071
12	50	-.73	0	-0.1652	+0.1186	-0.0512	-0.0270	-0.0003	-0.0046
13	50	+.73	0	-0.1666	+0.1144	-0.0241	+0.0677	-0.0019	-0.0050
14	50	0	0	-0.2069	+0.1192	-0.0343	+0.0194	-0.0003	-0.0042
17	50	0	0	-0.2050	+0.1237	0	+0.0204	0	0
18	50	0	-1	-0.1975	+0.1200	+0.0042	+0.0238	-0.0024	+0.0067
			0	-0.1975	+0.1165	-0.0258	+0.0237	-0.0013	-0.0032
			+1	-0.2094	+0.1165	+0.0172	+0.0238	+0.0016	+0.0021
			+2	-0.2164	+0.1165	+0.0597	+0.0229	+0.0031	+0.0022
			+3	-0.2221	+0.1165	+0.1154	+0.0197	+0.0054	-0.0013
			+4	-0.1936	+0.1165	+0.1861	+0.0178	+0.0079	-0.0081
			+5	-0.1535	+0.1183	+0.2516	+0.0143	+0.0101	-0.0173
			-7	-0.0998	+0.1219	+0.3705	+0.0114	+0.0152	-0.0371
			+10	-0.0277	+0.1174	+0.5214	+0.0298	+0.0215	-0.0600
19	50	0	0	-0.1949	+0.1736	-0.0312	+0.0290	+0.0019	-0.0087

Pitch angle was only slightly affected in the case of the Goldenrod. This would rarely be the case with cars of shorter wheelbase and greater bump and rebound wheel travel. Pitch forces are normally unstable on any vehicle without a horizontal tail surface. Nose pitch up at high speed, if severe, could easily more than double the lift forces. This could aggravate other forces and reduce steering and braking ability. There is little or nothing the driver can do under such conditions.

FINAL DESIGN & FABRICATION

Right after the wind tunnel tests, the electronic data was air-mailed back to Chrysler Engineering to be programmed on Chrysler's computers. This was a favor to us because of all the time it would save. The data was mailed along with written information as to its programming. In all fairness to the engineers who set it up, I want to point out that they had to do this strange program without benefit of person-to-person coordination. It also had to be sandwiched into their other work. In addition, this was occurring when key people were taking Christmas vacations.

When the data came back, parts of it looked a little strange to me. The drag data looked good, but I couldn't find consistency in the moment data. We had visions of an automobile bucking like a bronco at high speed, and this was the thing we thought had been carefully designed out of the car. In desperation, I began to see if I could stabilize it with a horizontal fin behind the driver. The more I used the data, the more I was convinced that something went wrong with the assumptions in the programming. By this time, Bob needed body information and could no longer wait. I wouldn't give it to him because I couldn't stabilize the car.

So he and I rushed out to see Bill Bettes at Cal Tech for a review of the wind tunnel data.

Bill agreed portions of the program were in error and began to spot erroneous assumptions. The Chrysler people were anxious to re-program as required, but there was no time. Bill took on the job and worked long and hard over a weekend. Anyone who has experience with computers realizes how easily programming can be in error. This is mentioned to point out the need for experience in interpreting this great mass of information that is subject to so much processing.

A number of changes were required in going from model to full-size automobile both as a result of the wind tunnel program and detail design problems. The major changes are listed here.

1. The overall length of the vehicle was increased 10%. Wheelbase and overhang front and rear were kept in proportion; each increased 10%. This change occurred because certain components were larger than we expected.

2. The front transmission had to be tilted up in front about 5° to get inside the nose contour on the underside. We used the droop nose to help this situation. The nose frame also had to be altered.

3. The rake angle (pitch down in front) was increased about one-third of a degree (.3°) to assist the nose down requirement of item 2 above and because we wanted a definite down load.

4. The air inlets were moved further aft and could not be given the direct original path to the vees between the cylinder banks. There was insufficient time to redesign the engine area, so we directed the air inlets to a mid point between the 1 and 2 engines and the

3 and 4 engines. This entailed more bends and vanes and some additional internal duct losses. This became another concern on the salt as we will see later.

5. Parachute cans required a little more room than we expected as may be seen by comparing model and car. The cans were kept as small as possible, stacked vertically and used all the space behind the cockpit.

These moments of change and redesign are a most hectic period of any project for the designers, the coordinating engineers and the shop people who are trying to build the vehicle. The designer is called upon to compromise his brainchild because of interferences that no one anticipated. Engineers find errors in their own or someone else's calculations and the shop people wonder why the people who make pretty pictures and play with numbers can't make up their minds. We certainly had our share of these problems, and we are happy to say that we are all still friends. Changes were made and everybody worked longer to meet the tight schedules.

ESTIMATED PERFORMANCE & POWER REQUIRED

Automobile performance calculation is relatively straightforward and reasonably accurate when good test data are available. Wind tunnel data can be accurate and rolling resistance data is available for tires on practically every surface except the Bonneville Salt Flats. Moisture content of the salt increases rolling resistance up to as much as several times the value for dry salt. This is the large unknown in calculations. I assumed that the lowest rolling resistance would occur on dry salt at 100 psi tire pressure. Tire pressure is normally much higher, but in my

---

HIGH PRAISE

Thrust SSC aerodynamicist Ron Ayers later declared that the *"Goldenrod is perhaps the most beautiful of all LSR cars, being both functional and elegant."*

He noted that the Summers Brothers' solution to stacking the greatest amount of power possible behind the smallest possible frontal area was:

"...breathtakingly simple. They achieved a bhp per square foot of frontal area nearly three times greater than Donald Campbell's Bluebird."

"If I had to design a wheel-driven record contender I could not improve on Goldenrod using piston engines."

One might consider that high praise indeed coming directly from the esteemed designer of the world's first supersonic land speed record car. - *JB*

From MotorSport Magazine - October 2001

GOLDENROD

Korff's notations are specific with regard to the highly streamlined scoops. A sharp splitter at the lower front of the scoop splits the boundary layer gently around the base of the scoop so it can remain attached and rejoin relatively undisturbed via the aft taper. This allows the scoop itself to run in clean air. The scoop opening is sized to feed engine demand (two engines) at speed. It is positioned above the boundary layer.

estimation, this will not lower rolling resistance. The salt then deflects instead of the tire. This is fine for the tire, but it doesn't reduce the power required to push it. When the lowest coefficients are used in a calculation, we must realize that we then get the highest performance estimates. Rarely will a machine go faster. It can only go slower. Wet salt accumulation on the body, particularly in critical areas, underbody, wheel fillets, etc., can trip the boundary layer and increase drag by unknown amounts. They cannot be kept clean during a run on wet salt, so this is a factor. Also, I am not in a position to prove my assumptions on rolling resistance, but will welcome any new data or findings.

Wind resistance was calculated as described in SAE Paper 649B, January 1963 - Korff, W. H. A sample calculation for wind resistance and rolling resistance at a velocity of 500 mph is shown (page 87). Note that rolling resistance is a result of aerodynamic down load as well as the weight of the car. It should be pointed out that aerodynamic down load is superior to weight or ballast because it does not add mass to be accelerated. For the 500 mph calculation we get:

Wind Resistance.. 749 HP
Rolling Resistance Due to Weight............ 1054 HP
Rolling Resistance Due to Down Load...... 109 HP
Total Horsepower Required.......................... 1912 HP

The large-mouth scoops used when setting the record had openings with nearly five times the area of the more aerodynamic Summers/Herda scoops. They were thought necessary to compensate for a perceived lack of inlet airflow.

Assuming 10% losses for the powertrain and 2,400 HP at the flywheels, we net 2,160 HP at the wheel hubs. This nets a bit more than the minimum required for 500 mph. It should be realized that absolute terminal velocity cannot be reached unless an infinite distance is available to accelerate in. The extra 248 HP is the amount left for acceleration.

> **Author's Note:** *The faster you go, the less time you have to accelerate in each mile approaching the timed mile. On a very long course, the cooling system would have to be further optimized to deal with the evolving heat load. - JB*

For all practical purposes, slightly over 500 mph can be assumed to be terminal velocity for the Goldenrod on dry salt for a long course. If run at sea level on a longer course, and with less rolling resistance on a harder surface, the speed should further increase. Some increase in power is also quite possible from these engines and would add to the speed. However, tires operate well on the salt, particularly if moist. A hard, dry surface would increase the tire hazard. It was assumed that duct losses plus altitude cancel ram air gains. Originally, ram air would have been a bit higher, but last minute changes increased the number of bends internally, so losses increased another 3-4%. It should also be realized that ram air is not available at low speed; it builds up slowly. Therefore, engines run richer and power is less at low speeds. Engine power cannot peak most of the time, only momentarily in each gear. Powertrain loss was assumed to be 10%. This is true only in high gear. More accurate figures might be first gear 87%, second gear 88%, third gear 89%. There is also a loss of time and distance with every shift.

Chrysler engineering figured acceleration in greater detail than I did by considering the gear ratios and efficiencies and the power curves for these engines at altitude. By comparison, my simplified approach is optimistic in speed and distance by about 4% for the Bonneville course. We did agree that the existing record could be exceeded in third gear. It was.

APPENDIX A: Power Required - Sample Calculations

The horsepower required to overcome aerodynamic drag and rolling resistance at a velocity u in feet per second is:

Equation A-1

$$HP_{Req} = u/550 \, (Drag_{Aero} + Drag_{Rolling})$$

where the aerodynamic drag and rolling resistance are given in pounds.

The aerodynamic drag is given by:

Equation A-2

$$Drag_{Aero} = 1/2 \, \rho_o \, \sigma \, u^2 \, S \, C_D$$

where:

ρ_o = mass density of air at sea level ~ slugs/ft³
σ = ratio of air density at altitude to sea level density (non-dimensional)
u = velocity (ft/sec)
S = vehicle reference area (frontal) (ft²)
C_D = drag coefficient (non-dimensional)

For the sample case considered, i.e. 500 mph run at Bonneville,

ρ_o = 0.0023769 slugs/ft³
σ = 0.882
u = 734 ft/sec
S = 8.53 ft²
C_D = 0.1165

and we have:

$$Drag_{Aero} = 1/2 \times 0.0023769 \times 0.882 \times 734^2 \times 8.53 \times 0.1165$$

$$Drag_{Aero} = 561 \text{ lbs.}$$

The tire rolling resistance is given by:

Equation A-3

$$Drag_{Rolling} = N \, [0.005 + (0.15/P) + (0.00403u)^2/P]$$

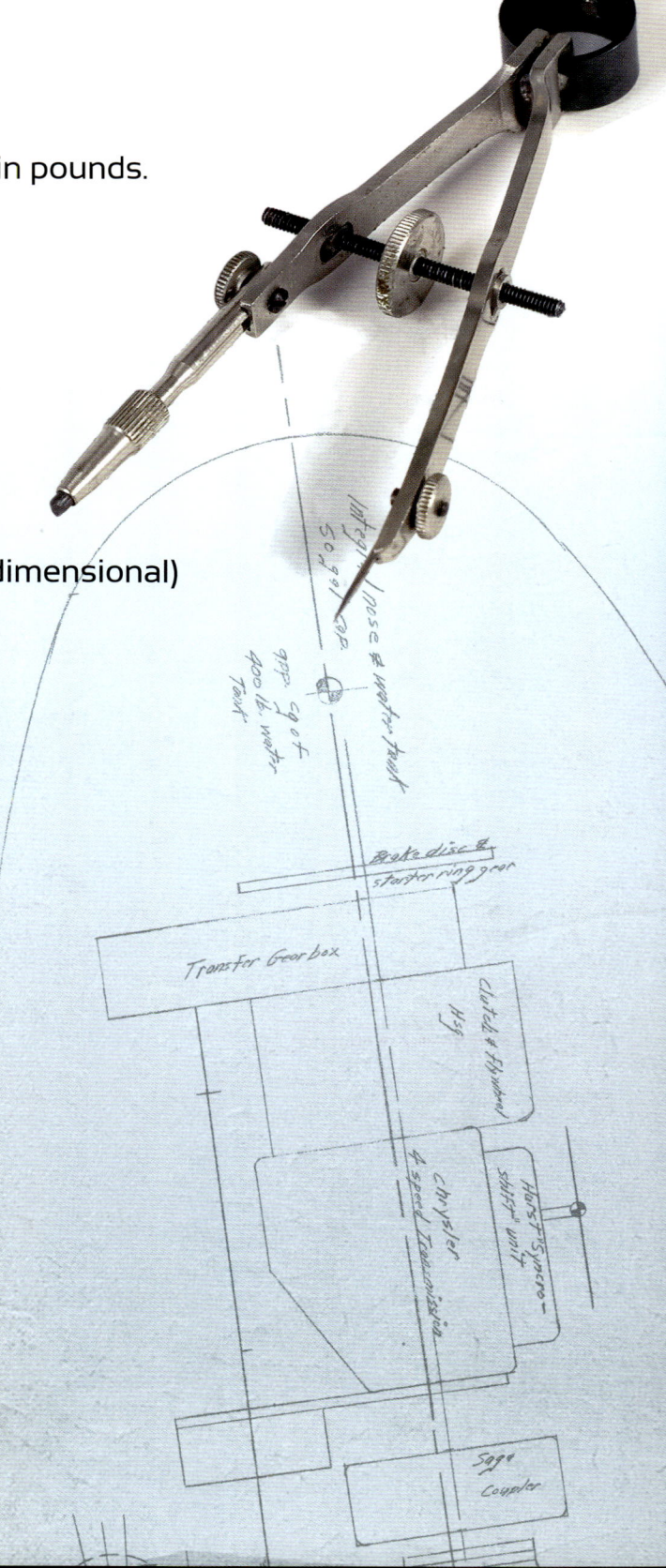

where:

N = normal load on the tires in lbs.
P = tire pressure in lbs/in^2
u = velocity (ft/sec)

For the present case a value of 100 psi is used regardless of tire pressure since the salt deflects if the tire does not.

The tire normal load is composed of two parts, the vehicle static weight, w = 8400 lbs. and the aerodynamic lift or down load, Lift$_{Aero}$

Considering first the effect of static weight, the previous equation yields:

$Drag_{Rolling_W}$ = 8400 [0.005 + (0.15/100) + (0.00403 x 734)^2/100]

$Drag_{Rolling_W}$ = 8400 lbs. x .094 = 790 lbs.

The aerodynamic down load is computed with Equation A-2 with C_D being replaced by the lift coefficient (C_L) which for this example is equal to -0.1806.

$Lift_{Aero}$ = 1/2 ρ_o σ u^2 $S C_L$

$Lift_{Aero}$ = 1/2 x 0.0023769 x 0.882 x 734^2 x 8.53 x -0.1806

$Lift_{Aero}$ = - 870 lbs.

The negative sign indicates an aerodynamic down load or addition to the tire normal load.

Using this value in Equation A-3 we realize:

$Drag_{Rolling}$ = 870 [0.005 + (0.15/100) + (0.00403 x 734)^2/100] = 870 x .094

$Drag_{Rolling_L}$ = 82 lbs.

Horsepower is now computed with Equation A-1.

HP_{Req} = 734/550 (561 + 790 + 82)

= 1.3345 x 1433

HP_{Req} = 1,912 HP

Note: With minor corrections for typos on the original handouts.

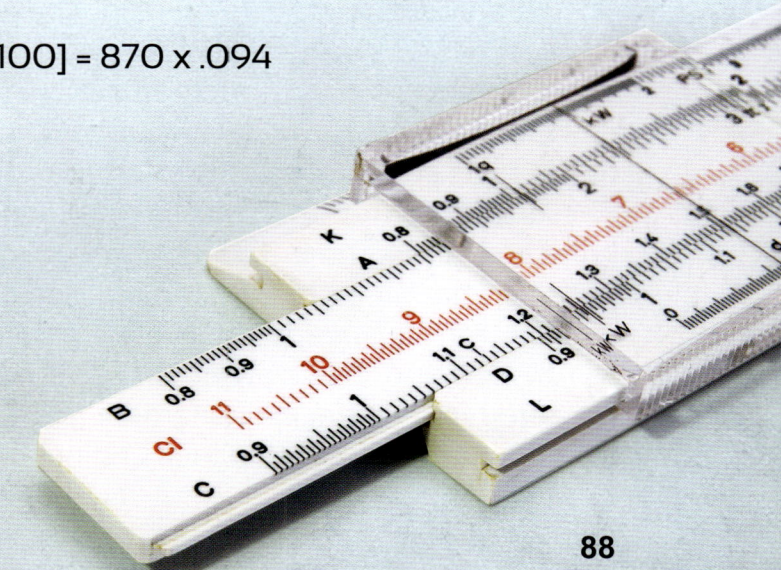

GOLDENROD

AERODYNAMICS:
THE AIR SCOOP CONTROVERSY

"The scoops used on the record runs were about three times the area of the original scoops. The original scoops, each of which was designed to feed two engines, had openings about 2½ to 3 inches high and 6 inches wide."

- Walter Korff

Goldenrod's record was set using the tall, large-mouth scoops specified by Chrysler engineers. These scoops were fabricated on site when a starvation problem was suspected and attributed to the high-speed scoops with smaller openings. The engineers felt that the streamlined scoops fabricated by Summers and Bob Herda were not passing enough air to feed the big Hemi engines at lower vehicle speeds, thus causing the engines to run rich and lose power. While responsibility for aerodynamic decisions largely lay with Korff, the engineers insisted that their engines would not

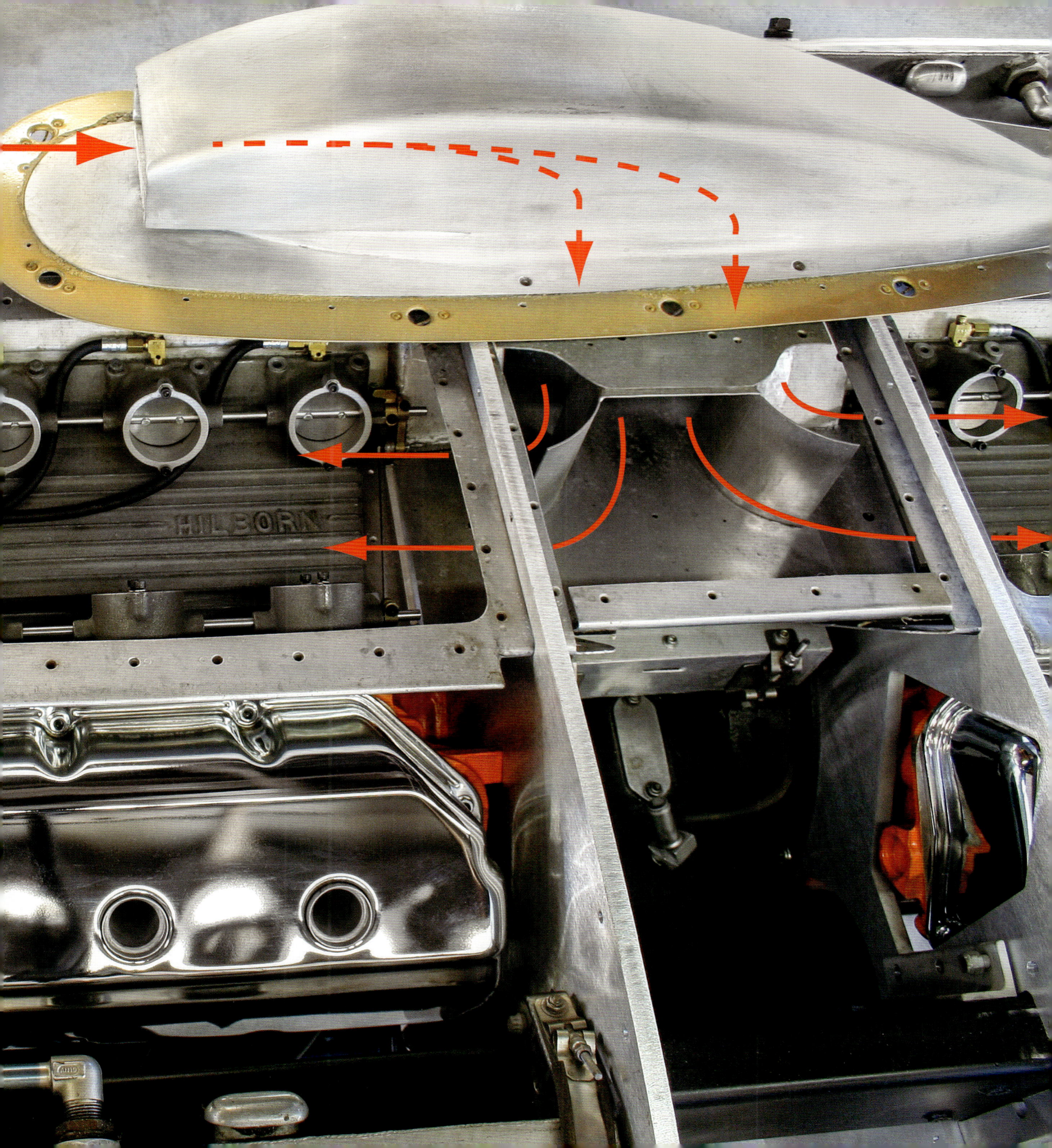

GOLDENROD

The crude but effective record scoops were an attempt to grab much more air at lower speeds. They worked, but incurred a significant drag penalty. The design of the aero scoops is based on a classic nacelle scoop shape seen on many prop-driven aircraft. The volume increase inside the center part of the scoop allows the air to lose velocity and make the turn into the intake feeder boxes. Air passing over the scoop flows smoothly off of the rear taper.

deliver the maximum available power unless the inlet airflow path was substantially enlarged to ensure adequate airflow at lower speeds.

The record scoops (409.277 mph) were a crude departure from the elegant design of the high-speed scoops which complemented the car's design perfectly. Both sets of scoops incorporated internal directional vanes to turn the air into the ductwork, but the streamlined scoops designed and fabricated with coaching from Korff featured a carefully calculated inlet opening to match predicted airflow requirements at elevated speeds. They also incorporated a gentle expanding arc as they tapered to the rear. This provided an area change allowing the incoming air to expand and slow down before making the turn into the ductwork. Whatever drag penalty that may have accrued with the large scoops was never quantified and they did prove effective enough to snag the long-standing record. With the high-speed aero scoops installed the car proved faster, with nearly a 15 mph increase the next morning. The 425.99 mph pass reinforced the effectiveness of the purpose-built scoops and also proved that the large-mouth scoops were likely unnecessary as the engines exhibited no breathing problems once all the calibration issues were solved.

Chrysler's Joe Nunez, seen here performing plug checks, was the factory performance engineer assigned to field operations with the Goldenrod project.

GOLDENROD

Korff has stated that ducting losses increased on the order of 4%, but it is hard to imagine a more elegant solution to feeding two big hungry Chrysler Hemis when they're breathing hard. This arrangement allowed the scoops to be positioned on opposite sides of the car so that both scoops could run in clean, unobstructed air. According to Crosby, they recorded a maximum ram pressure of 5 psi in the air boxes at speed.

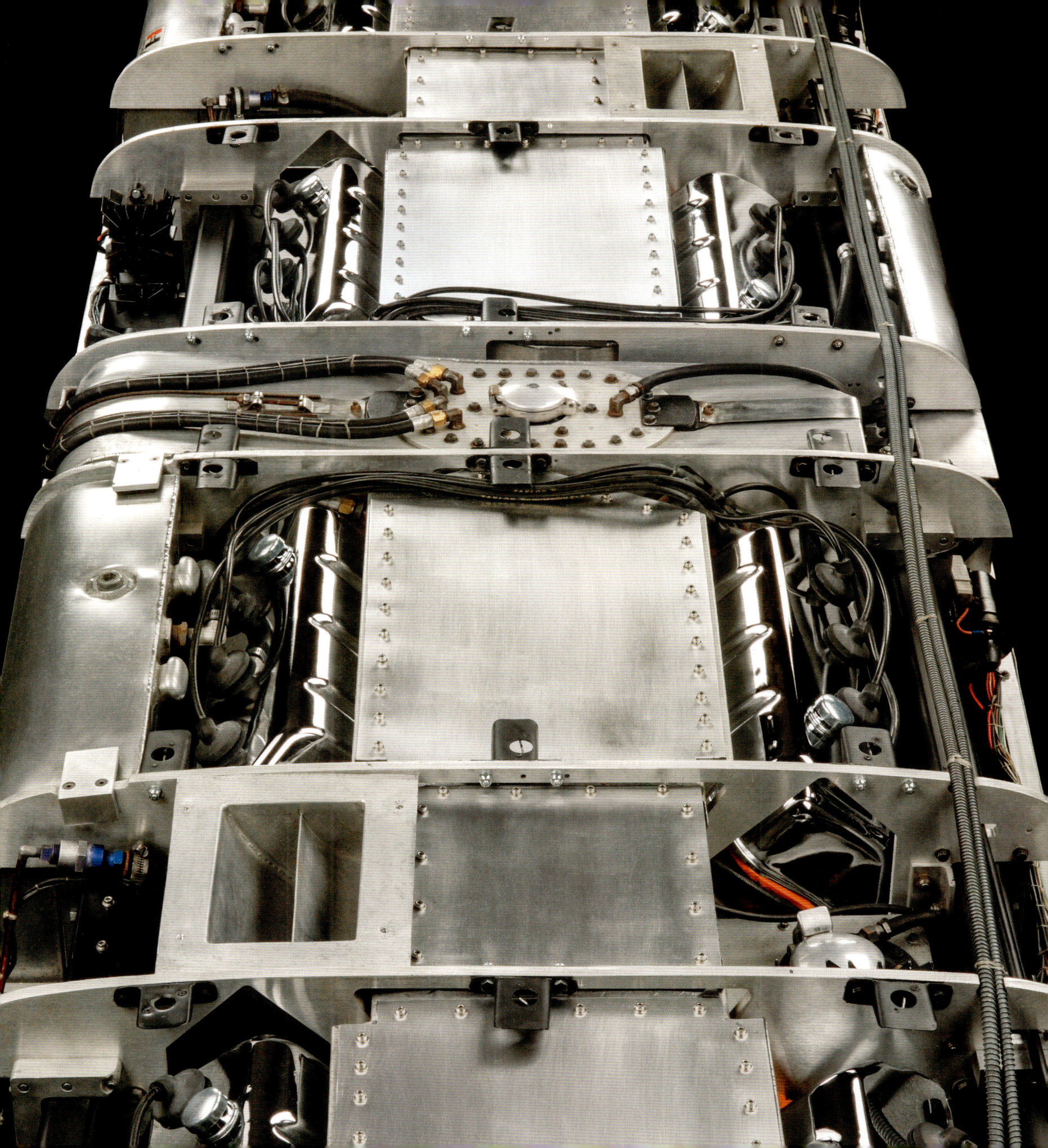

AERODYNAMICS:
JACK "Willie" SUTTON - MASTER FABRICATOR

Jack "Willie" Sutton never got the real recognition he deserved for hand-fabricating the Goldenrod's intricate multi-piece body panels from .064 3003 aluminum alloy provided by Harvey Aluminum.

Sutton, a master metal former, apprenticed at age 14, honing his skills in the British aircraft industry during WWII. Immigrating to America in the early fifties, Sutton made a name for himself fabricating custom bodies for Indy cars, custom cars, and racing vehicles. He worked on many cars for well-known luminaries such as Mickey Thompson, Ak Miller, and Max Bachowsky. He rode motorcycles with Steve McQueen and crafted the sleek, racy lines of Lee Taylor's Harvey Aluminum water speed record boat. Tasked with creating Walter Korff's wind-tunnel-honed Goldenrod body to exact scale, Sutton meticulously hand-formed every panel to perfection in his North Hollywood shop.

Master craftsman Jack Sutton forming the complex shape for the Goldenrod cockpit and rolling one of the under-body panels (below).

Willie crafted the Harvey Aluminum Indy cars and made the cover of *Hot Rod Magazine* when he created the stunning bodywork for Ak Miller's "Mille Miglia" sports racer. Max Balchowsky's spectacular "Old Yeller" race cars and the stunning one-off Ferrari nose above also sprang from his talented hands. Bob Summers sought the best in the business to fabricate the Goldenrod body, and it remains a fitting testament to Sutton's legacy of extraordinary craftsmanship.

AERODYNAMICS:
JACK "Willie" SUTTON - MASTER FABRICATOR

Sutton created external access doors for critical components so they could easily be accessed for service. As seen to the left, each opening accepted a door with a locking tab on one side and one or more Dzus fasteners to secure it.

Jack Sutton's metal mastery is seen on virtually every panel. All of the curves are perfectly matched, and all of the openings are rolled and stiffened, particularly around the tires and the exhaust openings.

Korff's design achieved exceptional stability with low drag by utilizing the tail and upper portion of the cockpit as an integral fin. Jack Sutton was challenged to create these compound shapes in metal, which he masterfully rendered as seen here.

Jack was meticulous in his metal craftsmanship, and he often worked and reworked panels to ensure the most perfect fit possible.

Riddled with the bullet holes of neglect, the stripped body panels revealed the extent of corrosion damage around all the openings and Dzus fasteners.

Flying Colors Aero Paints at the Riverside, CA, airport carefully stripped all the panels with aircraft stripper to prevent further damage to the metal. Every Dzus button on the bottom of the car had to be repaired and the adjacent body panel fully reworked and prepped for new paint.

From his aircraft and boat experience, Sutton was a master at forming large panels with perfect curves as seen here wrapping around the bulkheads.

Compound shapes like the wheel fairings are fashioned from multiple pieces of Harvey Aluminum welded together and hammered into their final shape.

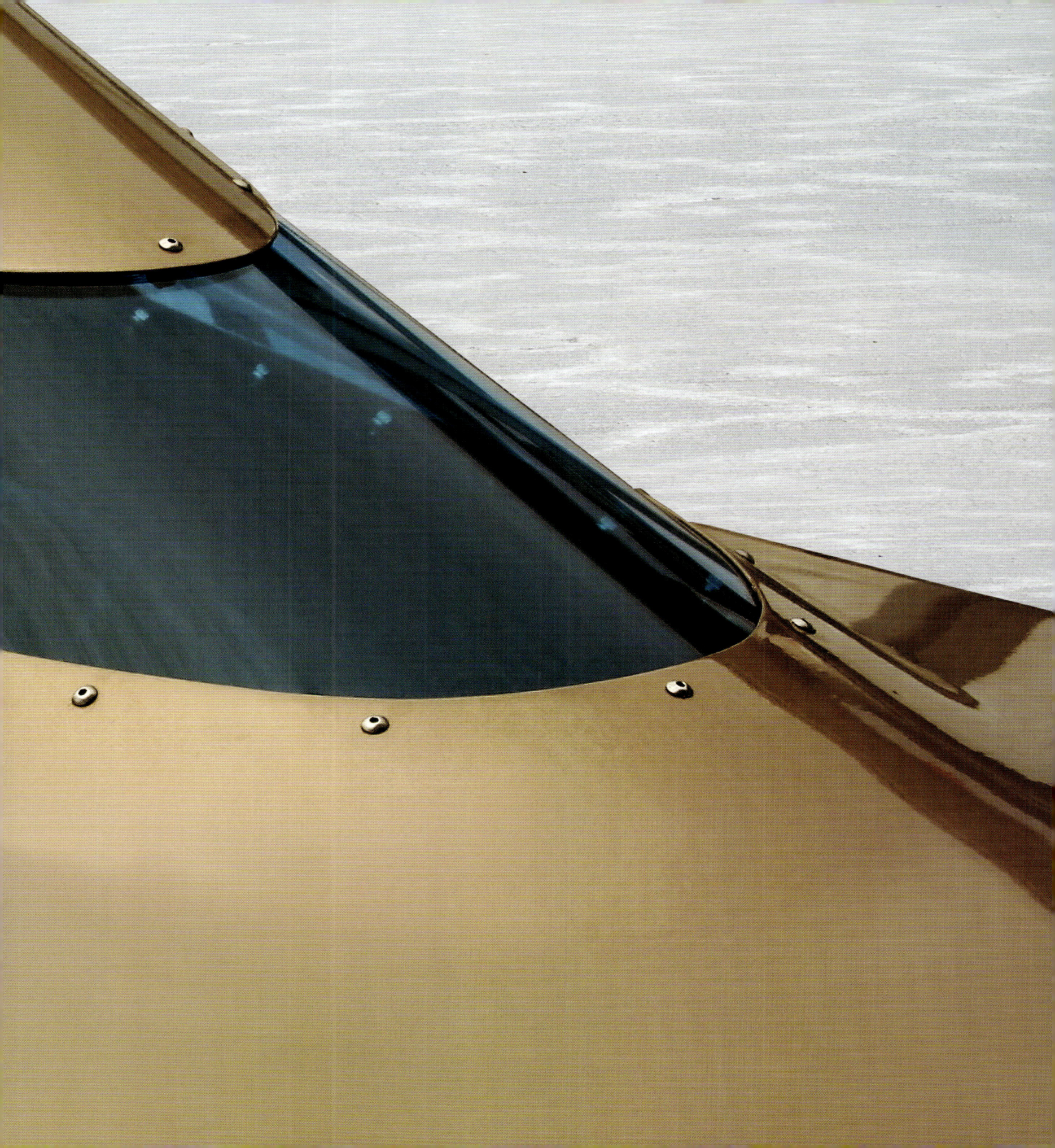

AERODYNAMICS:
RECORD BUSTERS IN THE NEWS

LOCKHEED STAR

December 16, 1965

RECORD ROD—Lockheed engineer Walt Korff, 74-51, left, stands with Bob Summers who drove the Goldenrod to a new world's land speed record at Bonneville Salt Flats. Korff designed car's body.

Shape of Record-Busting Auto Designed by Lockheed Engineer

When the rapier-like Goldenrod streaked across Bonneville Salt Flats to set a new world's wheel-driven land speed record there was no happier man than Walt Korff, a research engineer in 74-51.

The long (32 feet), low (28 inches) silhouette of the car that brought the record to the U.S. for the first time since 1928 proved out Korff's auto body design ideas in a 409-mph burst of speed.

Auto body design is the veteran Lockheed engineer's avocation.

Several years ago, youthful Bob and Bill Summers, a pair of accomplished hot-rodders from Ontario, approached him. They dreamed of building a car to attack the wheel-driven record. Would Korff help?

He did. Korff worked with the Summers brothers through preliminary design, 19 wind tunnel tests at CalTech, and final design.

Unlike many record cars for which a body shell has been designed around a chassis, principal designer Bob Summers designed the chassis to fit the body.

Chrysler — who supplied the four Hemi engines that deliver power to all four wheels—even redesigned the engines, replacing standard carburetion systems with low profile fuel injection so as to shoehorn the engines into the low, lean shape.

Firestone, Mobile Oil, and Hurst joined Chrysler and other sponsors to back the project.

With Bob Summers at the wheel, the Goldenrod barreled to the world's record of 409.277 mph last month. There is more potential in the car. The record was set in third gear.

Korff points out that engineering involved in the wheel-driven record car is somewhat more applicable to everyday cars than that involved in the jet-powered cars which now hold the absolute land speed record.

Korff points to what he feels were design breakthroughs:

The body in wind tunnel tests achieved the lowest drag coefficient (.117) ever recorded for an auto shape.

No directional fin is required for stability; the car actually has been driven hands off at 200 mph, Korff says.

Air flow forces the car down at high speed instead of lifting it as it does with a conventionally designed car.

How can such design results affect the cars we drive?

The answer to this question is contained in a paper on automotive aerodynamics Korff delivered to the Automotive Engineering Congress sponsored by the Society of Automotive Engineers at Detroit in 1963.

Proper streamlining of the cars we drive on the new non-stop expressways and freeways could:

Give us quieter cars with less wind buffeting.

Improve fuel economy. Korff predicts reduction of fuel bills by 35 per cent with no reduction in performance.

Eliminate lift which adversely affects stability and braking control.

Allow 25 to 35 per cent higher speeds from given horsepower.

And result in a lower cost car with equivalent performance because a smaller, less powerful engine and power train could be used with lighter chassis components. Initial cost of our cars could be lowered by 10 per cent or more, Korff estimates.

Right now Korff is working on an experimental sports car body and designing a formula road racer to provide further tests for his ideas.

AUTOMOTIVE
The Why Doesn't Matter; New Speed Record Does

BY BOB THOMAS, Times Auto Editor

It never pays to ask a mountain climber why he challenges a mountain. The answer is always the same. "Because it's there."

By the same token, never ask a man why he attempts to break the land speed record—or his neck. His answer will be as vague. He's not really sure either.

But, thank Heaven, the breed exists. And it has since "hot-rodder" Henry Ford became the first American to set a land speed mark in 1904—91 m.p.h.

Out of this ingenuity are born myriad things for a mobile age. The newest big names on this unusual speed horizon are a Southern California pair who are defying the jet age.

They're the Summers brothers of Ontario—Bob and Bill. A couple of "boy next door" types, they're confident that the general public are discerning enough to recognize what they're trying to do.

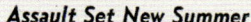

Assault Set New Summer

The Summers brothers are deep in the creation of a 400 to 500 m.p.h. piston-powered automobile for a special assault on speed next summer on the Bonneville Salt Flats.

They are doing it in the face of a series of much ballyhooed land speed record performances by jet-powered "cars" over the famed Utah salt flat. And they have no expectations of eclipsing the mark of 536.71 m.p.h. which was established there by Art Arfons of Akron in his jet engine on wheels, the "Green Monster."

But they are attacking their problem a bit more honestly perhaps—in the tradition of Ford, Englishman Malcolm Campbell in the 1930s (301 m.p.h.) and John Cobb in the 1940s (394 m.p.h.), Mickey Thompson in 1960 (406 m.p.h. unofficially) and the current axle-driven champ, Donald Campbell (403 m.p.h.), son of Sir Malcolm.

Difference of Jet and Wheel

"We want to do the ultimate in this type of car," said Bob, the 27-year-old builder-driver better known as "Butch."

"I sort of feel the public is aware of the difference," he continued in reference to the contrast between a wheel-driven and jet machine. "I'm sure they'll recognize what we're doing and I'm certain, too, they will appreciate what has happened if we can better the speed of Campbell."

Surprisingly, the odds aren't stacked as high against the Summers brothers as it might appear. They aren't taking the one-time hot rod approach of trial and error. Bob and Bill are in the midst of building a well-engineered, well-designed car with four engines!

They've also acquired some substantial support for their $250,000 project— Chrysler Corp., Firestone Tire & Rubber Co., Hurst Performance Products and Mobil Oil. The cost, incidentally, is dwarfed by the millions spent by Campbell.

Well-Known by 'In' Group

Bob and his 29-year-old brother, Bill, are not strangers to Bonneville or speed. They're well-known by the "in" group with 11 years of experience behind them. "A coupe, three roadsters and a streamliner," said Bill.

Bob has tasted high-speed driving as well—323 m.p.h. in his streamliner. The two of them are spearheading work that began in earnest last August.

The car itself is quite unusual. It is 32-feet long and 4-feet wide. It will literally slip through the air since the front end only stands 21 inches. The highest point, in fact, is a mere three feet off the ground. That is the canopy in the rear which will cover the tiny compartment that will hold slim Bob for the 11-mile (two minute) run over the salt.

Bill, a few pounds heavier than his younger brother, couldn't fit in the cockpit if he was inclined to drive. He insists that he's not.

Strong and Weak Assets

"I've got the strong right foot and the weak mind," quipped Bob.

They've taken a scientific approach to the design of the car. A one-fifth scale model was tested extensively in the wind tunnel at Caltech. The drag coefficient with nine feet of frontal area is .117. And, according to those who know, that's something.

Pre-construction research is important. At the speeds they're aiming for, one of the problems will be to keep the wheels on the ground.

"It should be good for 450 m.p.h.," said Bob about the car. "We found in the wind tunnel that it has great directional stability. And that's important. It would be quite easy for this thing to fly."

The hazards of this three-ton machine in flight are obvious. The design contrasts greatly with the locally built streamliner of Mickey Thompson, Challenger I, that went 406 m.p.h. in one direction but was unable to make the required return run fo a record.

Thompson's car also had four engines —Pontiac. Engine-placement was different. His car was two engines wide and two engines long.

The Summers Brothers' streamliner is only one-engine wide and four long. The four Chrysler hemispherical combustion chamber V-8s (426 cubic in.) are mounted in line, coupled in pairs, back to back.

"It's very simple," said Bill. "It's a lot like one great big V-32 engine. All the power will go to all of the wheels. Everything works together." A common driveline will run the length of the car.

One, Long Drag Race

The car, with independent suspension all the way, will have two transmissions —one at each set of wheels. Four speeds will be used.

"All it is is one long drag race," said Bill about the run. "If we had a longer run we wouldn't need all of those gears."

In concert, the four engines should produce at least 2,400 horsepower, 600 per engine.

The fuel supply, of course, will be limited—four gallons per engine. They'll burn a special racing gasoline provided by Mobil.

One trip across the salt amounts to 11 miles. The one in the middle counts most for it will be timed.

Crew-cut Bob doesn't really figure the ride will be especially tough—much easier, in fact, than his 323-m.p.h. run in the single-engine streamliner at Bonneville in 1963.

"I think it will handle better," said Bob about the new car, "which should mean a lot easier ride this time. We didn't have the old car in a wind tunnel."

He doesn't plan to do much steering. In fact, it will have a built-in range of only 14 degrees. "It will be real slow steering," explained Bill. "You don't want to correct too much—not at that speed."

3 Chutes Used in Stopping

And what does one do to stop at that speed? "Just use the chutes," said Bill. "The brakes won't be used except around the pits. We have a small chute to use first at high speed, then the final chute for 250 m.p.h. and below. We've also got an emergency chute."

The chutes, he added, will help if control of the car is lost. A chute would be popped, if necessary, to reinstate attitude.

There is no fear that a chute will snap loose as one did on Craig Breedlove's Spirit of America, the record-breaking jet car that wound up submerged in a ditch. Breedlove actually finished his record run freestyle.

"No, our chutes are designed to speeds of 550 m.p.h.," explained Bill. "So we have a good safety margin." It will take two to three miles to stop the car from top speed.

The streamliner was built with a frame of steel tubing and an aluminum body, hand-shaped by one of the few masters of the craft, Jack Sutton of Hollywood. The designer was Walt Korff, a Lockheed engineer.

Sponsors Sought for Year

Wheels and tires to accommodate both the speed and thrust are special products, too. The Hurst wheels are forged by Harvey Aluminum. They are 16 inches in diameter with a 6½-inch rim. Firestone has come up with special tubeless and treadless Nylon tires. They'll be inflated to 150 psi with a speed capability of 600 m.p.h.

The idea for such a car has been with the Summerses for years. It wasn't until a year ago, however, that they started rounding up sponsors.

"Credit George Hurst with getting the thing started," said Bob. "We couldn't have done it without him. He provided the money to get going last August and then helped line up other sponsors."

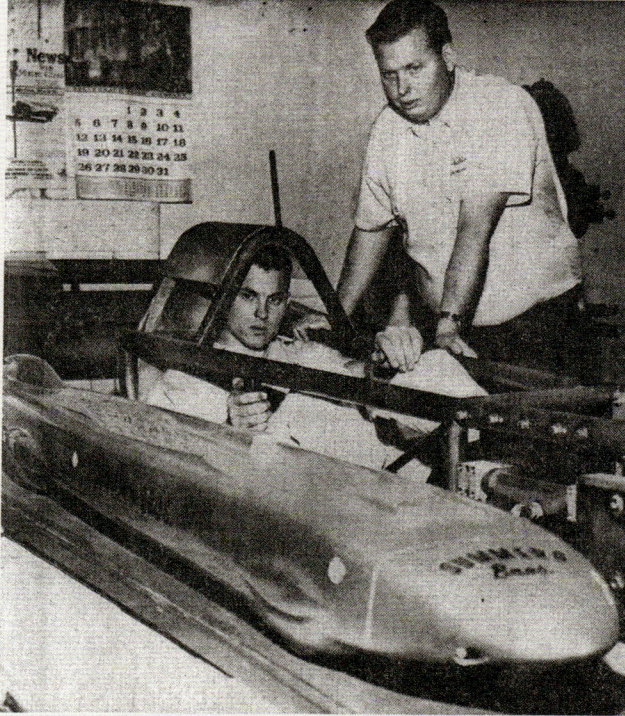

SPEED BREED—Bob Summers checks out cockpit for size with brother Bill on four-engine streamliner they're building for land speed record attempt. In foreground is one-fifth scale model used for extensive wind tunnel tests at Caltech.
Times photo

Countless man hours already have gone into the car. The brothers—both bachelors—couldn't come up with an estimate for the number spent since last August. And the hours are bad—2 a.m. to 5 p.m., seven days a week.

Odd Hours Avoid Interference

Why 2 a.m.? "To avoid interruptions," said Bill, alluding to the Southland's population of curious automobile buffs. "We couldn't get any work done if we tried to do it in the evenings. But at 2 in the morning nobody in his right mind would stop by to bother us."

Work will continue in their shop in Ontario with two buddies who are helping them, Glenn Ridge and Jim Crosby, until May or June when the car will be taken to Edwards for some dry lake testing. The Bonneville assault will be timed probably in July or August—with favorable salt and weather conditions.

Chevrolet builds a car everytime you blink an eye. The Summerses build one in a year. That's still progress, though.

★

Smog Control Regulations

Smog control laws, despite the buffeting they are taking in the State Legislature, still apply to many California motorists.

For instance:

All new cars, import or domestic, sold in the state must be equipped with an approved crankcase control device.

All gasoline-powered commercial vehicles registered in metropolitan counties, as far back as 1950 models, must have crankcase systems.

All used passenger cars (1950 or later) in the 11 metropolitan counties that change ownerships must have a device.

What 11 counties!

Alameda, Contra Costa, Marin, Santa Clara, San Francisco, San Mateo, Los Angeles, San Diego, Sacramento, Orange and San Bernardino.

For the time being at least, other used car owners are off the hook.

Bob Summers with Hilborn fuel injection installed without the air box for a fitment check. This was a staged photo for a press release, but there is no mistaking the intense look on his face. Goldenrod was his creation and he meant to own the land speed record.

GOLDENROD

The Chrysler Race Hemi

The elephant in the engine room was the A864/A865 Race Hemi and it's a damn good thing because the Goldenrod's engines were based on the upgraded and refined Chrysler Hemi engine reintroduced in 1964 as the "Race Hemi." The previous 426-cubic-inch RB-series wedge engine was refined with the addition of new Hemi cylinder heads and new induction gear to challenge OEM competitors on the nation's dragstrips and in NASCAR's Grand National stock car racing series. Two versions were developed and designated A864 and A865. The A865 was the drag race version equipped with an aluminum crossram intake manifold and dual four-barrel Carter AFBs. The A864 was the NASCAR single four-barrel circuit racing version. Both versions had iron cylinder heads with 12.5:1 static compression. They used the same valve gear and were essentially identical except for the induction system, oiling system, and camshaft timing.

A864 circuit racing engine on the dyno in the Chrysler engine lab in 1964. Except for the induction system, this engine was basically the same as the A865 drag race engine that was modified to suit the unique requirements of the Goldenrod. With appropriate modifications Chrysler engineers felt that its high power was well suited to the Summers Brothers' land speed record attempt.

GOLDENROD

Forty-five years later, Chrysler understood the value of supporting the Goldenrod restoration. They sent four new partial engine assemblies based on the currently available crate motor. The engines were complete except for rods, pistons and valve gear. We installed the restored induction systems and made replica dry sump oil pans to fit the lower body.

When Chrysler agreed to sponsor the Goldenrod effort, they stepped up in a big way. The sixties Hemi revival program was in its early stages, and it was folded into the Goldenrod development program without fanfare. It was given the same level of attention as the A864 NASCAR engines and the A865 drag racing engines; perhaps more since specialized parts had to be developed and validated for the unique application. Goldenrod Program Manager Pete Dawson coordinated a small team of engineers and technicians who were already waist-deep in Hemi development for NASCAR and drag racing engines.

While there were no major differences between the drag racing version and the oval racing version in terms of the cylinder heads and short blocks, the A865 drag racing version was ultimately chosen as the base engine for the Goldenrod program. Goals included power and durability development along with specific requirements unique to the Goldenrod. These included:

Dry sump lubrication so the engines could be mounted lower in the car's frame.

Mechanical fuel injection that could not exceed the height of the Hemi valve covers.

Camshaft-driven mechanical fuel pumps with special aluminum timing covers.

Most of these requirements were tackled within the confines of the Chrysler engine lab and most of the specialized engine components were engineered and fabricated by Chrysler people. Power testing was conducted with deep wet sump oil pans and it was recognized from the outset that specialized components would be required for the Goldenrod. Mike Buckel was the race engine development engineer who oversaw the development of the custom dry sump components and the unique mechanical fuel injection systems. His team brainstormed a unique setup for the application.

GOLDENROD RACE HEMI ENGINE SPECIFICATIONS

ENGINE	GOLDENROD
Piston Displacement	426 cubic inches
Development Output	575-580 horsepower @ 6400 rpm on gasoline with deep wet-sump dyno pan (1)
Race Output	Raced on methanol with dry sump lubrication. No power figures available. (2)
Bore Centers	4.80-in. center to center
Bore Diameter	4.25-in.
Main Bearings	Five, cross-bolted on the center three caps
COMPRESSION RATIO	
Compression Ratio	12.5:1
CRANKSHAFT	
Type	Fully-counterweighted, shot-peened, nitrided journals, undercut fillets
Material	SAE 4340 forged carbon steel
Stroke Length	3.75-in.
LUBRICATION	
Custom Dry Sump (Goldenrod)	Custom low profile with windage tray, kickout with 1-in. clearance to crank
Stages	2 scavenge, 1 pressure
Pump Type	3 stock gerotor pumps stacked with extended drive shaft on each engine
Pick-Ups	Stock pickup plus secondary pickup at the back of the dry sump pan
Drive	Cam-driven geared shaft w/intermediate plates and drive shaft extensions
CONNECTING RODS	
Type	I-beam
Material	Drop-forged steel
Length	6.861-in.
PISTONS	
Type	TRW high-dome
Material	Impact extruded (forged) aluminum alloy, tin-plated
Weight	852-grams
PISTON RINGS	
Description	Two compression, one three-piece oil control set
Number/Thickness	Three, 0.062-in., 0.062-in., 0.186-in.
Top Material Type	Cast-iron Dykes-type step-seal
Second Material Type	Cast-iron, tapered-face
CAMSHAFT	
Type	Iskenderian, 550-A Super Le Gerra (mechanical)(3)
Event Duration: Intake°/ Exhaust°	278°/282° @ .020 tappet rise, 250°/254° @ .050 tappet rise
Centerline	106°
Lift (Intake/Exhaust)	0.550/0.560
Drive	Single bolt double-roller chain and sprockets
Tappet Type	Solid/mechanical; flat-face, hollow
CYLINDER HEAD	
Type	Cast iron hemispherical combustion chambers
Description	Crossflow, fully-machined combustion chambers w/central sparkplug
Valve Diameter Intake/Exhaust	2.25-in./1.94-in.
Valve Springs	Isky dual, steel wire w/flat-wound surge damper
Rocker Arms	Forged steel, adjustable; 1.57:1 intake, 1.53:1 exhaust
INTAKE SYSTEM	
Manifold Type	Custom Chrysler-designed/Hilborn-manufactured mechanical injection
Throttle Bore Diameters (all)	2.08-in.
Fuel Pumps	Hilborn 150 mechanical, cam-driven
EXHAUST SYSTEM	
Headers	36-inch, 2-1/8-in. primaries, 3-1/2-in. collectors, fabricated by Gary Hooker
IGNITION SYSTEM	
Type	Prestolite, transistor
Distributor	Chrysler dual-point distributor

Chrysler engine specs courtesy of Al Kirschenbaum

CHART NOTES

Note 1: Initial testing was conducted with the crossram drag racing package. The car ran on methanol, but no power figures were established as the switch to methanol was made at Bonneville.

Note 2: Custom dry sump system was within a few horsepower of the deep wet sump dyno pan for power.

Note 3: Engineer Mike Buckel confirms the Iskenderian cam and matching valve springs, although the reduced duration and overlap from the standard A865 camshaft might have reduced peak power and increased mid-range torque delivery to help accelerate the heavy car at Bonneville.

GOLDENROD

The A865 drag racing engine used for the Goldenrod.

An A864 circuit racing engine used in NASCAR racing.

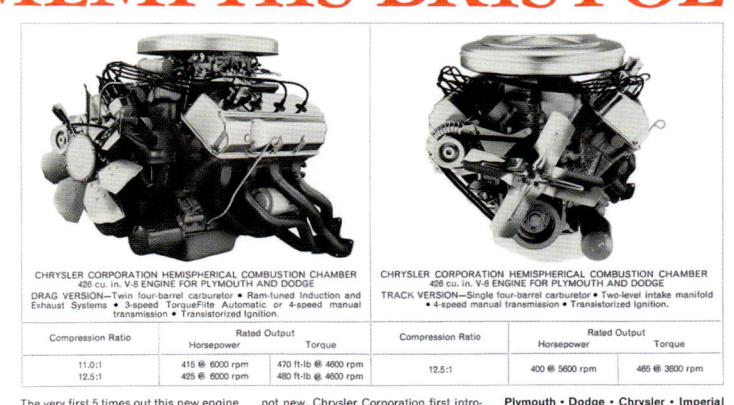

Chrysler introduced the new 1964 Race Hemi to the public with this two-page spread in performance magazines such as *Hot Rod* and *Motor Trend*.

GOLDENROD

The A864 NASCAR engine (above) was very similar to the A865 crossram drag racing engine used for the Goldenrod project. It had dry sump lubrication, and a single four-barrel Holley carburetor on a single plane intake manifold ('64-'65 first design). Chrysler brought its considerable engineering power to bear on this Hemi project which paid off handsomely by sweeping the field at the 1964 Daytona 500.

The circuit racing engine (1966 version) with a four-barrel Holley carburetor on a revised crossram style "bathtub" intake manifold that suffered fuel distribution problems in competition and didn't perform to expectations.

Dick Landy captured the first drag racing victory for the all-new Race Hemi by winning the Hot Rod Magazine Championships at Riverside Raceway on June 12th, 1964, with his SS/A 1964 altered-wheelbase Dodge Polara 330. The potent factory-prepped Hemi in Landy's Dodge foretold the tremendous success the engine would have on the dragstrip. Choosing it as the basis for the Goldenrod engine package was a natural for the Summers Brothers. A camshaft swap, new Hilborn fuel injection and dry sump oiling made it a formidable package.

This rare period photo shows a Holley-equipped A865 drag engine on the dyno. Goldenrod's engines were tested with a Carter AFB/crossram configuration and converted to fuel injection upon delivery to the Summers Brothers.

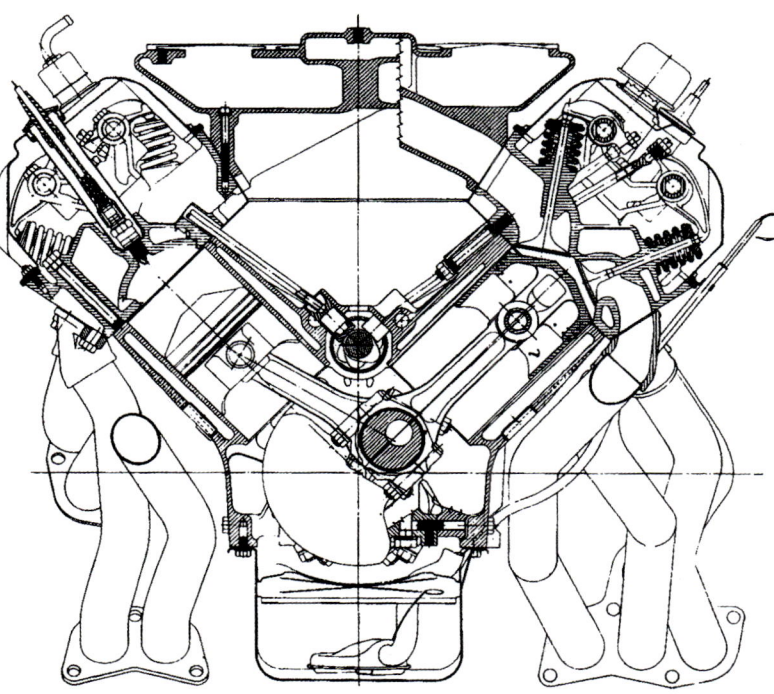

The A865 drag race engine was also internally similar to the A864 except for camshaft timing and crossram induction. It was fitted with an aluminum crossram intake manifold incorporating tuned length runners and dual Carter AFB carburetors that were later changed for Holley four-barrels.

Cutaway shows how the valve package was rotated 10° toward the intake side to shorten the exhaust rocker arm for better geometry and improved high-speed stability. It also permitted the use of a fifth head bolt via a stud off the bottom of the intake port secured by a nut on a boss in the lifter gallery.

CHRYSLER RACE HEMI ENGINE SPECIFICATIONS

ENGINE:	CIRCUIT RACE HEMI	DRAG RACE HEMI
Engineering Code	A864	A865
Displacement	426 cubic inches	
Output	400-hp @ 6000 rpm	425-hp @ 5000 rpm
Torque	480-ft.lbs. @ 4600 rpm	490-ft.lbs. @ 4000 rpm
Cylinder Block	Tin-alloyed cast-iron; stress-relieved	
Bore Centers	4.80-in. center to center	
Bore Dia.	4.25-in.	
Deck Height	10.725-in. (along bore axis)	
COMPRESSION RATIO		
Compression Ratio	12.5:1	
CRANKSHAFT		
Type	Fully-counterweighted, shot-peened, nitrided journals, undercut fillets	
Material	4340 forged carbon steel	1046 forged carbon steel
Main Journal Dia.	2.749-in.	
Rod Journal Dia.	2.374-in.	
Stroke Length	3.75-in.	
CONNECTING RODS		
Type	I-beam/Drop-forged steel	
Length	6.861-in.	
Big End Bore Dia.	2.375-in.	
Small End Bore	1.0945-in.	
PISTONS		
Type	High-dome	
Material	Impact extruded (forged) aluminum alloy, tin-plated	
Wrist Pin Material	High-manganese steel	
Wrist Pin Type	Press-fit in rod, floating in piston	
Wrist Pin Dia.	1.0935-in.	
Piston Rings, Type	Two compression, one three-piece oil control set	
Compression Rings	Two, 0.62-in., 0.62-in.	Two, 0.78-in., 0.78-in.,
Oil Ring	0.125-in.	0.186-in.
Top Ring	Cast-iron Dykes	Cast-iron, barrel-face
CAMSHAFT		
Type	Solid (mechanical) lifter	
Event Duration: (Degrees, Int./Ex.)	300°/300°	312°/312°
Overlap (Degrees)	76°	88°
Lift (Intake/Exhaust)	0.520/0.520	0.540/0.540
Drive	Double-roller chain and sprockets	
Tappet Type	Solid/mechanical; flat-face, hollow	
Tappet Dia.	0.9030-0.9035-in.	
CYLINDER HEAD		
Type	Hemispherical combustion chambers	
Description	Crossflow, fully-machined combustion chambers w/centrally located spark plug	
Material	Cast iron	
Valve Dia. Int./Ex.	2.25-in./1.94-in.	
Valve Stem Dia.	0.308-in.	
Valve Springs	Dual, steel wire w/flat-wound surge damper	
Rocker Arms	Forged steel, adjustable; 1.57:1 intake, 1.53:1 exhaust	
INTAKE SYSTEM		
Manifold, Type	Single 4-Bbl., dual plane	Dual 4-Bbl., crossram
Manifold, Material	Cast-aluminum or magnesium	Cast-aluminum
Carburetors	One Holley 4 Bbl.	Two Carter 4 Bbls.
IGNITION SYSTEM		
Type	Prestolite, transistor-type	

Chrysler engine specs courtesy of Al Kirschenbaum

GOLDENROD

ADAPTING AMERICAN V8 MUSCLE:
DRY SUMP OILING SYSTEM

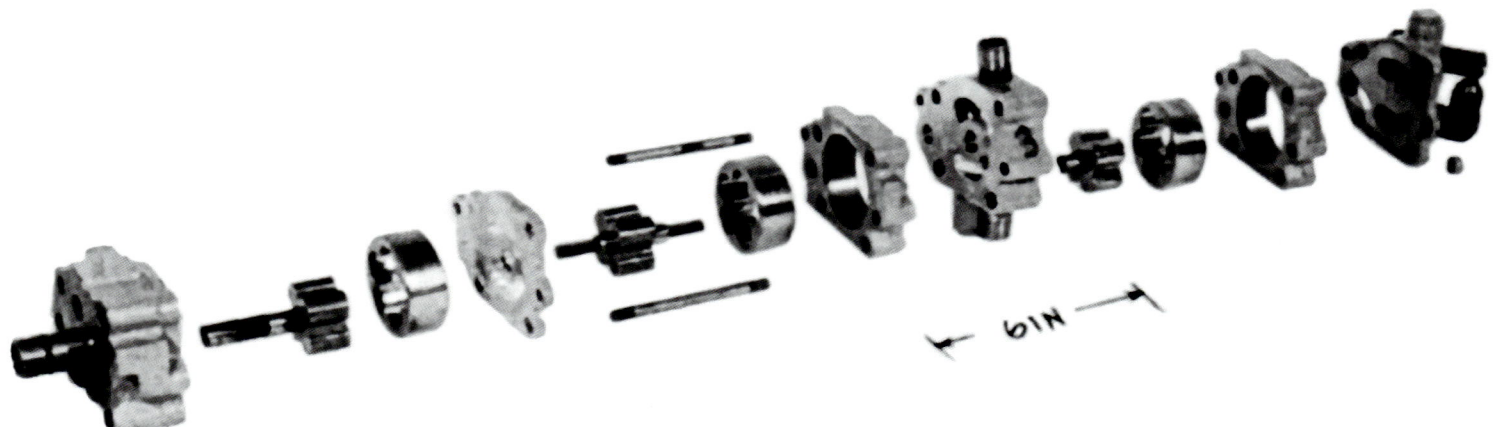

The oil pump stack incorporates three production oil pumps modified to form a custom dry sump system. An intermediate plate and a top cap make it work. Two scavenge pumps and one pressure pump make up the system. The intermediate plates ensure the proper flow paths to the pressure stage. These photos, scanned from Chrysler Chief Engineer Bill Weertman's original SAE paper, are nowhere to be found. We cleaned them up the best we could to show you how the Goldenrod dry sump system was set up.

Custom dry sump oil pans were fabricated by technicians Joe Trybus and Pat Brady and later modified by Crew Chief Jim Crosby. They were designed to leave one inch of clearance from the crankshaft with an integral windage tray and kickout. The pans were approximately three inches shorter than a production pan. A shortened stock pickup tube was used for one of the scavenge stages and a second scavenge stage was fed by a separate pickup point installed at the rear of each oil pan. Three production oil pumps were stacked on top of each other in the stock location on each engine. They were connected with

Goldenrod dry sump pan shows the unique kickout designed to funnel oil to dual pickup points. The windage tray is shaped to separate oil from the crankshaft. Note the stock pickup is used in the stock location and shortened to fit the shallow pan. The second pickup is at the rear of the pan, but it actually scavenges from the front of the pan via a full-length internal tube.

GOLDENROD

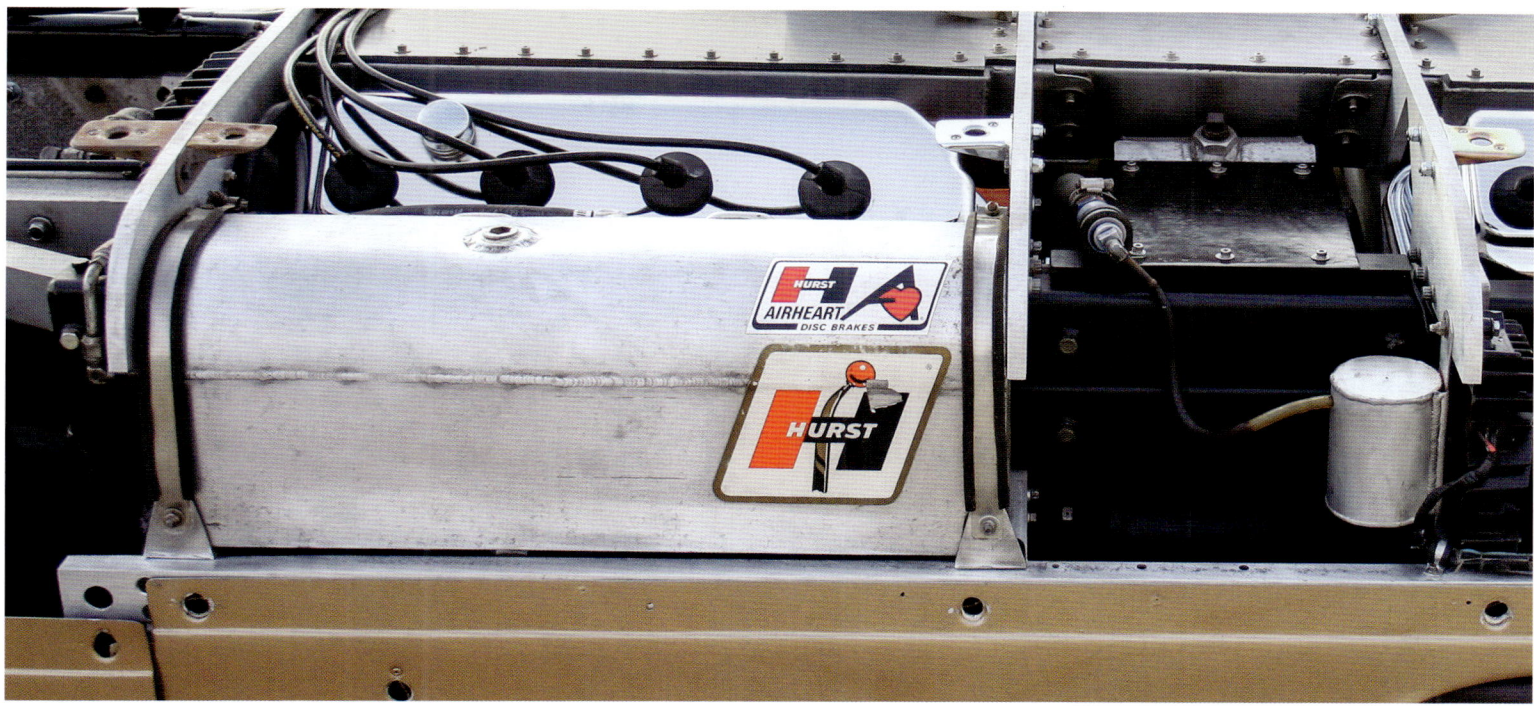

Dry sump oil supply tanks are mounted outside the frame rails for the center engines and inside the frame rails for the front and rear engines. The outrigger tanks are curved on the top to match the inner contour of the body panels. The tanks have a 16-quart capacity and are internally baffled for aeration control.

extension studs and intermediate plates to facilitate the desired flow paths. The stock gerotor pumps were modified with shaft drive extensions so they all turned in unison. Two pumps were used for scavenging, and the third pump served as the pressure stage. Each engine had its own oil storage tank holding approximately 16 quarts of Mobil racing oil. This provided a simple, yet elegant engineering solution that incorporated factory components while avoiding the more complicated chain-driven system used on the NASCAR engines. Bob Summers confirmed that the engine bays on the Goldenrod had sufficient room to support this approach. The NASCAR chain-driven system would have caused packaging problems at the front of each engine. In practice, the oiling system functioned flawlessly. The engines were run with 70 psi oil pressure and they experienced no starvation issues when accelerating or decelerating.

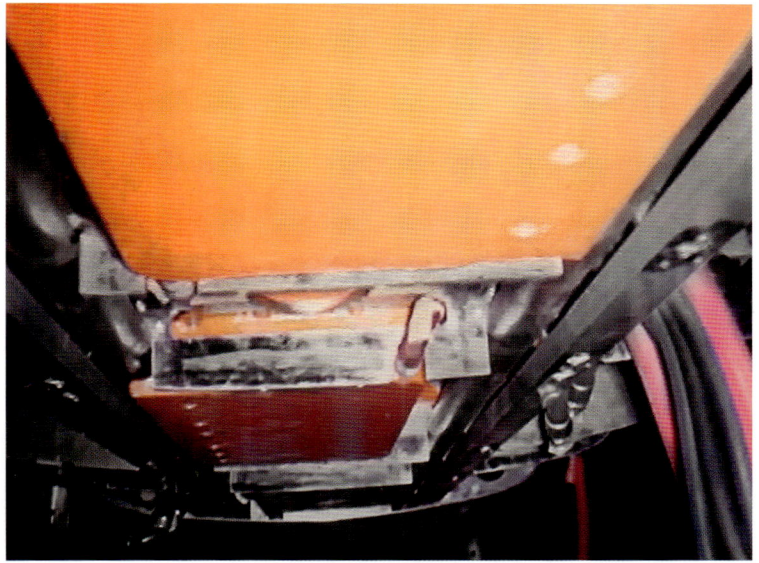

Crew Chief Jim Crosby's vintage snapshot of the oil pans from underneath the car. You can see the external pickup point on one of the pans. If you look closely, you'll see that the kickouts are on opposite sides because the engines are mounted back-to-back. Note the rows of pan bolts that go through the pans on opposite sides.

GOLDENROD

ADAPTING AMERICAN V8 MUSCLE:
FUEL INJECTING THE RACE HEMI

The ram tubes on the Hilborn fuel injection system are 7.5 inches long and 2.08 inches in diameter.

The fuel injection system was fully self-contained within the aluminum air boxes. This included the distribution block, the individual injector lines and nozzles, throttle linkage and the feed line from the front-mounted Hilborn fuel pump. With the dynamic pressure recovery of the Herda-designed scoops, inlet restriction of the tightly-packed stacks was likely nonexistent inside the pressurized air boxes.

GOLDENROD

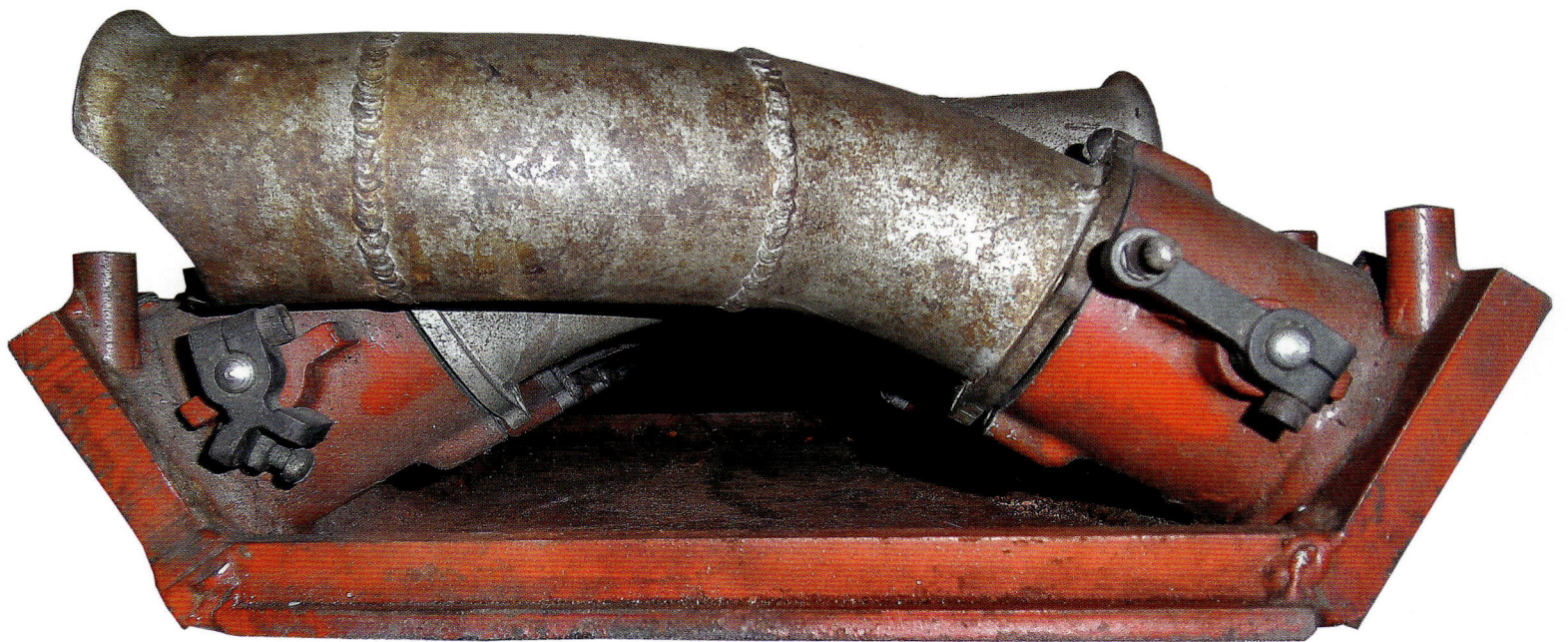

Gentle runner turn offered a reasonably straight shot at the valve along with potential blockage to airflow entering from one end of the air box at low speed. Positive ram pressure of 5 psi at higher speeds alleviated the problem. Air enters the air box from the same view that you see here with the sealed top barely a quarter inch above the tubes.

The fuel injection systems were also engineered for simplicity and proper ram tuning. According to Steve Baker, Tom Hoover performed the initial calculations and sonic testing to determine the most efficient use of the packaging restraints. Working with Hilborn, a low-ram manifold was designed to maintain the desired port entry angle while laying the ram tubes over horizontally to remain below the height of the valve covers.

The valve covers could not be changed; thus they dictated the design limit for the height of the car. Hoover specified 7.5-inch bell-mouthed ram tubes to provide effective air entry. These were then wrapped into custom aluminum air boxes. The air boxes were capped with flat plates to contain ramming pressure from the air scoops and promote a supercharging effect. They were open on one end to accept input from the air scoops. Each air box also housed the fuel injection distribution block and accompanying fuel lines. Their collective engineering efforts reduced the height of the engines by a considerable sum allowing Korff and Summers to maintain a vehicle hood line only 28" tall for the entire length of the car except the cockpit area which was shaped to resemble a fin. The air boxes were thought to be restricting airflow at low speeds, but that later proved incorrect as excess weight caused low-speed sluggishness.

The dry sump pans matched the deep sump dyno pans on the dyno, and the induction system proved effective at matching power levels achieved by the NASCAR engines. By supporting a significant reduction in the aerodynamic drag signature these efforts effectively made more power available to drive the car. *(See the Aerodynamics chapter for Korff's calculations.)*

Mike Buckel, the Race Engine Performance Development Engineer, confirmed that the race engines were built with Isky 550 Super Le Gerra solid lifter camshafts and Isky-specified valve springs. He noted that they were testing many

GOLDENROD

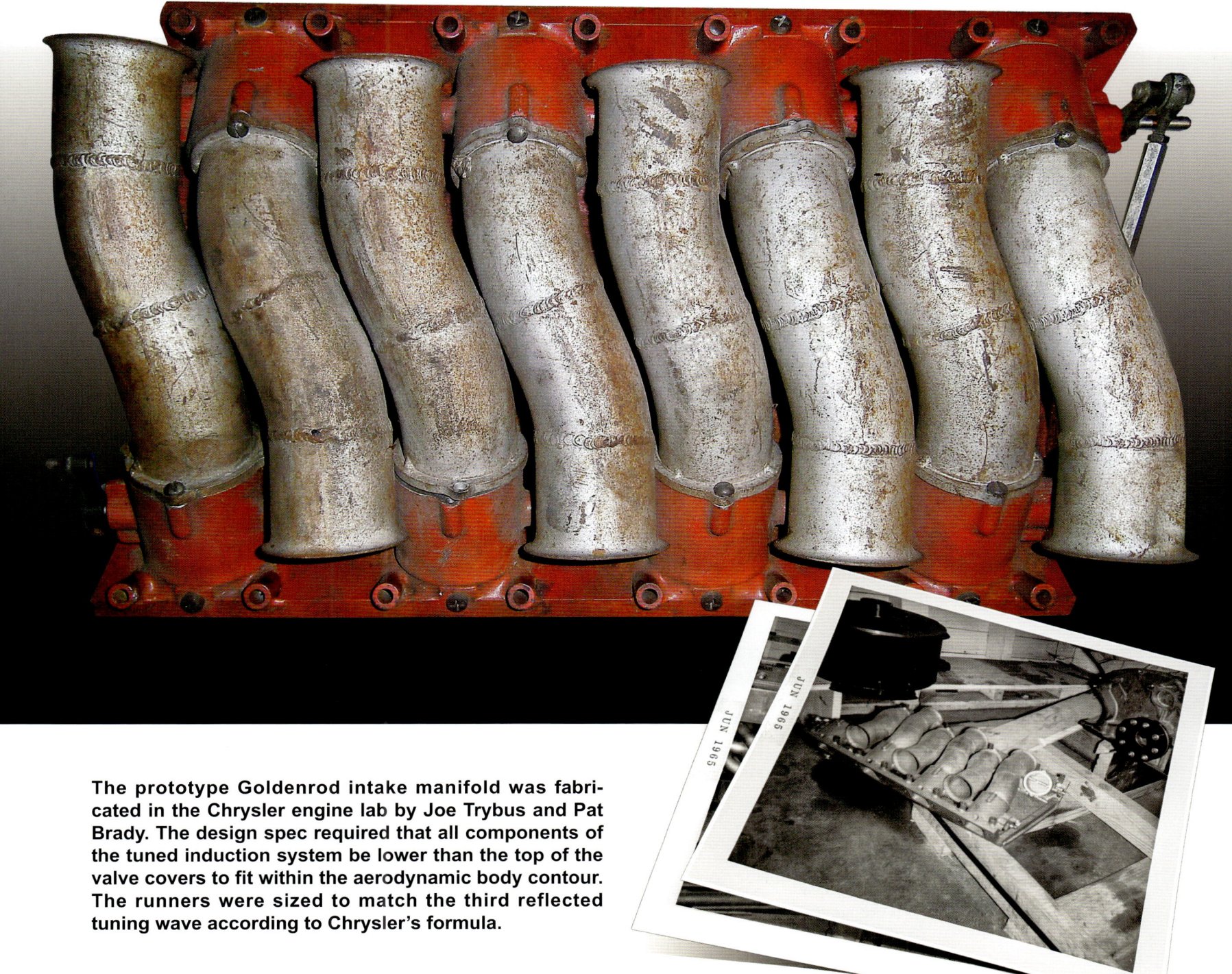

The prototype Goldenrod intake manifold was fabricated in the Chrysler engine lab by Joe Trybus and Pat Brady. The design spec required that all components of the tuned induction system be lower than the top of the valve covers to fit within the aerodynamic body contour. The runners were sized to match the third reflected tuning wave according to Chrysler's formula.

Crosby's album photo above shows the prototype on a pallet in the Summers' garage with a date of June, 1965.

different camshafts in that time period and they selected the Isky grind because it made the smoothest and broadest power curve. A contemporary Racer Brown grind made more power, but it was deemed too aggressive and thus hard on the valve springs for extended high-rpm use.

GOLDENROD

Fuel Injection #426-CH-8C is the Hilborn pattern number for the Goldenrod intake manifolds. When we told Stu Hilborn that one engine was missing a manifold during the restoration, he told us that he still had the patterns and he would cast us a new one to replace it. He made two more, and the additional one was later sold to a collector.

CHRYSLER GOLDENROD ENGINEERING TEAM	
Peter Dawson	Program Manager
George Wallace	Driveline Engineer
Bob Mullen	Inlet Systems Engineer
Mike Buckel	Race Engine Development Engineer
Steve Baker	Engine Assembly and Dyno Testing
Joe Nunez	Track Liason at Bonneville
Pat Brady	Intake Manifold and Dry Sump Fabrication
Joe Trybus	Intake Manifold and Dry Sump Fabrication
Forrest Pitcock	Dyno Operator

A flurry of activity within the Chrysler engine lab was supporting all of the drag racing and circle track racing efforts. Baker said they were working around the clock on everything and the Goldenrod project was given equal attention. These are the engineers and technicians who directly worked on the Goldenrod project.

Close-up of the runner pattern showing the throttle linkage mounts and the mounting boss for the screws that secure the ram tubes.

The aerodynamic packaging requirements made it quite difficult to achieve the most efficient flow paths for the intake system. In the end, Korff convinced Summers that the aerodynamic profile would more than make up for the necessary restriction in the induction system. His assertion proved correct as Summers achieved the 425.99 mph speed and never got the car into fourth gear. Summers believed the car was capable of 450 mph.

It is a well-proven fact that these cars will go faster with a 100 horsepower drag reduction than they will with a 100 horsepower addition under the hood, partly because there is no traction required to apply the 100 horsepower drag reduction. It actually frees up that amount of power to increase the acceleration rate all the way to the end of the timer, but it increases the theoretical terminal velocity since the car has the same amount of potential traction-generated thrust on the ground with less aerodynamic drag. Assuming there was adequate power to overcome both the aerodynamic drag and acceleration rate within the available track distances, the 1.19:1 third gear ratio and direct fourth gear ratio would make the 425 mph run in third into a 506 mph terminal speed.

Acceleration becomes the real show stopper in this assumption as those final miles are going by at less than eight seconds each, so there is not much time for the excess power to actually speed the car up, especially when the car weight is over 8,400 pounds. Power quickly decreases as the aerodynamic power consumption increases with the cube of speed, so 506 mph uses 1.68 times the power that 425 mph required.

GOLDENROD

Grasping for Glory

The longest-standing speed record in land speed racing history almost never happened. Punctuated by an exponential degree of difficulty, it was also burdened with incessant interference by those devilish gods of speed who seemed delighted to find new challenges for the Summers Brothers to overcome. The brothers, resolute and ever practical racers, had already experienced big speed with meager means. They overcame extreme financial challenges and mustered the support of major sponsors including the Chrysler Corporation, Hurst Corporation, Firestone Tire & Rubber, and Mobil Oil with additional support from Champion Spark Plugs to build the car. Extraordinary effort went into the design and construction of the new land speed record challenger, and now it had to prove its worth.

Prior to the first real test at Riverside Raceway, the brothers conducted an impromptu local engine test outside the shop in Ontario. The engines were fired, and the car was driven down Mission Boulevard. The local sheriff was not impressed, but he wasn't a bad guy. He made them take it back to the shop and promise not to do it again. Then he stuck around to check it out.

The subsequent Riverside test was more inclusive, and it provided the long back straightaway for Bob to work the car up to a bit of speed with the body off while chased by the family station wagon with observers. The session identified minor problems and also helped them test and observe the car's various systems in action. Adjustments, calibrations, and minor changes were corrected before the car went to the salt.

RIVERSIDE RACEWAY TEST

Goldenrod's initial test at Riverside Raceway offered the world's first look at this extraordinary mechanical masterpiece. These two photos were taken in almost the exact same spot. Eric Rickman's Hot Rod Magazine shot unveils the car's brilliant design and tightly-packaged features with four new fuel-injected Chrysler Hemi race engines and supporting components including fuel and oil tanks.

The snapshot above is from Crew Chief James Crosby's album. Note the track centerline for the back stretch at Riverside and the Champion crossover bridge in the background. Crosby is seen in the Hot Rod photo bending over to inspect the front of the car.

GOLDENROD

The photo to the left offers an interesting contrast with local helpers pushing the car into the refurbished and recently repainted black and gold horse/race trailer that was long enough to accept the car. Beneath that we see uniformed crew members with sponsor reps and technicians unloading the car at the Riverside track in a similar photo. A crowd of friends and curious locals assembled to watch the proceedings. A vehicle of this advanced sophistication was particularly impressive, and onlookers nodded approval with appropriate ooh's and aah's.

The team swarmed over the car checking fasteners, fittings and fluid levels. Technicians and engineering reps from each of the major sponsors were keen to examine and recheck the various components and services they had provided for the car. It evolved into quite a jubilant occasion as the car's initial performance suggested the very real potential for legendary accomplishment on the salt flats.

GOLDENROD

The Summers Brothers suffered no lack of race day support as representatives from the major sponsors attended the initial test session to examine the car's construction and provide technical advice.

Mobil Oil representative Ray McMahan sizing up Goldenrod's technical sophistication. Gotta love the can of Mobil oil sitting at the lower left. Looks like Ray is getting ready to top off one of the dry sump supply tanks.

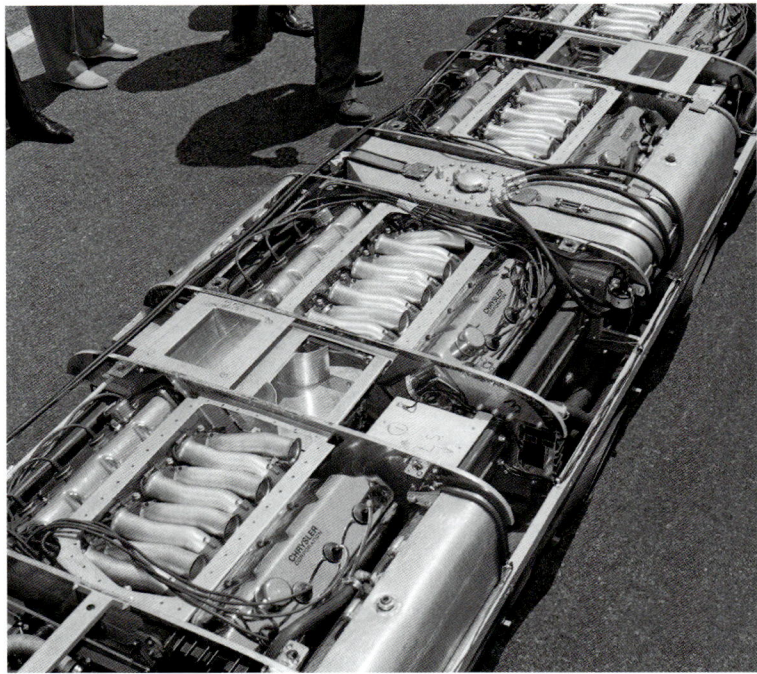

Goldenrod's tightly-packaged powertrain with four injected Chrysler Hemis, attending fuel and oil tanks, and stunning tuned induction system.

The black cable in the foreground is the tachometer drive cable that is driven off the front of the rearward facing number four engine.

GOLDENROD

This view shows the hydraulic clutch slave cylinder above the rear transmission. It operates the clutches for both transmissions via a common pressure line. A transmission vent is seen at the top left.

Dual surplus coolant pumps were powered from a localized battery source at the nose of the car. Two pumps were used to provide redundancy in case of a failure, thus ensuring uninterrupted coolant flow.

Crew Chief Jim Crosby (center right) directs preparations for the initial trial runs on the back straightaway at Riverside Raceway. Sharp looking crew in their team shirts.

Here you can see the front driveline coupler that failed, leaving a tell-tale dent in the lower frame rail. Its replacement ultimately proved satisfactory.

GOLDENROD

Among the specific goals to be accomplished at the Riverside Raceway test were vital concerns such as the seamless integration of the engines and the multi-part driveline. While seemingly simple in concept and execution, the transfer cases and lengthy driveshaft arrangement left plenty of room for misalignment misery. The test was conducted with all the body panels off so the operation of these components could be further observed from the chase car.

The engines, now fitted with Hilborn fuel injection, had been retested on the dyno at Keith Black Racing Engines and pronounced sound and powerful. It was important to verify that all systems were functioning properly. That included the lengthy and complicated throttle shaft mechanism with its multiple rods and bell cranks providing numerous opportunities for binding and failure to open all 32 throttle blades equally and evenly. Then there was the hydraulic clutch system, and the cable operated Hurst shifter that incorporated dual twenty-foot Morse cables. The cooling system was unproven, and the proper function of the dry sump lubrication systems needed to be verified. Wheels, tires, and braking were also part of the testing regimen, and with few discrepancies, the Goldenrod passed its initial baptism by fire with flying colors. The test was deemed so successful that plans were made to head up to Bonneville at the earliest opportunity.

Pay close attention to this photo — the wheels were manufactured by Hurst Corporation with final machine work by Larry DeVeny. Few photos show the wheels with the Hurst logos on them. In this photo from the Riverside test, the armor plating on either side of the driver has not yet been installed, but note the driver head restraint on Summers' helmet; a relatively advanced idea for the time period. The hydraulically operated clutches were activated by the round pedal seen just above Bob's feet. Surprisingly, Goldenrod had no onboard fire extinguishing systems as all of the interior volume was filled with power delivery systems and supporting components. The chassis was unpainted at this time.

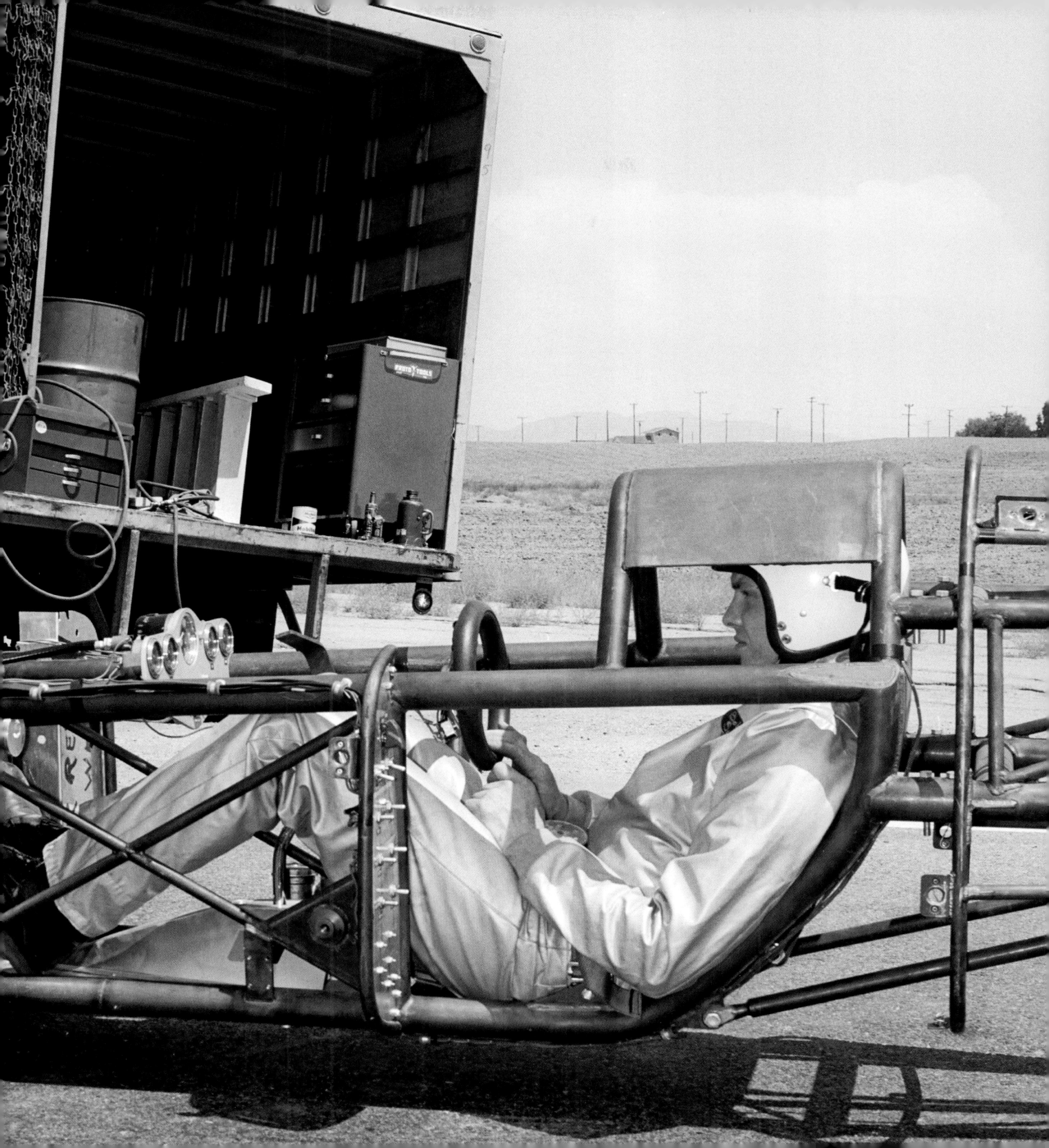

GOLDENROD

Surplus water pumps from G&J Aircraft salvage in Ontario, CA, were used to circulate the coolant water carried in the 50-gallon nose tank. Coolant was pumped into the right upper frame rail and distributed to each engine via appropriately located hose bungs. Coolant returned via the left frame rail. The pumps were battery operated.

An interesting perspective about the Goldenrod is the degree of mechanical refinement which tempered its design. In a period where evolving electronic sophistication was fully integrated into military and civilian aviation, the Goldenrod primarily incorporated simple, proven hot rodding methods and techniques to accomplish its mission in straightforward fashion. With the exception of gauges and electronic ignition amplifiers, the Goldenrod was an elegant mechanical device configured to excel at a singular mission. Bob Summers believed in high function drawn from simplification and the avoidance of excessive complication. No part of the Goldenrod escaped lengthy contemplation in Summers' active mind before anything was fabricated.

Prior racing experience with the Pollywog and the Summers' roadsters provided ample knowledge of how to approach the car's requirements. Summers and Crosby were both competent machinists, and they utilized their skills to great effect. Military training also played a role by providing the discipline and work ethic to persevere despite all setbacks. Bill Summers was an Army veteran, and Bob served in the Navy, where he absorbed valuable mechanical and machining skills. Some of those military contacts hung on well into the future, and it is interesting to note that when they finally set the new record, Bob received a congratulatory telegram from his former commanding officer; an unexpected, but well-deserved accolade for a job well done.

GOLDENROD

Top: Rare Summers smile anticipating his first powered test at Riverside Raceway. Below: Note camshaft-driven Hilborn 150 mechanical fuel pump on the front of the engine.

A Firestone Tire & Rubber Company representative checks over the high speed tires. Even down on one knee he is still considerably taller than the Goldenrod's long, low profile.

GOLDENROD

Primary sponsor Mobile Oil dispatched company engineer Ray McMahan to accompany the car every time it ran. The Goldenrod only made a total of eight runs, achieving the record on runs number six and seven. McMahan was responsible for fuels and lubricants and ultimately approved the switch from Mobil premium racing gas to methanol.

The test at Riverside Raceway validated the overall design concept and proved the functionality of Goldenrod's complicated drivetrain with Bob making multiple passes up and down the back straightaway to work out the bugs.

Next stop, an empty hangar at Wendover Airfield that became the team's operational base during the multiple trips to and from the Bonneville Salt Flats.

136

The large WWII hangar at Wendover was a welcome advantage for clean working conditions out of the weather. With body panels removed, the Goldenrod assembly occupied a sizeable portion of the floor.

CHASING THE RECORD AT BONNEVILLE

Confidence and excitement swelled in anticipation of the forthcoming record challenge. On the first of September, 1965, the Goldenrod crew, support teams, and officials assembled on the salt flats for the record attempt. The first run was anti-climactic. Bob Summers squeezed into the cramped cockpit, and brother Bill eased the station wagon push car up to the rear of the Goldenrod, pushing it off with the Hemi engines roaring to life. Almost immediately, Summers revved the engines, clutched it and coasted to a stop, declaring that it had felt like only three of the engines were running.

One engine had failed to fire because its throttle linkage failed to open the throttle blades. The problem was quickly remedied and Goldenrod executed its first pass down the salt, stopping six miles away after posting a

GOLDENROD

The converted horse trailer parked outside the service hangar with its snappy black and gold paint scheme adding an aire of professionalism to the budget-built Goldenrod effort. This hangar has played host to many legendary land speed racers over the years.

speed of 218.66 mph. Optimism grew as no major issues presented themselves. They prepared the car to make a run for 300 mph. At 4 pm they were ready, but a gentle breeze suddenly grew to a 22 mph crosswind and chief timer Joe Petrali called a hold. Summers remained in the car as the wind grew to nearly 40 mph with a light rain. It was a long wait. At 6:33 the wind subsided to 12 mph, and Petrali released the car. Summers gunned it down course, but the speed proved disappointing; only 244.9 mph as he was unable to shift the car out of second gear. As darkness approached, they trucked the car back to town to trace the problem and come up with a solution.

The twenty-foot-long shifter cable was sticking inside its housing. It was worked loose and lubricated. Summers worked the linkage in the car and found it working properly. The next morning it seized again. It would take weeks to obtain a new cable and Bob was willing to keep trying by working with the existing cable. Other obstacles arose to challenge their patience. Vibration dampers on the driveshafts were distorting, and failure seemed imminent. Bill Summers sped back to Ontario to have them reinforced. Four days of their reserved track time vanished before the dampers were reinstalled. Time was running out. The engines were revved, and the drivetrain was observed for problems. Almost immediately the front damper and u-joint exploded, scaring nearby crew members and leaving a sizeable dent in the lower frame rail.

They were out of time. Mobile field engineer Ray McMahan advised the brothers to take the car home and fix the problems. Racer's stubbornness emerged. It was imperative to test the car under challenging real-world conditions that only

existed at Bonneville. They could go home and fix it, but if other problems existed, they wouldn't learn of them back in the shop. Summers opted to stay there and make new driveshafts with a revised design. An order for special driveline parts was placed and received a week later only to learn that they had been machined too short. More new parts were made and finally installed. Other racers occupied the salt, but the rain was forcing delays.

Summers remained concerned about power. He queried Peter Dawson, Chrysler's program manager for the Goldenrod project, suggesting that the engines were not performing up to par. Dawson assured him the engines were sound and capable and suggested that they likely needed larger air inlets to aid breathing at lower vehicle speeds. Such was the origin of the large-mouth scoops that were on the car for its record runs. Bob Summers also proposed switching to methanol fuel for more power. This would require recalibration, and worse, it might present a problem for a major sponsor. Mobil Oil already had a film crew in place anticipating a record on Mobil premium gasoline. Dawson concurred and then turned to Mobil's Ray McMahan for his take. McMahan well understood that alcohol would raise the power level and he also knew that Mobil was in too deep at this stage to back out. If a record were indeed certified, the commercial would have to praise the power of Mobil racing fuels and relate it to Mobil's street pump gas. The culprit in the power struggle was eventually traced to the additional 2,400 pounds of weight that had slowly attached itself to the car during construction. With a 6,000-pound initial design weight, the car had morphed to over 8,400 pounds, presenting a more difficult challenge for

"The ends were fairly wet. The middle was nice and dry although there were a few bumps."

- Bob Summers

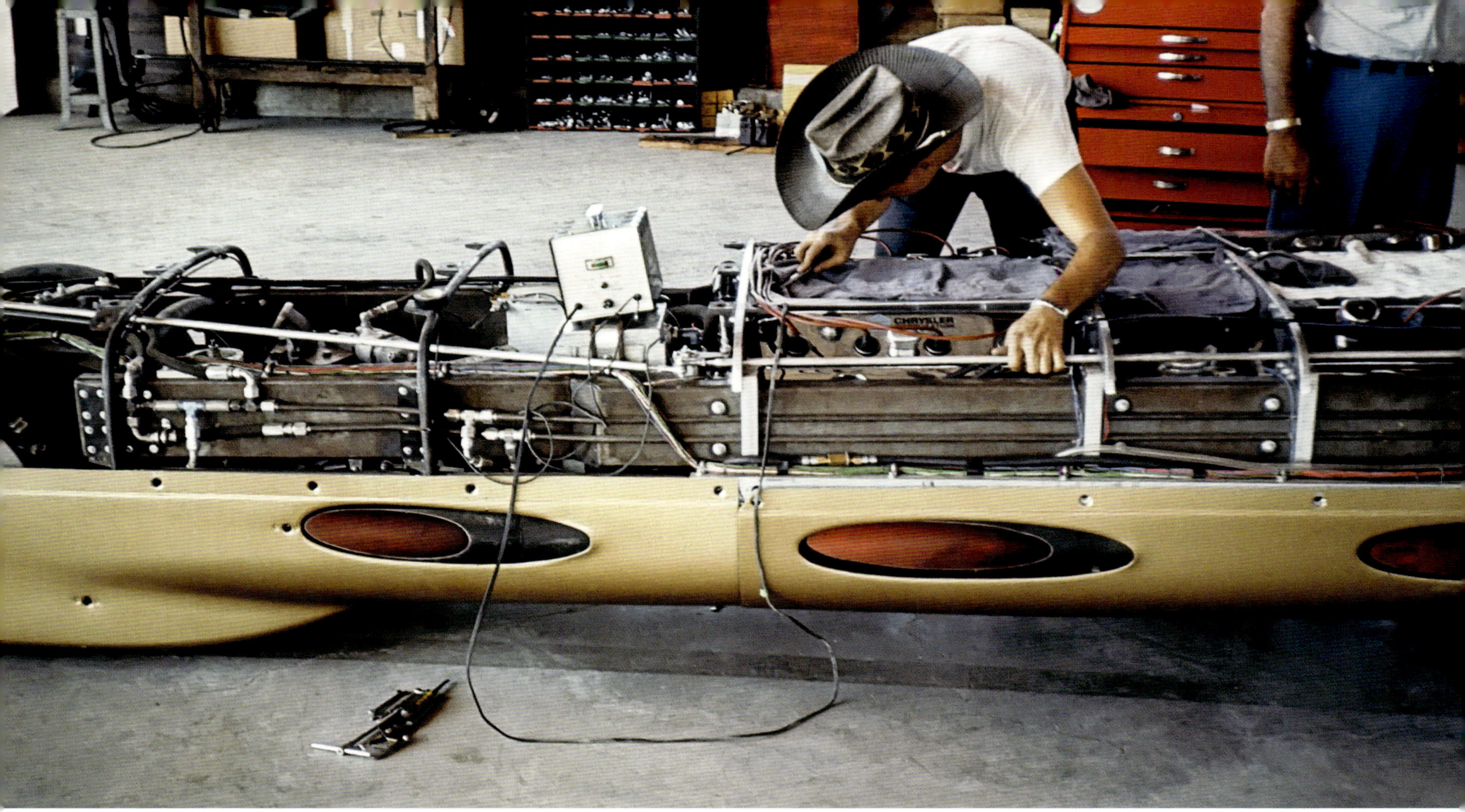

the engines. Dawson remained unconcerned, and McMahan approved the fuel change.

They labored intensely to ready the car to run on September 16th, only to endure a full deluge on the evening of September 15th that flooded the salt flats. It seemed their best efforts were ruined. The financial burden was mounting, and sponsor pressure loomed. Bill convinced Bob they had to stay and roll the dice, insisting that a record would easily forgive all debts.

Finally, on September 25, they got some open time on the course and made a run at 269 mph. They were encouraged. The next morning Bob made a run and was elated to find that he could shift the car and it seemed to gain stability the faster he went despite the course being soft. A confirming voice over the walkie-talkie removed all doubt, announcing a speed of 367 mph. They were in the game, but fate is a cruel mistress.

The 3-1/2° angle on the front driveshaft challenged Bob Summers to incorporate a fully functional driveline system within the limited confines of Korff's aerodynamic body requirements.

A torrential downpour greeted them in the morning, and it was clear they would not be able to run again. A long, quiet drive back to California was accompanied by silent thoughts of the record that had eluded them. It was a bitter pill.

Nearly a month later, Joe Petrali called to announce an opportunity to run if they could get there immediately. They hit the road and arrived on the salt on October 23, finding the course short, soft and treacherous, but they were determined to try. The next morning the Goldenrod was pushed off, and Summers let her rip to the tune of 400.667 mph for the flying mile and 405.095 mph for the kilometer. It was only the third 400 mph plus run by a wheel-driven car at the Bonneville salt flats. John Cobb and Mickey Thompson had previously achieved 400 mph runs. Jubilation ensued, but there was still no record. The task remained, and it was formidable.

The electric coolant pump nearest the front tire was wrapped in rags to protect it from the salt. In similar fashion, the extra batteries were wrapped and taped to protect the connections.

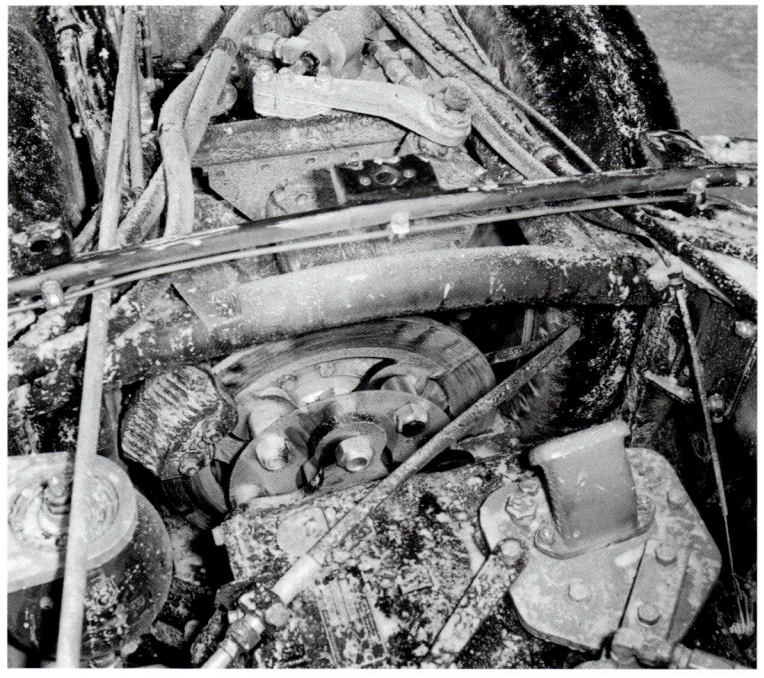

Post run inspections always found the car well covered with clinging damp salt. This had to be washed off after every pass to prevent damage to the car's various systems.

Bob reported breathing difficulties despite the use of a respirator and he noted that his goggles and the canopy had fogged up. But he wasn't quitting. The car was prepped for the return run. The engines and tires were serviced, and the tanks were refilled with fuel. With 15 minutes to spare, Goldenrod was ready to sprint the other way and into the record books. Bill pushed her off and his wheels spun hopelessly on the soft salt. The heavy Goldenrod had sunk into the salt up to its belly pan. A second push car failed to help, and finally, the fuel truck was used to tow the Goldenrod free with only minutes left.

It sped back down the course chasing glory, only to be cruelly denied by the gods of speed who were not yet in a favorable mood. The car decelerated through the final mile, recording a speed of 368 mph for the mile and 365 mph for the kilo. Summers knew something was wrong. Disappointment shrouded them with the heavy fog of failure. In much the same manner as every land speed racer that had gone before, the gods intended to make the team earn it the hard way. But they had seen the shiny side of 400 once, and they were confident they could flip that coin.

A dent formed in the nose tank due to a pressure change and expansion from overheating. More seriously, the power transfer gears between the front two engines had disintegrated, allowing the number two engine to over-rev and destroy itself. The left front wheel bearing had also burned out. The 600-mile trip back to California with the injured Goldenrod proved ample time to relive the experience and ponder the extent of the repairs necessary if Goldenrod was ever to run again. Somehow the road home seemed bumpier than ever, and the gods of speed were no doubt amused.

Goldenrod was unloaded and inspected, and the team gloomily contemplated their fate. They

Burned up wheel bearings hinted at looming problems. They were changed and all the bearings were adjusted looser to avoid further complications.

GOLDENROD

would have to get back to their day jobs and forget about racing for a year even if their sponsors didn't abandon them. Dark days were short, however, as Art Arfons called on November 2nd announcing that he had reserved a week of track time beginning on November 7th to challenge Craig Breedlove's new 555 mph jet record and they were welcome to share it if they could make it. Racing spirit swelled again. The brothers and Crew Chief James Crosby sprang into action to repair the car and install a replacement engine.

With Herculean effort, they made it and arrived on the salt ready to run on November 11, 1965. Arfons had already raised Breedlove's record, and Breedlove was due back on the salt on the 14th to make a try at Arfons' new record. The Summers Brothers were slotted into a narrow window between the dueling jet jockeys like an intermission act. Only they knew their effort was just as serious and could potentially stun the world if they succeeded. Arfons' generosity opened the door, and Goldenrod was poised to rush through it.

Precisely at 12:50 pm the car was moved to the starting line and Bob throttled it through despite foul air and a foggy windshield. The result: 400 in the mile and 404 in the kilometer. During the turn-around, Bob found that both rear wheel bearings had burned up. They were done for the day, but new bearings could be acquired and installed before the next day. Chief timer Joe Petrali advised them to adjust the wheel bearings looser as they only had to run 25 miles. It was good advice.

November 12th was their Hail Mary day. They were out of time with their backs to the wall again. Under cloudy skies and intermittent raindrops, Summers determined to make it happen no matter what. He stayed in the throttle through 7,000 rpm. With the chute out, he coasted five miles to a stop where a course steward met him and handed him a timing slip: 412.7 in the mile and 409.2 in the kilometer with an exit speed of

The genius of Bob Summers is widely acknowledged and never challenged. Former *Car Craft Magazine* editor Rick Voegelin told me, "Bob Summers had the Right Stuff. He was the closest thing to an Apollo astronaut I've ever known." Summers was an intense, but generous and humble man and broadly admired. His wife Becky told us that he invited her out to dinner on their first date and took her to McDonald's. Later, at the drive-in movie, a newsreel came on the screen detailing the Goldenrod's extraordinary achievements. Bob simply said, "Oh yeah, I forgot to tell you about that."

GOLDENROD

Goldenrod on the vast expanse of America's premier racetrack, the Bonneville Salt Flats. The car is framed by the fuel truck, team support truck and a Ford Mustang pony car.

417 mph. During the turnaround, bright sunlight suddenly broke through the clouds hinting quite strongly at a brighter result. Goldenrod was pushed off with five minutes to spare, engines running clean and strong. Summers wouldn't be denied this time. No faulty parts or unfortunate consequences would be permitted to interfere.

The day brightened further as he cleared the mile, Goldenrod flashing like a gleaming golden spear thrust into the heart of the record books. Petrali arrived to personally show Bob the timing slip. Summers examined it and nodded yes, accepting the new World's Land Speed Record of 409.277 mph in the mile and 409.695 in the kilometer. The gods of speed were satisfied that the Summers Brothers had earned their respect and the world took note.

From England, fellow land speed racer Donald Campbell called to express congratulations and admiration, remarking, "I have unbounded admiration for any man who can design, build and drive any automobile at any speed over 400 mph."

It was a glorious day for the young hot rodders who parlayed a minimal amount of capital and thoughtful application of available engines and performance hardware into a world record machine. Sponsors reaped their just rewards, and the brothers secured a staggering achievement that would easily last a lifetime.

But there's a postscript to the story. A nagging suspicion suggested that a good deal more speed was lurking under the Goldenrod's lengthy hoodline, and Summers was keen to have a go at it. That night they swapped the large bulky scoops for the streamlined scoops designed by Summers and Bob Herda and adjusted the calibration. The next morning they were given time on the course while Craig Breedlove made his final preparations. Summers adjusted his driving technique to ease the engines through the crucial low-speed period and let them sing their sweet song with high-speed ram air power. The reward was a staggering 425.99 mph blast that trumpeted Goldenrod's potential in no uncertain terms.

Goldenrod on the starting line wearing its record scoops. It is accompanied by two other legendary racers, the Bob Herda streamliner (lower right) and the Markley Brothers bellytank (upper right).

RECORD RUN: 409.277 MPH - November 12, 1965

"I knew we could do it. I was confident all along. I knew the car had the capabilities. It was just a matter of getting all the minor mechanical problems ironed out."

- Bob Summers

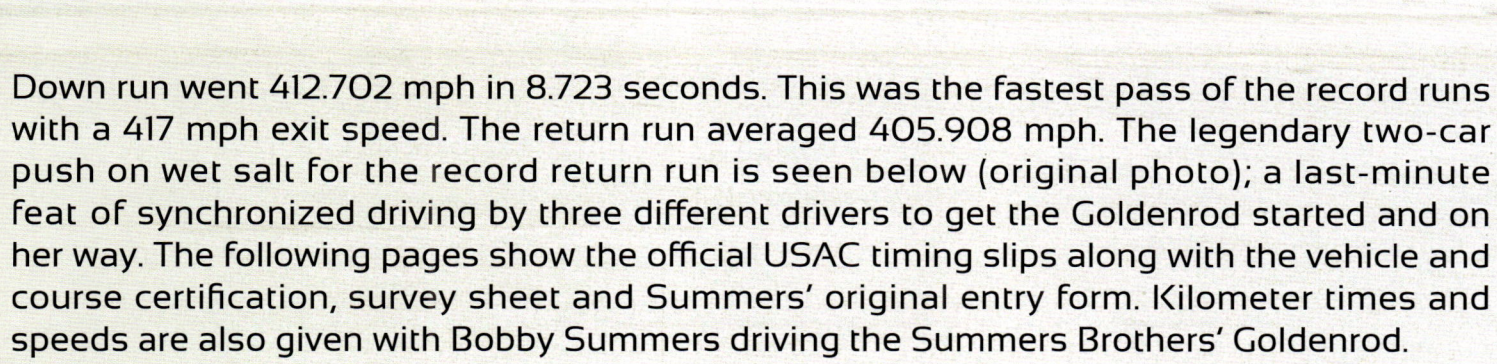

Down run went 412.702 mph in 8.723 seconds. This was the fastest pass of the record runs with a 417 mph exit speed. The return run averaged 405.908 mph. The legendary two-car push on wet salt for the record return run is seen below (original photo); a last-minute feat of synchronized driving by three different drivers to get the Goldenrod started and on her way. The following pages show the official USAC timing slips along with the vehicle and course certification, survey sheet and Summers' original entry form. Kilometer times and speeds are also given with Bobby Summers driving the Summers Brothers' Goldenrod.

"The shifting was good. I shifted from first to second gear at 180 mph. And then from second to third at 300 mph. That last shift will be at 425 mph when we get a little more power."

- Bob Summers

Excerpt from USAC Chief Timer Joe Petrali's notebook from the day of the record run. It shows a 2.5 mph wind from the north and 51 degrees on November 12, 1965. Runs were made in the morning at 9:25 and 10:17 respectively with the start and finish of the timed mile noted. Both mile and kilo times are shown with the calculations indicating a 412 mph down run (south) and a 405 mph return (north).

November 12, 1965
Summers Bros. to run at 07:30 AM Timers on at 06:30 AM

1st Run South   Time 09:25 AM   Wind 0   Temp 43°

Mile Fin 2:55:35.144   Kilo Fin 2:55:31.887
    St 2:55:26.421   St 2:55:26.421
    TT   8.723 – 412.702 MPH   5.466 – 409.245 MPH

2nd Run North   Time 10:17   Wind 2½ N   Temp 51°

Mile Fin 3:47:02.131   Kilo Fin 3:47:02.131
    St 3:46:53.262   St 3:46:56.678
    TT   8.869 – 405.908 MPH   TT   5.453 – 410.220 MPH

Average Mile 8.796 – 409.277 MPH   Kilo 5.460 – 409.695 MPH

GOLDENROD

Steaming and sweating like a true thoroughbred, Goldenrod wears it's salt colors proudly, having run its race and conquered the world record. Forty years later these glorious trappings would become the source of considerable frustration to the restoration crew.

Damp salt spray penetrated everywhere on the car, and the crew was forced to tape up the firewall in front of the cockpit to keep salt from entering the cockpit and affecting Summers' vision.

"It handled just beautifully, just great. We went out at 9:00 and had the record by 10:20 AM."

— *Bob Summers*

GOLDENROD

Happy day on the salt with safety and parachute specialist Jim Deist, Bill Summers, George Hurst, and Bob Summers. They wrote the new record on the tail and with tape above Bob's name. Note the patch on Summer's firesuit: Hurst, Firestone, Chrysler, Champion.

FÉDÉRATION INTERNATIONALE DE L'AUTOMOBILE

Certificate of Record

this is to Certify that
Bill and Bob Summers "Goldenrod"
with Bob Summers driving
achieved
F.I.A. International Records
Category A, Group I, Class 11
"The World's Fastest Automobile"
One kilometer - Flying Start - 659.341 K.P.H.
- and -
One mile - Flying Start - 409.277 M.P.H.
at
Bonneville, Utah Salt Flats, U.S.A.
on
November 12, 1965

FÉDÉRATION INTERNATIONALE DE L'AUTOMOBILE

The Goldenrod Crew

Jim Crosby's wife Lorna had the foresight to write the names of all the crew members on the back of this photo. These are the California hot rodders that labored tirelessly to gain the world's wheel-driven land speed record.

Left to Right:

"Oinker" Dietz
John Veenstra
Murph Ryan
Wayne Brandon
John Sprinkle
Jim Brown
Glen Ridge
Jim Crosby
Bob Summers
Bill Summers
Bill Cox
Larry DeVeny
Roy "Malty" Aldrich
Don Borth
Bill Duncan

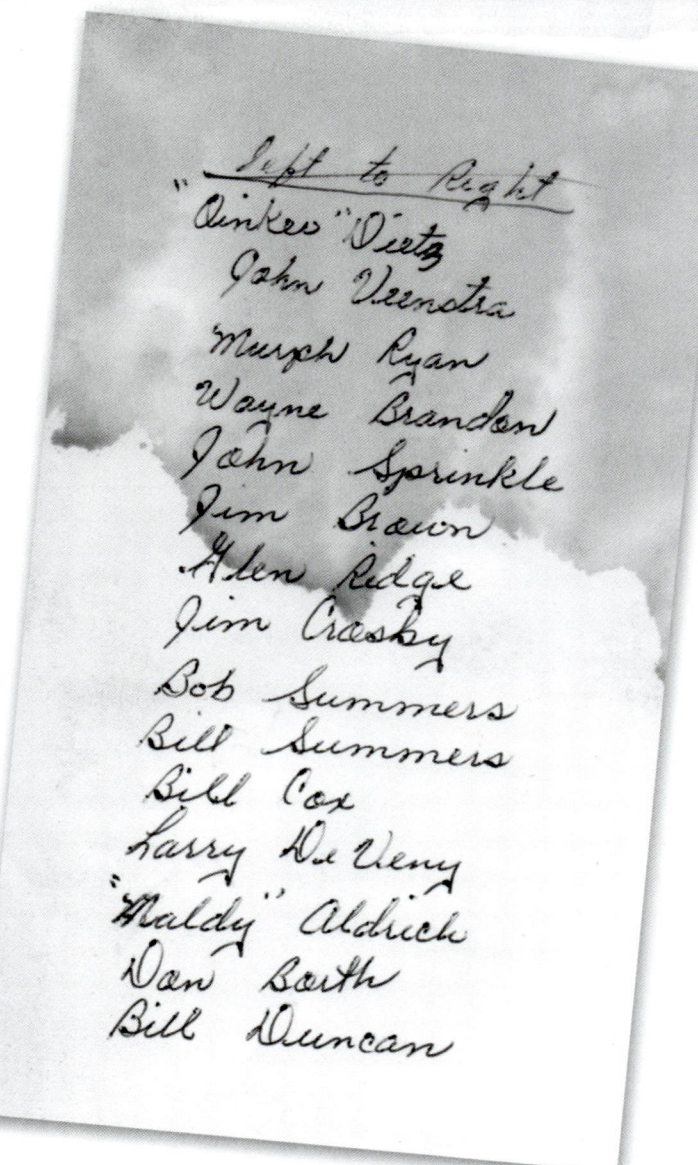

GOLDENROD RECORD DOCUMENTATION

UNITED STATES AUTO CLUB
FEDERATION INTERNATIONALE de L'AUTOMOBILE

NATIONAL & INTERNATIONAL
CLASS __UNLIMITED__
SPEED TRIALS

BONNEVILLE SALT BEDS – UTAH – USA
Date __NOVEMBER 12, 1965__
USAC Sanction No. __65 SR 7__
F.I.A. Listing ____

GOLDENROD	11 MILE STRAIGHTAWAY	BOBBY SUMMERS
Automobile	Course	Driver

FLYING 1 MILE
Distance

North Run	10:17AM	Recording	Time	Speed M.P.H.
Finish Time		3:47:02.131		
Start Time		3:46:53.262	8.869	405.908
South Run	09:25AM			
Finish Time		2:55:35.144		
Start Time		2:55:26.421	8.723	412.702
Time – – Two Directions			8.796	

Official Average __409.277__

We, the undersigned, served as the regularly appointed officials of the Contest Committee of the United States Auto Club and Federation Internationale de L'Automobile, in connection with the above times and record run of __BOBBY SUMMERS__ driving the __GOLDENROD__ under United States Auto Club Sanction __65 SR 7__ and we HEREBY CERTIFY that the above times and speeds are correct as shown and were made in accordance with all Rules and Regulations of the United States Auto Club Contest Committee and the Sporting Commission of the Federation Internationale de L'Automobile.

Joe Petrali
Chief Steward, Member Contest Committee
United States Auto Club and
Federation Internationale de L'Automobile

T. Ben Torres
Chief Observer, Contest Committee, United States Auto Club
and Federation Internationale de L'Automobile

John S. Wetton
Chief Timer, Contest Committee, United States Auto Club
and Federation Internationale de L'Automobile

Johnny Caswell
Chief Scorer, Contest Committee, United States Auto Club
and Federation Internationale de L'Automobile

GOLDENROD

UNITED STATES AUTO CLUB
FEDERATION INTERNATIONALE de L'AUTOMOBILE

NATIONAL & INTERNATIONAL
CLASS __UNLIMITED__
SPEED TRIALS

__BONNEVILLE SALT BEDS - UTAH - USA__
Date __NOVEMBER 12, 1965__
USAC Sanction No. __65 SR 7__
F.I.A. Listing _____

GOLDENROD	11 MILE STRAIGHTAWAY	BOBBY SUMMERS
Automobile	Course	Driver

__FLYING 1 KILO__
Distance

North Run	10:17AM	Recording	Time	Speed M.P.H.
Finish Time		3:47:02.131		
Start Time		3:46:56.678	5.453	410.220
South Run	09:25AM			
Finish Time		2:55:31.887		
Start Time		2:55:26.421	5.466	409.245
Time - - Two Directions			5.460	

Official Average __409.695__

We, the undersigned, served as the regularly appointed officials of the Contest Committee of the United States Auto Club and Federation Internationale de L'Automobile, in connection with the above times and record run of __BOBBY SUMMERS__ driving the __GOLDENROD__ under United States Auto Club Sanction _____ and we HEREBY CERTIFY that the above times and speeds are correct as shown and were made in accordance with all Rules and Regulations of the United States Auto Club Contest Committee and the Sporting Commission of the Federation Internationale de L'Automobile.

Joe Petrali
Chief Steward, Member Contest Committee
United States Auto Club and
Federation Internationale de L'Automobile

Ben Torres
Chief Observer, Contest Committee, United States Auto Club
and Federation Internationale de L'Automobile

John S. Wetton
Chief Timer, Contest Committee, United States Auto Club
and Federation Internationale de L'Automobile

Johnny Bennett
Chief Scorer, Contest Committee, United States Auto Club
and Federation Internationale de L'Automobile

GOLDENROD

UNITED STATES AUTO CLUB
FEDERATION INTERNATIONALE de L'AUTOMOBILE

NATIONAL & INTERNATIONAL
CLASS __UNLIMITED__
SPEED TRIALS

F.I.A. Listing
USAC SANCTION NO. __65 SR 7__
DATE __NOVEMBER 12, 1965__
__BONNEVILLE SALT BEDS - UTAH - USA__

ORIGINAL-OFFICIAL TIMING MACHINE TAPE OF CONTEST COMMITTEE, UNITED STATES AUTO CLUB ELECTROMATIC TIMING MACHINE.

Time			Description	Chief Steward U.S.A.C. & F.I.A.	Chief Timer U.S.A.C. & F.I.A.	Chief Scorer & Computer U.S.A.C. & F.I.A.	Time		
2:55:26.421	2:55:31.887	2:55:35.144	U.S.A.C. Sanction No. 65SR7 November 12, 1965 Original Timing Machine Tape of the U.S.A.C. Electromatic Timer (Beckman) as approved by U.S.A.C. & F.I.A. Records Flying 1 Mile & 1 Kilo Unlimited Class	*Joe Petrali*	*John A. Wetton*	*Johnny Bennett*	3:46:53.262	3:46:56.678	3:47:02.131

We hereby certify that the timing machine tape attached hereto is the original and official tape of the Contest Committee of the United States Auto Club Electromatic Timing Machine and that the impressions thereon were caused by the passage of the _____GOLDENROD_____ on the record runs certified to in this report; and we further certify that the timing machine was **STARTED** and was in OPERATION from __06:30 AM__ __2 HOURS 55 MINUTES__ hours prior to start of the official record attempt.

Joe Petrali
Chief Steward, Member Contest Committee
United States Auto Club and
Federation Internationale de L'Automobile

T. Ben Torres
Chief Observer, Contest Committee, United States Auto Club
and Federation Internationale de L'Automobile

John A. Wetton
Chief Timer, Contest Committee, United States Auto Club
and Federation Internationale de L'Automobile

Johnny Bennett
Chief Scorer, Contest Committee, United States Auto Club
and Federation Internationale de L'Automobile

GOLDENROD

BONNEVILLE SALT BEDS - UTAH - USA

Date NOVEMBER 12, 1965

UNITED STATES AUTO CLUB
FEDERATION INTERNATIONALE de L'AUTOMOBILE
TECHNICAL COMMITTEE REPORT

SANCTIONEE HURST, CHRYSLER, MOBIL & FIRESTONE

DRIVER BOBBY SUMMERS

CHIEF MECHANIC BOBBY SUMMERS

CAR GOLDENROD

COURSE 11 MILE STRAIGHTAWAY

ELEVATION 4228

ENGINE SPECIFICATIONS:

      4 CHRYSLER HEMIS
 BORE 4.250
 STROKE 3.750
 CYLINDERS 8   --- PER ENGINE
 Cu. In. 426

SPARK PLUGS CHAMPION

OVERHEAD VALVE YES

TIRES- FRONT FIRESTONE 6:50 X 16   REAR FIRESTONE 6:50 X 16

WHEELS HURST

BRAKES AIRHEART DISC

TRANSMISSION SPICER

GEAR RATIO 1 to 1

MOTOR OIL MOBILOIL 30

GEAR BOX OIL MOBIL VISREX R.C.

REAR END OIL MOBIL VISREX R.C.

TEMPERATURE 43 to 51 WEATHER CONDITION CLOUDY WIND VELOCITY 0 to $2\frac{1}{2}$

J. D. Tobey
United States Auto Club and
Federation Internationale de L'Automobile
Technical Representative

GOLDENROD

UNITED STATES AUTO CLUB
FEDERATION INTERNATIONAL de' AUTOMOBILE

NATIONAL & INTERNATIONAL
CLASS UNLIMITED
SPEED TRIALS

BONNEVILLE SALT BEDS, UTAH, U.S.A.

DATE NOVEMBER 12, 1965

USAC SANCTION NO. 65 SR 7

FIA SANCTION NO. _____

I, L. T. (BEN) TORRES, and my other assistant observers were stationed equidistantly at inside points on the STRAIGHTAWAY 11 mile course to observe BOBBY SUMMERS drive his GOLDENROD on his attempt for NATIONAL & INTERNATIONAL Class UNLIMITED Records. I HEREBY CERTIFY that all rules were complied with, and at no time during the course of his run did he deviate from the true course. I further certify that in establishing the record claimed, he drove the car in both directions of the course.

L. T. Ben Torres
Chief Observer--Contest Committee
United States Auto Club
Federation Internationale de' Automobile

GOLDENROD

UNITED STATES AUTO CLUB
FEDERATION INTERNATIONALE de L'AUTOMOBILE

ENGINEER'S CERTIFICATE

I hereby certify that on **Sept 1 1965** I measured the **1 Kilo and 1 Mile** distances along the record course at **Bonneville Salt Beds Utah ~ U.S.A** and established points for the beginning and end of these distances at **3280.83 feet** and **5280.00 feet**. I also certify that the gradient of the entire course is less than **one percent**.

S.G. Hook
Calif R.E. #1281

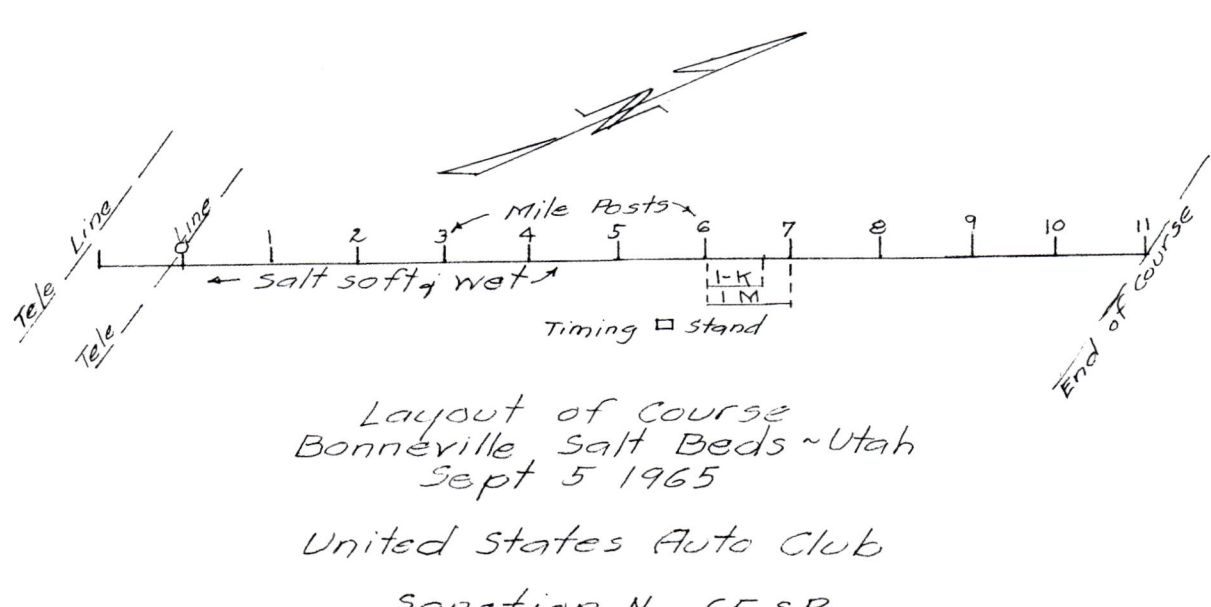

Layout of Course
Bonneville Salt Beds ~ Utah
Sept 5 1965
United States Auto Club
Sanction No. 65-SR-

S.G. Hook
Calif. R.E. #1281

GOLDENROD

SANCTION NO. GRANTED __65 SR 7__
(To be filled in at office)

Application for Official Sanction Grant for

AUTOMOBILE RACING CONTEST

Under the Rules and Regulations of the United States Auto Club

P. O. Box 24001, Speedway 24, Indiana

SANCTION REQUESTED FOR:

Date __July 26th 1965__ Time_____

Place __Bonneville Salt Flats Wendover Utah__

Name of Track_____ Size_____ Surface_____

Type of Event __National and International Worlds Record Attempts__

Program of Events_____

_____

_____

_____

Total Purse to be Posted_____

Promoter __Firestone Tire Co, Mobil Oil Co, Chrysler Motor and Hurst Co.__

Sanction Fee __250.00__ pd 8-2-65   Benevolent Fee_____

__Timing Fee 250.00 first day and 150.00 per day thereafter.__
pd 8-2-65

Application must be made at least thirty (30) days prior to the date of the event for which sanction is requested. Cancellation of an event less than thirty (30) days prior to the date of the event will be cause for forfeiting sanction fee, unless such cancellation is approved by the United States Auto Club. Application for sanction is not complete unless accompanied by sanction fee, and no contest shall be advertised as a United States Auto Club event until sanction has been granted by the United States Auto Club, Inc.

Form S-4

In Making Application for Sanction of this Race Meet by the United States Auto Club, the Undersigned Hereby Agrees:

(1) That if sanction is granted the events will be conducted under, and subject to, all rules and regulations of the United States Auto Club.

(2) That track herein named will be put in, and maintained in, a suitable condition and will be subject to an inspection by a United States Auto Club representative.

(3) That the business transactions of the undersigned will in no way bring discredit upon automobile racing or upon the United States Auto Club.

(4) That a duplicate of all entries be made available to the United States Auto Club.

(5) That the United States Auto Club in consultation with the promoter will select the list of officials. This shall be mailed to the promoter not later than 5 days prior to the event. The chief steward shall be the Representative of the United States Auto Club. The arrangements for these officials will be the promoter's responsibility.

(6) That all advertising and publicity for the event will carry the name, insignia, or some other means to identify the United States Auto Club as the official sanctioning body.

(7) That suitable precautions will be taken to provide safety for both spectators and participants and adequate track safety equipment as prescribed by the United States Auto Club will be provided.

(8) That the chief steward appointed by the United States Auto Club shall have the right to regulate or alter the program as conditions warrant.

(9) That the promoter agrees to make available to the United States Auto Club representative the amount of the benevolent fee assigned this meeting. In consideration of this benevolent fund fee received from the promoter plus entrant contributions, the United States Auto Club agrees to provide life and accident insurance covering all drivers, owners, crews, officials and other official personnel.

(10) That the amount of the guaranteed purse be made available to the chief steward or United States Auto Club representative at least 24 hours prior to the scheduled contest in the form of cash, certified check or suitable bond.

(11) That participants in the race meeting are to be limited to those in good standing with the United States Auto Club.

The undersigned understands and agrees that the connection of the United States Auto Club with the promotion of this race is purely advisory; that its regulations are promulgated for the improvement and stabilization of the activity and are without responsibility or profit and, in applying for this sanction, formally agrees to be bound by the Official Competition Rules of the United States Auto Club and by any modifications of them and, therefore, in consideration of the granting of this sanction, releases and discharges the United States Auto Club and their respective officials and representatives from all liability for personal injuries that may be received, and from all claims and demands for damages to personal property or to any agent or employee of his (or theirs), growing out of or resulting from the race, races, or any other events whatsoever, contemplated or held under these regulations or caused by any construction or condition of any track or tracks, equipment, cars or devices used therefor, or resulting from any act or failure of any official serving in connection with this race.

Date_____ Applicant's Signature _William R Summers_

Sanction Granted _Frank J Bani_ Date _8-2-65_

Sanction Number Assigned _65-SR-7_

(Sanction applications should be filed in triplicate, all three copies signed, forwarded to the United States Auto Club office, P. O. Box 24001, Speedway 24, Indiana. When sanction is approved, one copy will be signed by USAC representative and returned to the promoter. One copy will be sent to Zone Supervisor.)

PARTING SHOT:
425.99 MPH - NOVEMBER 13, 1965

Eight total runs to accomplish the developmental testing and set the FIA record is an amazing testament to Summers' design process, construction, workmanship, and crew discipline in operating a complex car. It also demonstrates the driver skills that Bob brought to this project in addition to his design and fabrication expertise. Getting comfortable in this car in that small number of runs is quite an accomplishment in itself.

The long unanswered question is why the Goldenrod never made another record attempt. According to Bill, Chrysler Corporation recalled the engines for testing and evaluation. The intent was to find more power in case their record was broken. It wasn't, and the engines slowly disappeared into the corporation. Some were revised and found their way into drag cars. The last surviving engine that remained intact was in the possession of Chrysler engineer

Bill Hancock. He later passed it to a Chrysler collector who was unresponsive to inquiries.

The morning after Goldenrod's record-setting performance, Summers made a stunning test pass at 425 mph using the reduced drag aero scoops that he and friend Bob Herda had originally designed for the car. The Goldenrod's staggering performance potential was swiftly revealed. "I didn't even shift into fourth gear," Summers remarked. "I would say this car is good for 450 mph. And that's what we'll go for next year when we try to raise the record." That record attempt was never made, but the Goldenrod's superior speed established an unmatched performance legacy that remained unbeaten by a normally-aspirated, piston-driven car for 44 years, 10 months and 9 days. Knowledgeable racers have suggested that the Goldenrod, with modern upgrades, would still be fully competitive today.

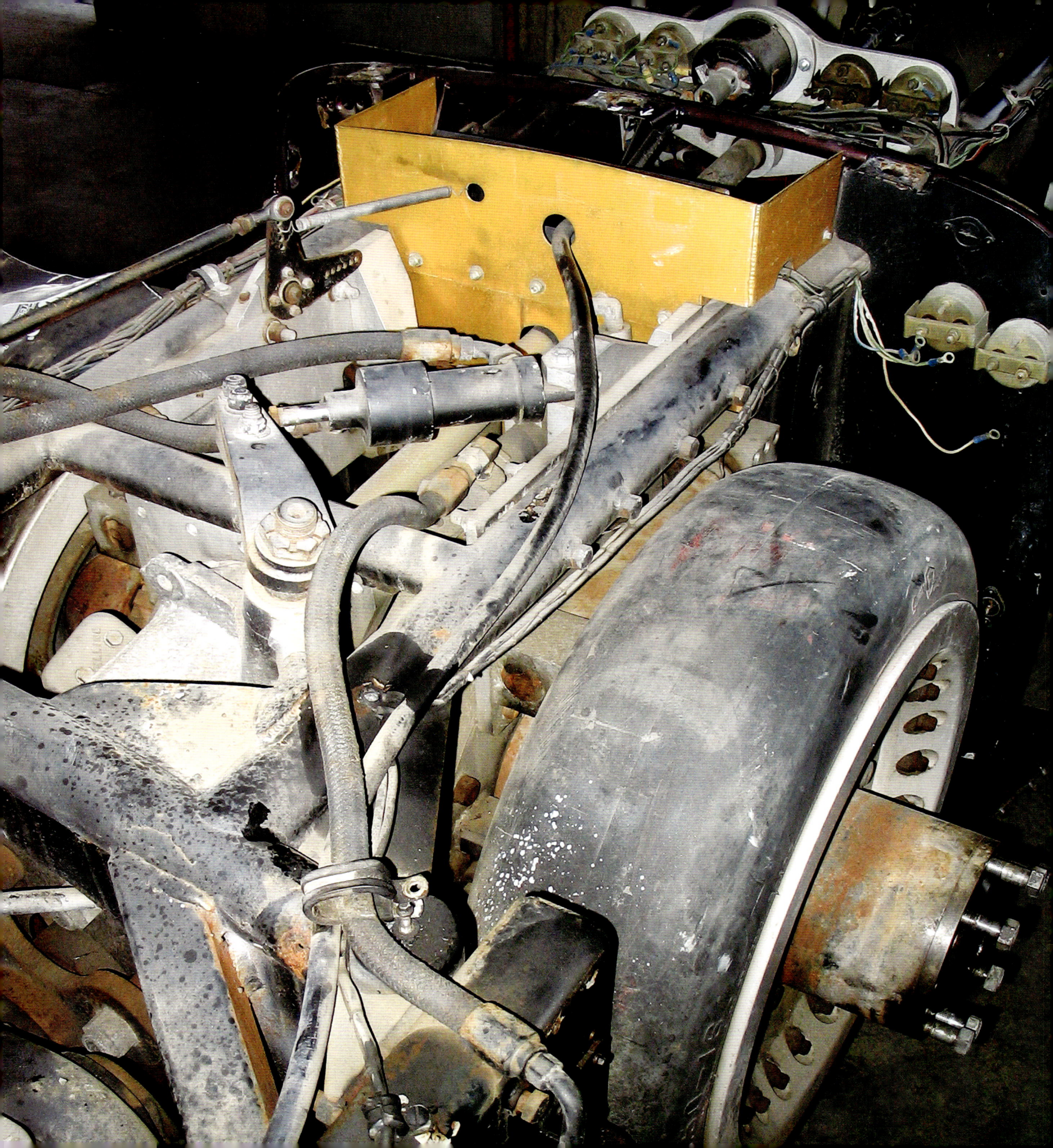

A Fine Mess

Thirty-eight years after that resounding record performance by the Summers Brothers team, I hitched up the Goldenrod in front of the NHRA Museum and towed it back to my shop to perform the detailed examination that Henry Ford Museum Curator of Transportation Bob Casey had agreed to when I approached him about photographing the car's technical details for a book. The Goldenrod, purchased by The Henry Ford, was awaiting transportation to the museum in Dearborn, MI, and this was my chance to get my hands on it. For a while at least, the Goldenrod was all mine. I could strip it down, photograph it…maybe even sit in it and imagine the glorious feeling that Summers experienced piercing the mile faster than any human before him. A certain reverence overcame me as I stood alone in the shop with an icon I had admired since high school. I sat on a stool and stared at it for a long time.

It was difficult to evaluate the car's true condition after almost four decades of weathering. Telltale signs hinted at the cancerous decay lurking within. Old, cracked and weathered plug wires plunged into murky water-filled plug tubes

Patient on the gurney arriving at the emergency room. Can she be saved? Body panels coming off for a first look at what ailed this legendary vehicle. A preliminary driveway inspection revealed a very sick patient.

GOLDENROD

Professional inspection party included from left to right: Bill Summers, Art Chrisman, Stu Hilborn, Manual Maldonado, Doug Kruse, along with Chrysler engineers Bob Mullen and George Wallace. Front row: Al Teague, John Baechtel and Tom Habrzyk.

The shop lift was taxed to the max supporting the car which was suspended via chains and eight 1,500-lb. tie-down straps while Tom Habrzyk fabricated the initial teardown stands equipped with casters for easy movement.

Once the supports were built the car was much more secure, and we could begin a more thorough exploration of its problems. All accessible bolts were repeatedly coated with penetrating oil while we surveyed the damage.

GOLDENROD

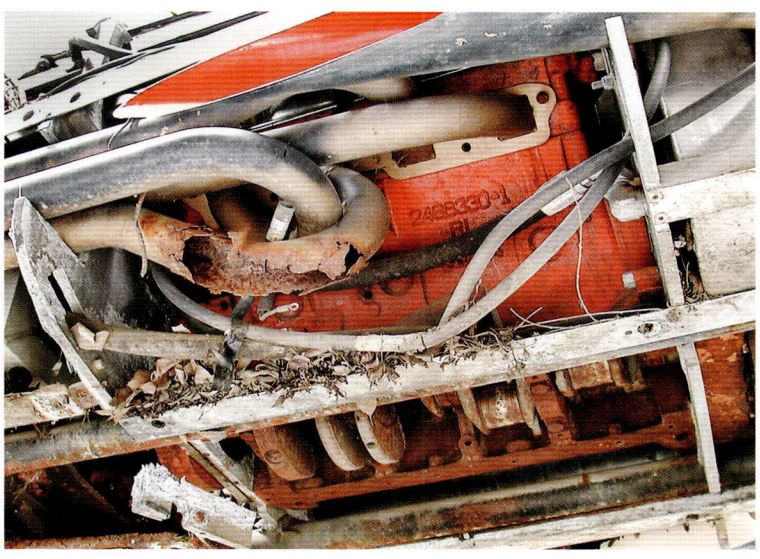

Dropping the belly pan sections revealed this unwelcome collection of dirt, leaves, twigs and assorted mouse droppings. High-speed flotsam that was most likely not along for the ride during the record runs.

Even more distressing was the condition of the exhaust headers which had quite clearly filled with water from the exposed dummy engines. Frame rail and bulkhead corrosion was severe and widespread.

in the valve covers of the two exposed engines. Hardware around and on the engines was rusted and corroded. The body seemed solid, but pieces were missing, and they revealed even greater distress. At this point, my friend, SCTA President Mike Cook, had no idea I was doing this and how it might affect him later. I was beginning to wonder if I had any idea what I was about to get myself into. I was on my own with only the support of museum representatives Bob Casey and Malcolm Collum, shop tech Tom Habrzyk and the beaming encouragement of my lady Leann Furgerson who simply commented, "Why don't you restore it?"

Bob Casey and Malcolm Collum took photographs, and we took turns anointing rusty bolts with sacrificial penetrating oil to see if it had any effect. None was noted. They caught a flight back to Detroit, and we backed the trailer in under the lift so we could suspend it to construct a pair of heavy-duty front and rear teardown cradles. At this point, we didn't even know if we would be doing the work as the museum was still required to put the job out for bid.

Before anything else was done, I decided to solicit the opinions of some knowledgeable people in terms of what it would take to perform a complete restoration of the vehicle while preserving as much of the original car as possible. The initial intent was to clean and repair, but not replace unless absolutely necessary. A small party seemed in order, so I called a caterer for some refreshments and began calling my guest list.

The first calls went to Bill Summers and Mike Cook. Mike was already committed elsewhere, so I called legendary racer Al Teague, and then Art Chrisman, as I knew he had been there when the car originally ran. I asked Stu Hilborn to help examine the induction systems, Eric Dahlquist for the historical perspective from a previous *Motor Trend* editor, fabricators Doug Kruse and Manual Maldonado, along with two Chrysler engineers who worked on the project back in the day, Bob Mullen and George Wallace. I could have brought in more, but I was not aware of some of them at the time.

GOLDENROD

GOLDENROD

These photos and those on the adjacent page show the extraordinarily grim state of disrepair that greeted us when the body panels were removed and the leaves and debris swept away. No component escaped the ravages of time, neglect, and creeping salt corrosion.

GOLDENROD

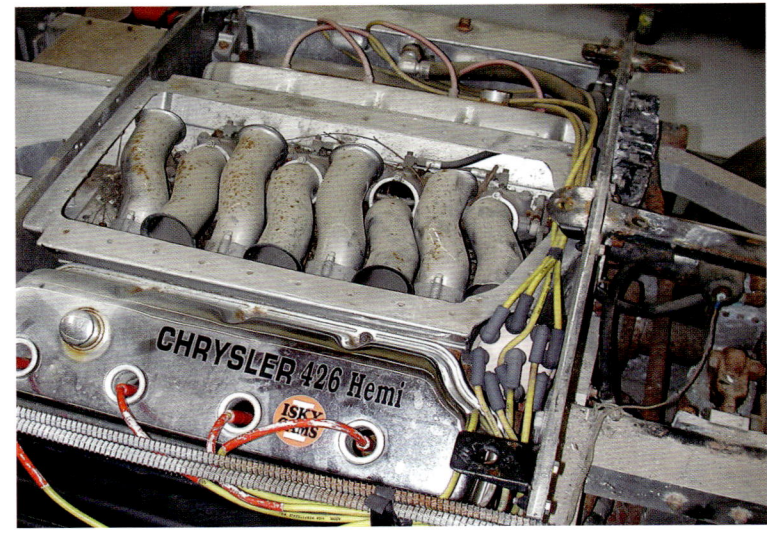

 **LANDSPEED RESTORATIONS**

4752 B, Felspar, Riverside, CA 92509

Bob Casey
Benson Ford Research Center
20900 Oakwood Blvd.
Dearborn, MI 48124

Dear Bob,

The accompanying CD contains photographs detailing the abysmal condition of the Summers Brothers Goldenrod land speed record car. The car is nearly impossible to move and neglect has taken its toll on one of the greatest land speed record legends. The car has spent most of the past 38 years exposed to the elements. It is heavily rusted and some of the main bulkheads are so corroded the primary frame rails are flexing under the weight.

All four engines are dummies and various fuel injection components are missing from each of them. The dummy engines are salvageable to display condition, but they will require some replacement parts. The body panels and scoops are in pretty good condition, but one of the engine covers is missing and the rear parachute cover is gone. Bill Summers still has one of the other engine covers. Both of the air scoops are in good condition.

The chassis and associated driveline parts are the worst. Most components are rusty and corroded and generally in poor condition. The good news is that it is all repairable if the car is disassembled and reconstructed carefully. It will have to be done bay by bay to inventory the good parts and determine parts that have to be remanufactured and/or replaced. It may be possible to have some of the original vendors remake or restore some of their products, but the bulk of the expense will fall under time and materials.

It will take some time to estimate the cost of restoring the car to a condition worthy of your fine museum. Until we can raise the car off the trailer we can't get the rest of the body panels off to fully determine its condition. A cosmetic restoration is pretty straightforward and we are fully equipped to handle it. Most of the industry that created the car is still located right here around us. Bill Summers himself is just down the road and has indicated he would help.

After viewing these photos, I think you will agree that a restoration is necessary. Since the car is such a significant piece of history, recapturing the land speed record from the British after nearly twenty years, I think it is important to restore it to exhibit condition, but not running condition. This is critical, since the British have taken such good care of their land speed record cars, and in light of the fact that this car still holds its record.

I assume you would display the car with some of the upper panels off so the engines and drive train can be viewed. With a complete restoration, the panels could be changed from time to time to freshen up the display. There is an extraordinary degree of innovation on display under the body and one can hardly imagine the nerves of steel it took to drive it.

I am presently trying to track down the original wind tunnel model from Cal Tech and I have gathered a lot of original material for the book I am doing. To give you a restoration estimate at this time is probably premature, but I wouldn't be surprised if it exceeds $200,000, even with parts contributions and help from the original hot rodding community. I'm hoping that you will be able to visit us in the near future to make personal observations and see the car's condition first hand.

Best regards,

John Baechtel

John Baechtel // Landspeed Restorations

GOLDENROD

It was a small but enthusiastic group of people that crawled over, under and around the car pointing out problems and various things that were missing such as ignition boxes, fuel pumps and so on. Stu Hilborn graciously offered to restore the fuel injection manifolds and fuel systems, and he also agreed to cast another manifold to replace one that had gone missing. Nearly forty years after the fact he still had the pattern. Based largely on these gentlemen's well-studied opinion, a basic plan was developed and I was able to pencil a bid for Casey to consider if we did the work.

My ace-in-the-hole was the local proximity of experts who were familiar with the car and a backup cadre of volunteers who were all familiar with land speed cars. Collectively, we represented a core group well equipped to render a proper restoration of a landmark land speed record car. Then there was the not small matter of expense and whether the museum really wanted to front the entire cost after already shelling out a considerable sum to purchase the car in the first place. Armed with a formidable collection of photos and written estimates, curator Casey penned a brilliant proposal to the U. S. government's Save America's Treasures program. His compelling arguments resulted in a generous government grant that covered more than half the expense of restoring the car. It was a clever and impressive move, and Casey deserves major credit for ram-rodding this project to completion. By this time, my buddy Mike Cook knew what I was up to, but he still didn't know how severely I would try our friendship by tossing a large portion of the job in his lap along the way. I didn't plan it that way, but unforeseen circumstances conspired to throw us both under the bus. Luckily, trooper that he is, Cook never flinched and attacked his portion of the task with determination and vigor.

GOLDENROD

A hidden eco-system was flourishing inside the intake manifolds, so we snapped this picture before firing up the leaf blower to clear it out.

The body panels were loaded up two and three at a time and carted over to Flying Colors Aero Paints, an aircraft repaint facility at the Riverside airport. Owner Steve Kelishes offered their services to strip all the panels to bare metal so they could be repaired and prepped for new paint and lettering.

GOLDENROD

Bob Summers did an incredible job of packaging the drivetrain within the narrow confines of the frame rails. Each engine has a front and rear bulkhead and the bulkheads are spaced closer together between paired engines to accommodate the narrower transfer cases for the drivetrain. To remove an engine, the C-clips for each bulkhead had to be removed or loosened to gain clearance for the engine to move upward.

GOLDENROD

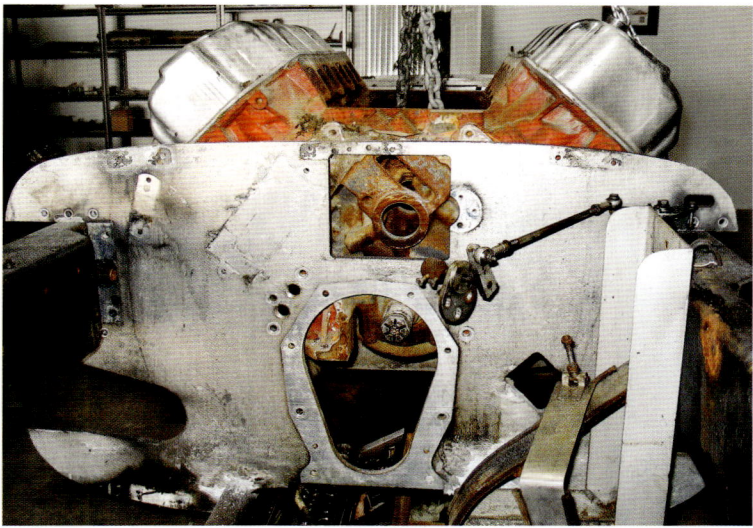

Bob had designed aluminum timing covers to hold the camshaft-driven Hilborn mechanical fuel pumps. Gary Cole of DC Waterjet in Las Vegas reverse-engineered a surviving original cover (left) to create a duplicate for one that was missing.

GOLDENROD

The original seat insert was recovered and sent to the museum for repair. Note the row of bolts securing the cockpit side armor to the frame rail. The dash panel and instruments were also sent to the museum for restoration.

After the record, Bob told friend Royce McClintick to choose a souvenir from the car. He chose the steering wheel, so they gave it to him on a plaque.

GOLDENROD

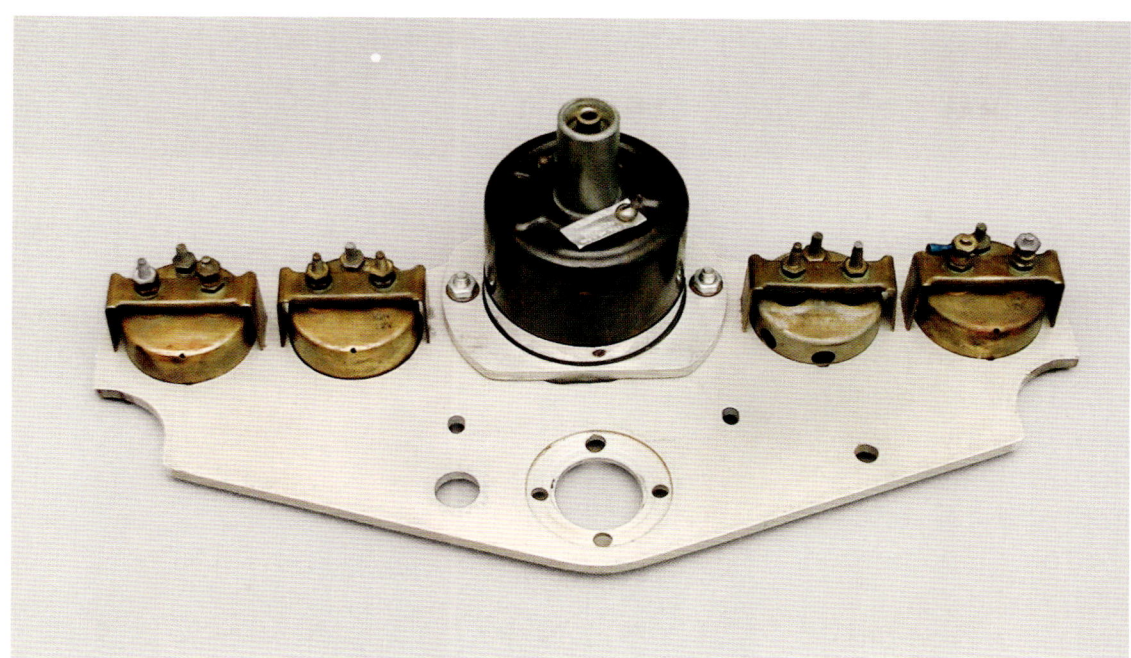

In-house conservators at the museum took on the difficult job of making the gauges look original. After restoration at the museum's Dearborn facility, the dash panel was returned in near new condition with all gauges functional.

The gauges are all original, but the gauge panels had seen better days. Museum specialists would make them look authentic again.

GOLDENROD

A FINE MESS:
THE TEAR DOWN BLUES

After a prolonged waiting period, museum curator Bob Casey finally secured the necessary funding and the project commenced. In the interim, preliminary research was performed, and important contacts were established. Advice from the original evaluation team proved to be invaluable in determining a course of action. Museum officials were keen not to over-restore the car, and we agreed to make a concerted effort to reuse every original nut and bolt we possibly could.

Chrysler Corporation's retired Goldenrod project program manager Peter Dawson was located and brought on board to consult. To facilitate a more dedicated work space, a 3,500 square foot empty building down the road was leased for the duration. It provided plenty of room for what soon became a very dirty job. The Goldenrod was in far

Right front hub assembly displays the extent of corrosion that attacked suspension members exposed to the salt. The bearings were fine, so they were cleaned and reused upon reassembly.

The expression "Oh, my god..." was never more appropriate. What we discovered after stripping most of the components from the car was horrifying, but we pressed on despite our reservations.

GOLDENROD

The Summers-designed center section was discovered in good shape. It mounts to the lower frame rail via the aluminum plate. The bolts were seized, but heat and penetrating oil eventually freed them.

Direct coupling mechanism connecting the rear transmission to the rear gearcase incorporated a custom Airheart disc brake rotor to provide driveline braking under 100 miles per hour.

The rear transmission was angled to gain clearance for the steering box and cable-actuated shifter mechanism on top. Body braces and lower supports were badly rusted, but salvageable.

GOLDENROD

The upper portion of the frame is narrowed ahead of the front bulkhead where the 2 x 6-inch side rails end. The front transmission, gear casing, and transfer case are cantilevered forward in a narrowed structure. Summers fabricated these beefy triangular braces to anchor the arrangement securely at the front bulkhead.

worse shape than even the experts had estimated and we were concerned with the enormity of the task ahead of us.

If you thought it looked bad in the preliminary inspection, you probably need to be sitting down for the next few pages. The photos pretty much speak for themselves. Severe corrosion and rust were everywhere. Not many components were missing, but some were so far gone it was clear they would have to be replaced. The eight aluminum bulkheads are a primary example. It quickly became clear that the car would have to be stripped to the bare chassis. In the bottom photo to the far right, museum conservator Malcolm Collum absorbs the dismal assessment I'm presenting and wholeheartedly agreed with the plan. Every picture tells a story and it's a sad tale indeed when you see the conditions in the heart of the beast. One can argue that it should never have been allowed to deteriorate so badly, but it was still saveable, as you will see.

Some components seemed almost beyond repair. The front coil-over shocks were frozen solid and could not be loosened. The aluminum adjusters had delaminated to the point that they were falling apart and could not be turned at all. The rear shocks were in better shape, but the mounts were equally distressed. The ravages of time and neglect were daring us to try to fix it.

GOLDENROD

The throttle linkage assemblies were intact and functional, but the bolts in the C-clamps that secure each bulkhead to the upper frame rail (right) proved troublesome and required heat to remove them.

Once we got it off the trailer and back on the stands, the dreadful task of disassembly loomed large. To make it easier to separate and catalog all the pieces, we separated the car into engine bays, transmission bays, cockpit and so on. A trip to the local Costco cleaned them out of all their multi-level shelf kits to line the walls of the shop.

GOLDENROD

The front transmission coupler was also equipped with an Airheart disc brake rotor. Here the transmission has already been removed and you can see the uprights that connect to the top frame rails and the aluminum plate Summers fabricated to position the front driveshaft bearing. The CV joint, suspension members, and hub assembly have been removed in the lower photo.

GOLDENROD

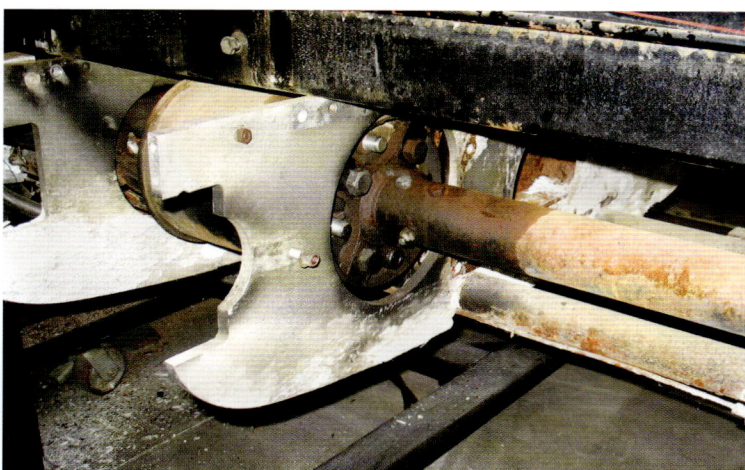

The driveline down the left side of the car consisted of four transfer cases; one between each pair of engines to transmit power out to the driveshafts and one at the front and rear to direct power back to the centerline for the transmissions. The narrow section between the center two bulkheads in the upper photo is a space between the two pairs of engines. It is occupied by the main center fuel tank which supplied engines two and three.

GOLDENROD

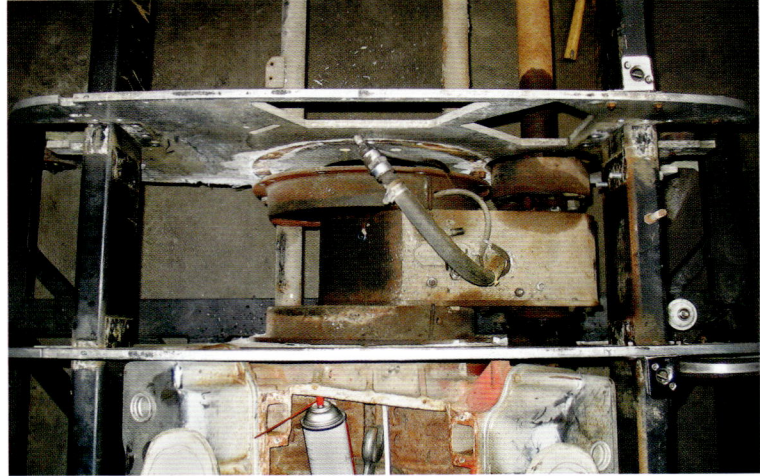

Top left view shows how the transfer case between paired engines transferred power out to the driveline assembly running down the left side of the car. Center views show details of the same assembly between the bulkheads. The bulkheads were machined with large holes to accommodate the anti-vibration couplers. As seen at the lower right, it was easier in some cases to remove entire units together to disassemble them outside the car.

GOLDENROD

These views all reveal the sad and often hidden condition of components found all over the car. It was even worse than it looks. Everything you see here was pretty much seized up solid. Fasteners did not want to turn, and some pieces literally were falling off the bottom of the car. The body mounts and lower supports were particularly distressed and a few support members were actually found lying in the bottom panels upon removal.

GOLDENROD

The two bulkheads in the foreground sandwich a transfer case between two back-to-back engines. The V-configuration of each engine dictates that the right-hand cylinder head sits farther back, hence the cutout in the bulkhead to let the cylinder head and valve cover protrude into the bulkhead space. So you see a similar cutout in each bulkhead, only on opposite sides because of the reversed engine. The larger cutouts at the top center are for the inlet air box entry points. On the far bulkhead, the square opening accommodates a bulge in the aluminum air box for the end ram tube on the intake manifold. The machined opening to the right of it provides space for the distributor to rotate. You can see an old distributor still in place on the dummy engine.

GOLDENROD

More carnage from days gone by and years of neglect. Everything exposed to the salt was badly corroded. All of the suspension and drive components directly exposed to salt spray were particularly susceptible to corrosive damage. Note the flange on the rear center section (center right) crumbling and breaking along with heavily-rusted fasteners and the left rear hub arm seized in its aluminum mount (center left).

GOLDENROD

Hydraulic lines for the front clutch and brake run along the right side main frame rail. In this picture, you can see how the aluminum bulkheads bolt to tabs on the lower frame rails and attach to the upper frame rail with the large C-clips. You can see the full setup with the dummy engine to the left. The bulkheads have U-shaped cutouts on the bottom, so they also sit saddle-like on two of the lower frame rails. Above: Note the built-in front caster for steering stability.

GOLDENROD

The sturdier material of the driveline components withstood the ravages of the salt better than the fragile aluminum bulkheads which had long since surrendered to decay.

Rear transmission with clutch housing and transfer case was in great shape due to isolation from any salt spray. The oil in the transmission still had color.

The vertical rear dry sump storage tank holds the same capacity as the side-saddle tanks for the center engines. Note the throttle linkage neatly tucked along the bulkhead to the left of the tank.

Battery box filled with brackish water from countless rain storms. Despite this, many of the pieces were ultimately cleaned and restored, although in some cases heavily pitted from corrosion.

GOLDENROD

The bulk of the teardown stage was performed by just two people working night and day; myself and Leann Furgerson. A surprise master with a torch and a can of penetrating oil, she also accomplished disassembling most of the driveline all by herself.

Teardown took many long months. We had to be extremely careful not to cause more damage. Most bolts required heat, lots of penetrating oil or heat with wax to remove them. Then they had to be cataloged, cleaned and prepped for final installation. Every effort was made to save and reuse as many original nuts and bolts as possible. The success rate was near perfect, and there are very few new fasteners anywhere on the car.

Among the volunteers who stepped up was a guy who had a suspension shop. He claimed he could repair the shocks and make them look original. After some discussion, we agreed to let him try, and he took them with him when he left. Long story short, he was never seen again. The phone number on his card was no good. We had no way to track him down. One of the other volunteers knew him, but he couldn't find him either. We don't know if he was a souvenir hunter scamming away with some pieces or maybe he just never got around to doing the work. For all we know, the parts are in a landfill somewhere or still lying around on the shelf in some shop. For expedience, solid bars were added to replace the shocks. As the car is rarely displayed with the panels off, the museum showed little interest in finishing off some of these minor details that we as perfectionists feel are necessary for authenticity. For reference, here's how they looked when the car was originally constructed (right).

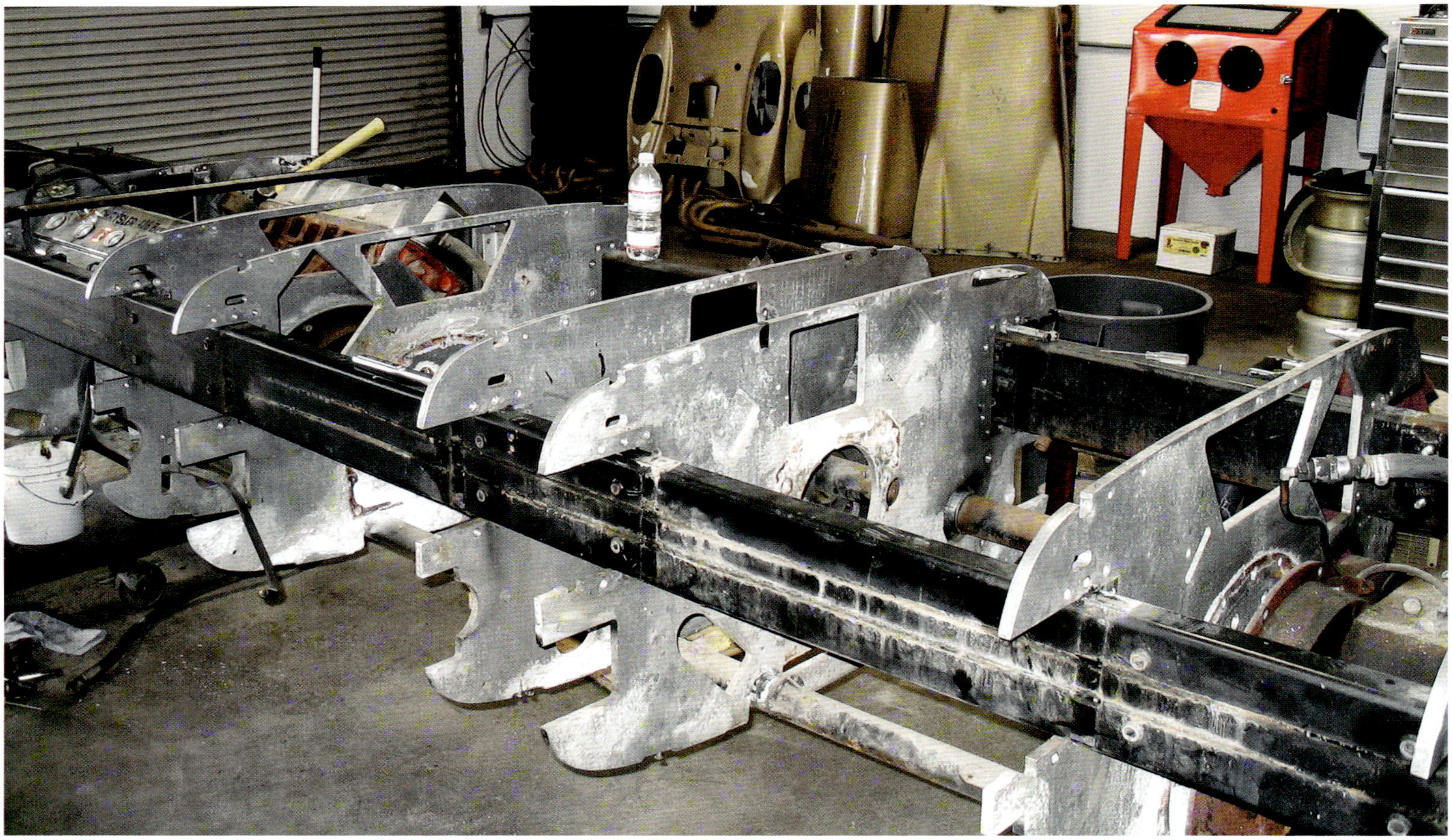

GOLDENROD

The aluminum bulkheads were the most seriously decayed pieces on the car. We knew immediately that we were going to have to replace all of them. You can see the advanced state of decay they suffered from decades of salt corrosion. The heavy-duty dollies constructed by Tom Habrzyk provided good access to the car and made it easy to push it around for shop cleanup while providing work space for individual projects. Note the rusty crankshaft that fell out on the floor.

GOLDENROD

At the top left, you can see part of the front steering mechanism and a cut off water hose that reveals the location of the coolant flow return outlet on the left upper frame rail. Coolant flowed down the right side upper frame rail and returned to the nose-mounted coolant tank via the left side rail. The lower frame rails were heavily pitted and seemed unsalvageable. After blasting, the rails and shock mounts (lower right) cleaned up reasonably well, but rusted up again almost immediately. Re-blasting and chemical corrosion treatment were required to make them ready for sealer and paint.

GOLDENROD

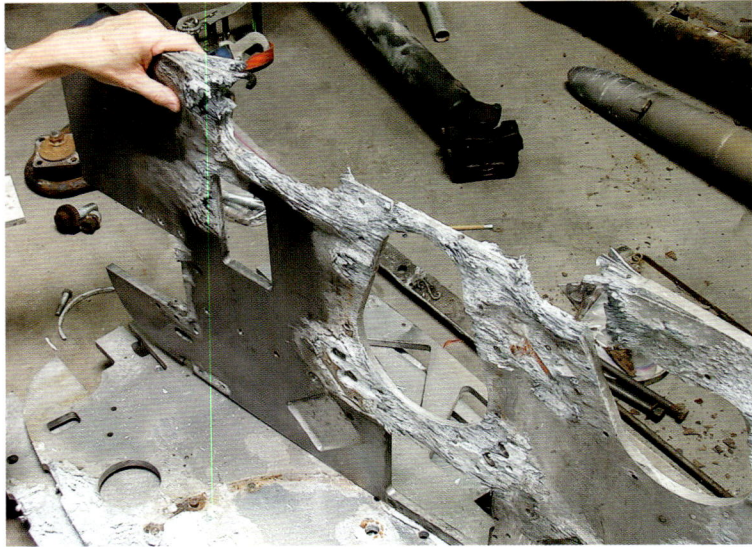

The aluminum bulkhead damage was severe and beyond reasonable repair. In the photo above you can see that the U-shaped saddles for the lower frame rails and the cutout for the oil pan rail have completely disappeared with no possibility of restoration.

Every bulkhead on the car sustained damage critical enough to warrant replacement. As you might expect, the problem was particularly severe wherever aluminum and steel parts mated. Below: museum conservator Malcolm Collum surveys the damage firsthand before the bulkheads are removed from the frame.

The bulkheads were cataloged "A" through "H" from front to back. No two bulkheads look alike, so each one was a custom piece painstakingly machined by Summers and Crosby. Take a close look at the details to see how the aluminum was slowly delaminating from corrosion. In a few places, remnants of the bulkheads remained bolted to the lower frame rail tabs while completely separated from the bulkhead itself.

With side frame rails removed the skeleton is fully exposed. The bulkheads were plucked off and put aside to be copied, and the bare frame was sand blasted twice. The blasting company did a particularly exceptional job, flipping the chassis over multiple times to make certain that they didn't miss anything.

The frame required multiple sand blastings to remove all the embedded rust. It was finally treated with a sealer and a primer prior to repainting.

The Goldenrod was accidentally dropped by dock workers on a trip to England, and the frame broke. We ground the broken weld, pulled it back to square and rewelded it.

Author with Henry Ford Museum Curator of Transportation Bob Casey examining old magazine articles and disassembly photographs to confirm assembly details. The piece on the table is the front upper frame for the transmission, gear case and suspension mounts and the front clutch and transfer case. It is upside down, but you can see the short vertical tubes that connect to uprights on the lower frame rails. The crossmember has a central mount for the front transmission, and both side rails have separate mounts for the opposite end of the transmission. The splayed plates in the foreground are mounts for the front transfer case and the nose cone framework. The frame rails terminate at the other end where they bolt directly to the front bulkhead with 3/4-inch bolts. On the floor, you can see the original dummy engines that were removed, plus a cylinder head and two of the transfer cases that have not yet been restored.

The side-saddle dry sump storage tanks sit on shelves attached to the main frame rails. Here the tank has been removed, and you can see the strap clamps used to secure it. The aluminum channel running across the outside of the bulkheads is the beltline mount for the body panels. Note the Dzus fastener mounts. Many of the small screws holding the bar to the bulkheads were frozen and required heat to remove.

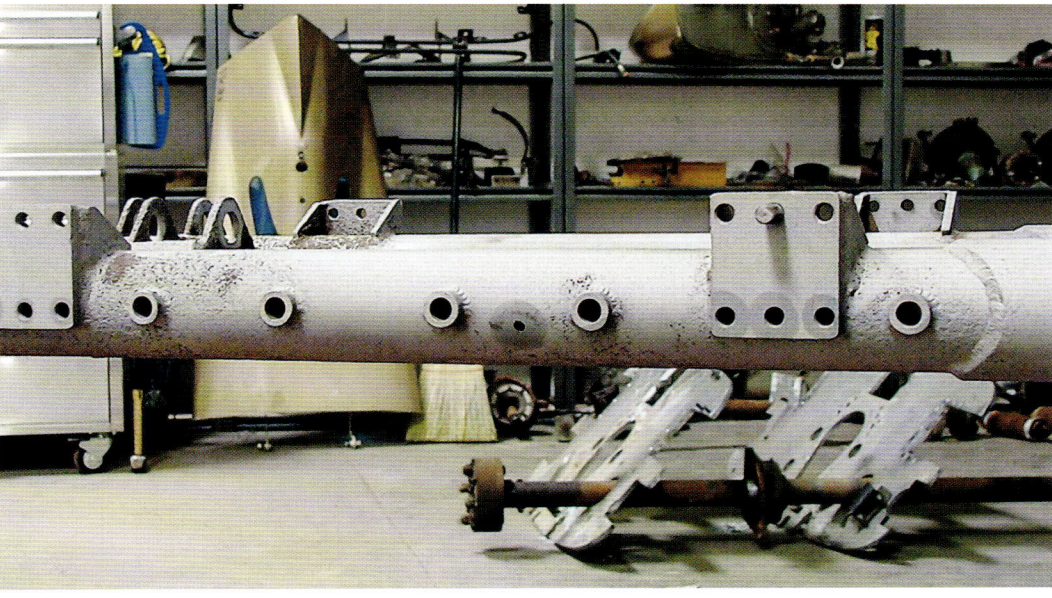

Close-up of the front upper frame extension with upper control arm mounting brackets shows the extensive pitting on the frame rail tubing. All the mounting holes for the aluminum gear case mounts use welded reinforcement tubes for maximum strength.

GOLDENROD

A FINE MESS:
BULKHEAD REPLACEMENT

Digital technology and industrial might combine to make all-new aluminum bulkheads for the Goldenrod.

One of the most perplexing problems of the restoration was the severe degradation of the eight aluminum bulkheads. A rescue angel came in the form of a Faro articulating arm that took precise digital measurements of each bulkhead and rendered a detailed digital file that could be read by Duane Cole's waterjet cutter in Las Vegas.

Faro rep Jeff Squibbs brought the advanced measurement technology to the Landspeed Restorations shop and performed a hands-on demonstration for a group of engineering students hosted by the Society of Automotive Engineers (SAE) via Doug Kruse. Every bulkhead had the same basic shape, but with different openings to accommodate whatever support components were fitted at that station on the car.

Armed with the digital bulkhead maps, we trucked to Las Vegas where Bonneville racers Duane and Gary Cole of DC Waterjet cut us a

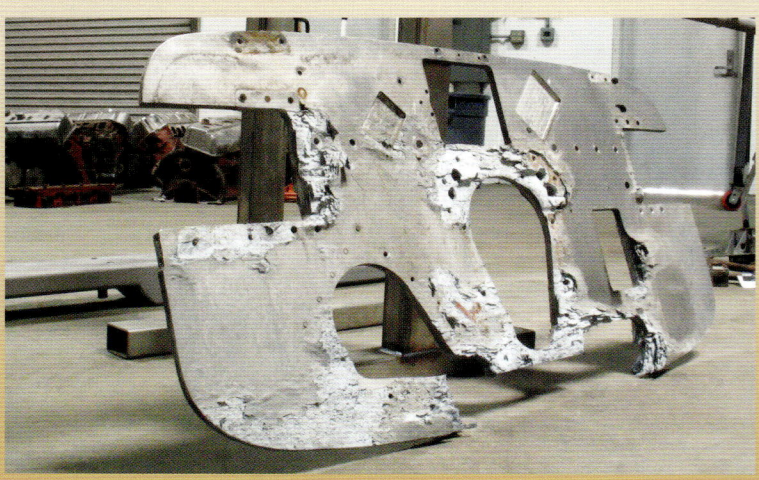

perfect set of eight new bulkheads with their waterjet. The combined precision of the Faro scanner and the waterjet cutter was spectacular as these two evolving technologies combined to save the day.

But there was still one more problem. To provide clearance for linkages, valve covers, and other components, the Summers had milled assorted notches into some of the bulkheads, something the digital waterjet was not able to duplicate. Fortunately, there is a lot of depth within the land speed racing community. Engineer Bob Robe from Gale Banks Engineering eyeballed the task and had us load everything into his vehicle. He took them to his home shop and milled perfect copies.

GOLDENROD

Note the high precision of the water jet cutter as it renders each bulkhead an exact copy of the original. A 4' x 8' sheet of 1/2-inch aluminum yielded 4 bulkheads. Two sheets were required to replace all eight. All of the bulkheads have square notches on each side to accept the large 2 x 6-inch side frame rails. A pair of smaller half-round notches at the bottom allow them to sit on the lower frame rails where they are bolted to supporting tabs.

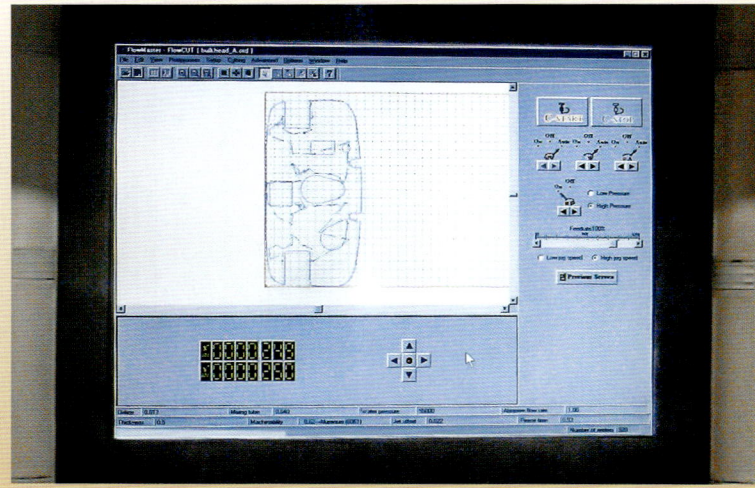

The digital file created by the Faro articulating arm scanner is loaded into the water jet computer, and the cutter software is linked to the program. The automated program will run to completion according to the file.

The program checks its work as it goes and pauses when necessary. The cutter uses a fine slurry of sand and water at 60,000 psi to cut perfectly straight, smooth lines and holes with very close tolerances.

GOLDENROD

An honored guest at the SAE tour, Chrysler retiree George Wallace (left), one of the original Chrysler engineering team assigned to the Goldenrod project in charge of driveline engineering, was presented an award recognizing his contribution to Goldenrod's success.

The SAE shop tour was a memorable experience as SAE members from the Orange County chapter were treated to a detailed demonstration of the Faro arm's measurement capabilities applied to a real-world application where precision was essential.

Note the valve cover and distributor clearance notches milled into the bulkhead by Bob Robe. The waterjet is also not capable of cutting an angle as seen on the square opening at the upper center. Robe added the appropriate angle to accommodate the linkage. At the right, you can see how Summers fabricated C-shaped aluminum blocks to capture the frame rail when bolted to the bulkhead.

GOLDENROD

A FINE MESS:
TRANSFER CASE RESTORATION

The enormity of the restoration task brought a lot of selfless and talented volunteers to the effort. David Basham and a small crew from Basham Motorsports in San Bernardino took on the difficult challenge of restoring the driveline transfer cases. Their hearty effort resulted in this remarkable preservation of the original geartrain and supporting components.

Front transfer case prior to removal from the car. It was externally rusty, but gave little indication of the dismal conditions lurking inside.

GOLDENROD

The gears were heavily rusted, and most of the bearings had seized. Following a lengthy cleanup, all new bearings were installed, and the transfer cases were restored to fully-functional, ready-to-run capacity. When finished, the entire driveline turned freely and easily. Top photo shows the mounting brace for the nose water tank.

GOLDENROD

A FINE MESS: HEADER REPAIR

Sitting outside unprotected for many decades caused the near destruction of Gary Hooker's beautifully fabricated headers as they repeatedly filled with rainwater. Former Hooker Headers lead design tech Tom Dawson masterfully repaired the damage while carefully preserving the integrity and layout of Hooker's original design.

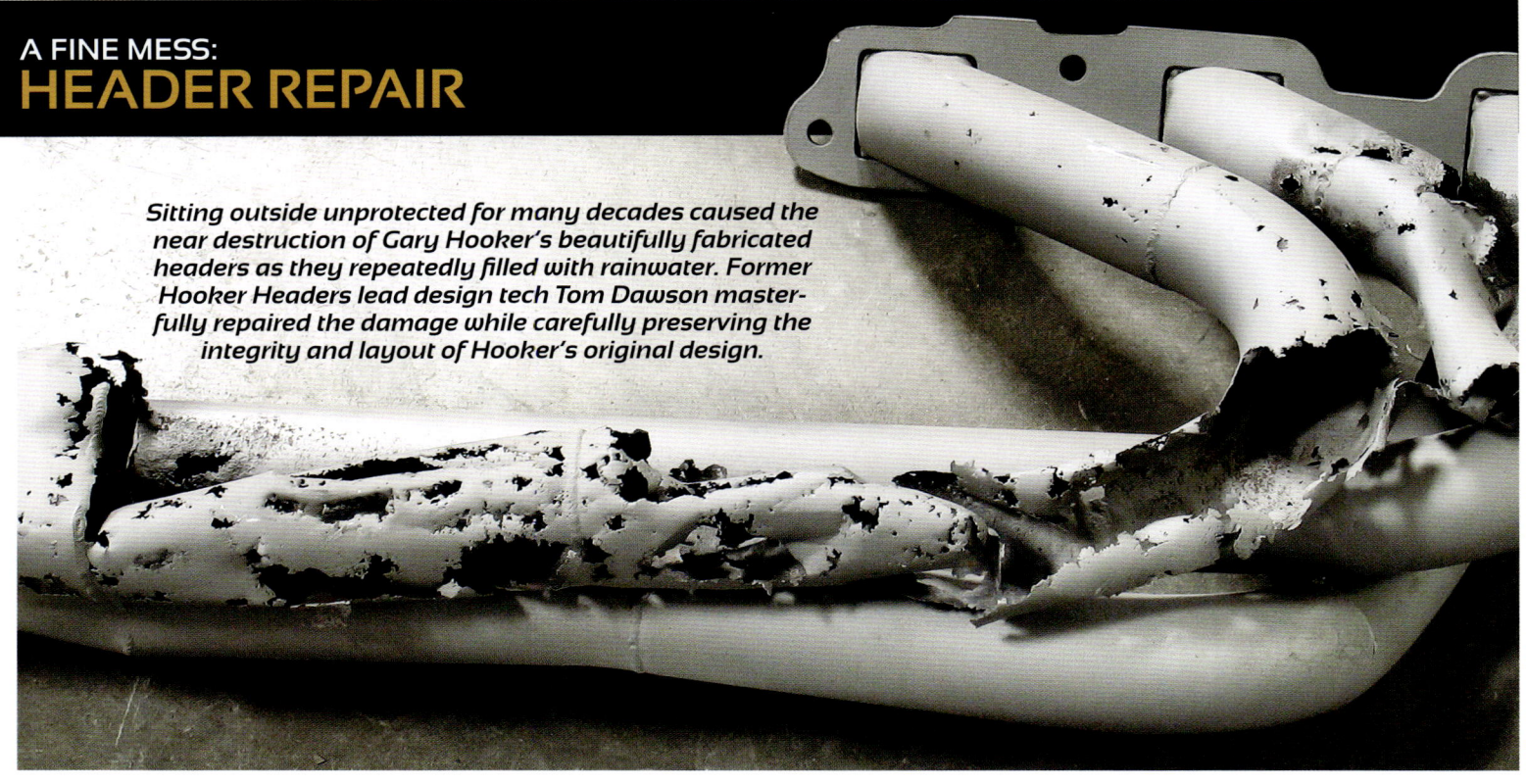

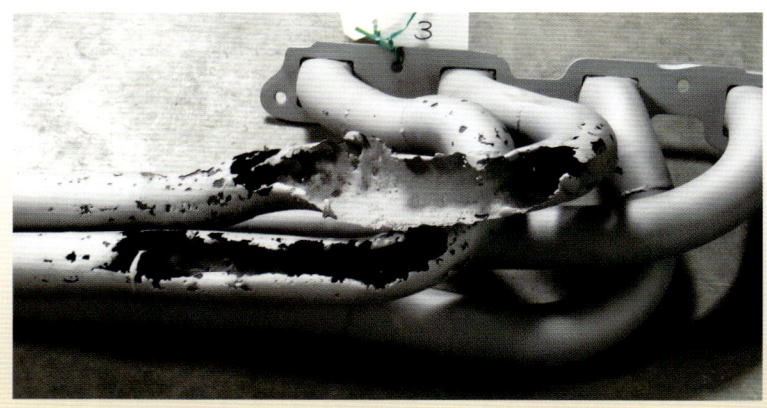

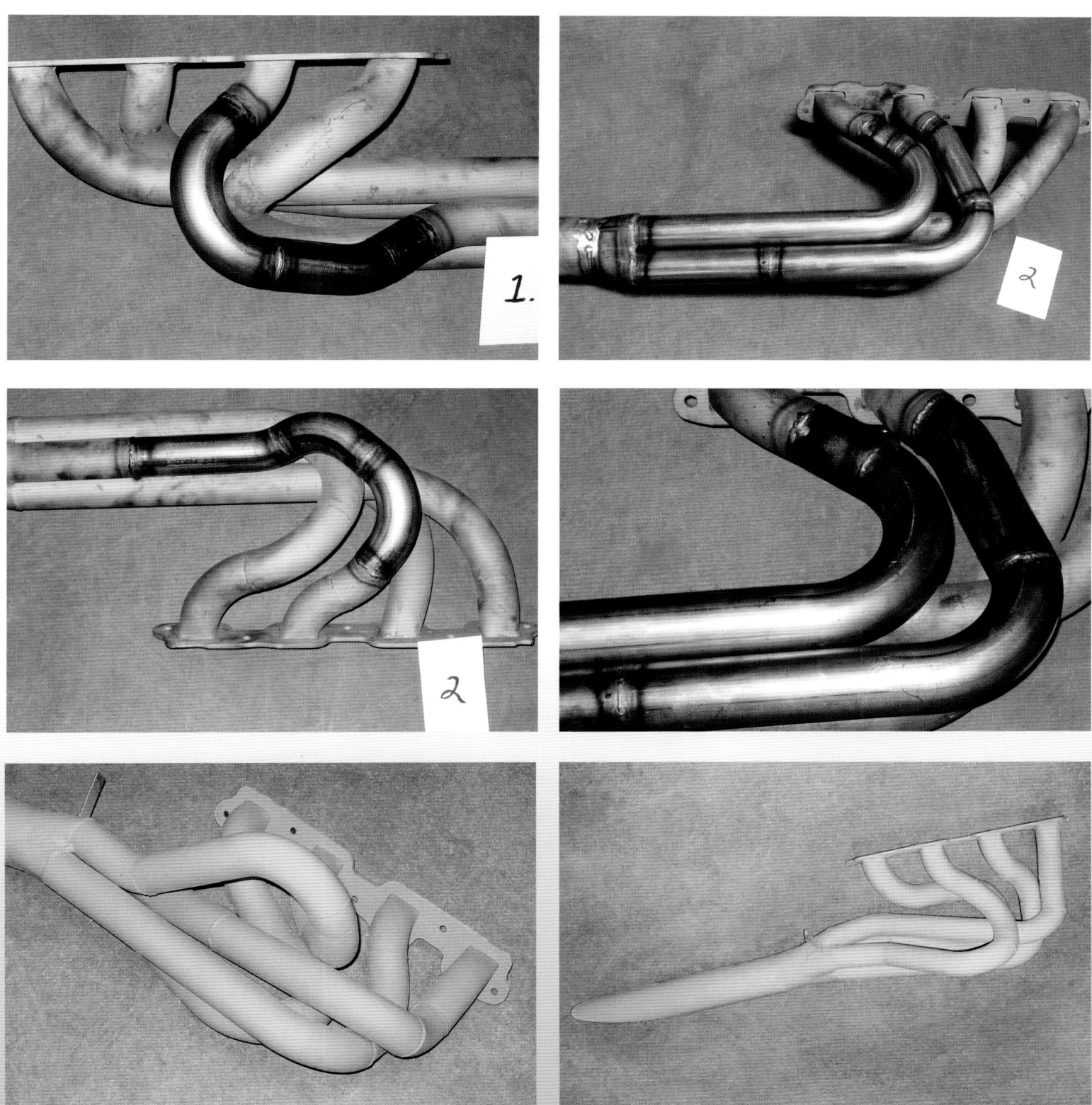

After the initial repairs were completed, the headers were primered and repainted. Museum conservator Malcolm Collum specified a spray treatment that could be periodically sprayed in via the collectors to preserve the inside of the tubes and prevent the return of rust and corrosion.

GOLDENROD

A FINE MESS: SOME ASSEMBLY REQUIRED

Rear view shows two lower rear crossmembers. The one in the foreground has mounting brackets for the rear coil-over shocks. The next one forward has a center mount for the front of the rear facing transmission. Beyond that, separate brackets on the lower frame rails accomplish three-point mounting of the rear transmission and clutch housing assembly.

We have all taken something apart at one time or another and ended up with parts left over after we put it back together. Even with careful cataloging and a extensive photo record we frequently contemplated the pile of parts we might have left over once these shelves were emptied and the car was reassembled. Luckily, we found a home for every piece, but getting there from here was a rough journey despite the carefully mapped trail we had laid out during the disassembly.

GOLDENROD

The final transition period occurred once the main frame had been sandblasted twice, sealed, primed and painted. The beginning of the reassembly required the installation of the front and rear transmission and attending driveline components, clutch housings, and transfer cases. Here the prepped main side rails await some muscle to lift them into place.

All three of the aluminum parachute canisters were in excellent condition, requiring only minimal cleanup with an aluminum wash prior to re-installing them into the rear framework of the chassis.

The electrical discharge device that triggered the charge to blow off the tail cone was like new. The original charge overcame small snaps that held the cone in position until Summers triggered the release.

Goldenrod Reborn

After what seemed like an eternity, it was finally time to put the gold back in the Goldenrod. The teardown, parts cataloging and cleanup process had taken eleven months, but all the parts were now clean and the sub-sections ready to go, and we looked forward to picking up the pace. The new bulkheads would be ready in a few days, and we anticipated a trip to Vegas to pick them up from fellow racers Duane and Gary Cole. Dave Basham and his small team completed the reassembly of the transfer cases, so I decided to go ahead and reinstall the front and rear transmissions with their respective transfer cases.

This was an easy task as the Spicer transmissions were completely refinished and ready to install. The front transmission went in first, and the upper frame support was attached and bolted to the upright connectors. This made the front frame assembly ready to accept the number one aluminum bulkhead when it arrived. The front transfer case was also installed and aligned. That put enough weight on the front of the frame that we could then install the rear transmission and attending components which also fit within a box-like support structure.

While awaiting the new bulkheads, we prepped the primary side rails for installation once the bulkheads arrived. Note the coolant hose bungs on the frame rails and how the upper and lower front frame is connected by uprights.

THE REBIRTH: FRONT TRANSMISSION INSTALL

Installing the transmissions and drive components was easy, but it soon became apparent that finishing the car in a timely manner was going to require a lot more help. With museum reps becoming anxious, it was time to call the cavalry in the form of Mike Cook and a team of Cook Motorsports volunteers that he called together specifically for this job.

When bolted together, the upper and lower frame tubes form a rigid box structure enclosing the front transmission, the clutch housing and the front transfer case attached via the aluminum plate at the extreme front.

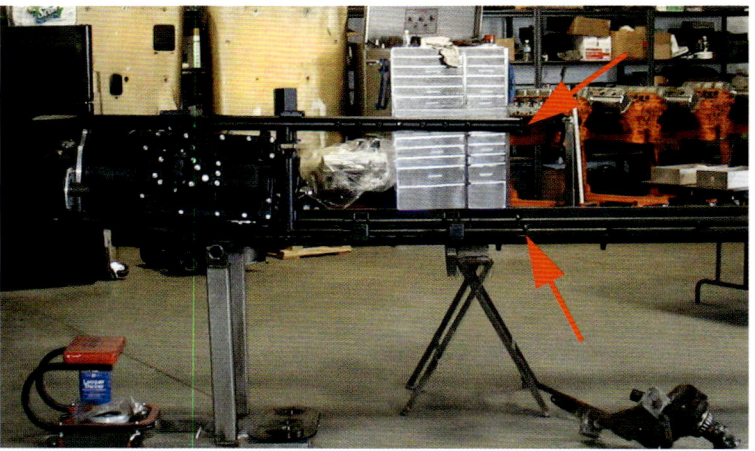

The ends of the upper frame tubes attach to the front bulkhead (not shown). The lower portion of the bulkhead attaches to the bottom frame via small tabs (arrow). This forms a rigid box structure around the front gear casing.

The front transmission sits in a tubular framework cantilevered off the front of the car. The transfer case and clutch housing are at the extreme front. In this picture, you can see the hydraulic slave unit for the clutch and one of the two electric water pumps. Body supports surround the assembly.

While seemingly simple enough, keeping four engine crankshafts and two transmission main shafts in perfect alignment over a length of twenty feet and doing the same with four transfer cases and multiple driveshafts operating at different angles and working in concert with the engines and transmissions is no easy feat. Summers was capable of seeing all this in his head and translating it to functional hardware with little trouble and lots of precision machine work. Restoration team members were able to clean, repair and restore the entire driveline so that it turned easily upon completion. The resto-engines are dummies with functioning crankshafts, so the whole system turns in unison.

These uprights from the lower frame connect to the upper front frame rails to help form the box structure around the transmission. Behind the coupler, the transmission is bolted to the lower crossmember.

GOLDENROD

Tabs on the lower frame rails anchor the clutch housing at the front. Similar tabs are used to attach the upper frame rails. Summers fabricated a mounting plate adapter to mate the clutch housing to the transfer case which has not been installed in this photo (see below).

Aluminum adapter plate mates the clutch housing to the transfer case. Getting all of this properly aligned required great precision on Summers' part.

A rigid framework surrounds the primary structure of the car to position and reinforce the body panels. Note all the Dzus fastener tabs used to hold the body secure on the body hoops. Flat channel provides a solid supporting surface for the upper and lower bodywork. The entire body consists of upper and lower panels so the top can be removed for service.

An unwritten caveat of any project is that you can never take enough pictures, measurements or video recordings of how stuff comes apart and goes back together. For the most part, we stacked parts and components that went together on separate shelves and maintained a fairly extensive photographic record to help ensure that we put everything back where it belonged. This approach was useful and saved the day on many occasions where the exact configuration of things was not readily apparent. Even for experienced land speed racers who already know their way around these cars, the photographs were frequently consulted for backup.

Gary Garcia consults the photo record to ensure accuracy.

THE REBIRTH:
REAR TRANSMISSION AND DRIVE HUB INSTALL

Rear transmission uses three-point lower mount with two tabs on the frame rails and one on the crossmember at the rear. The large flat plates to the left are the primary mount and secondary brace for the 2 x 6-inch upper frame rail.

The drive hub on the transmission is drilled to accept a multi-part adapter to the rear axle flange. Note how the transmission is laid over on its side to reduce its height in the car and maintain the low hood line. The main hoop is heavily reinforced for rigidity and forms the front half of the box structure for the rear axle assembly.

The transfer case for the rear transmission attaches to the clutch housing via the aluminum adapter, the same as at the front. Along the lower frame rail are various tabs for the body hoops and (lower center) one of the half-round mounts that hold the lower portion of the aluminum bulkhead (not shown here) in place.

View from the left side of the car provides an indication of where the driveline is located in relation to the upper and lower frame rails. One concession we made with the transfer cases was the installation of all new bearings to ensure longevity and smooth operation. Note rear hub at the far right.

222

GOLDENROD

Summers formed a rigid mount for the rear gear case using aluminum plates attached to the upper and lower frame rails. These plates are further employed as mounts for the upper and lower rear hub control arms.

Serious corrosion had affected the CV joint assemblies (note pitting), but we were able to disassemble, clean and re-lubricate them without much trouble. It was often difficult to imagine that this whole layout was not the work of an entire engineering team rather than just Bob Summers with the help and advice of friends.

GOLDENROD

GOLDENROD

These photos show the complete left rear floater assembly as it goes together. The lower left photo shows the CV joint installed in the drive hub for the center section. The right-hand photo is looking through the floater hub support toward the splines in the drive hub.

GOLDENROD

Detail of the upper rear control arm mount. Note original bolts and hardware were wire-brushed and wax-coated to preserve their surface finish.

The driveline coupler between the transmission and the gear case also incorporates a disc for an Airheart disc brake caliper.

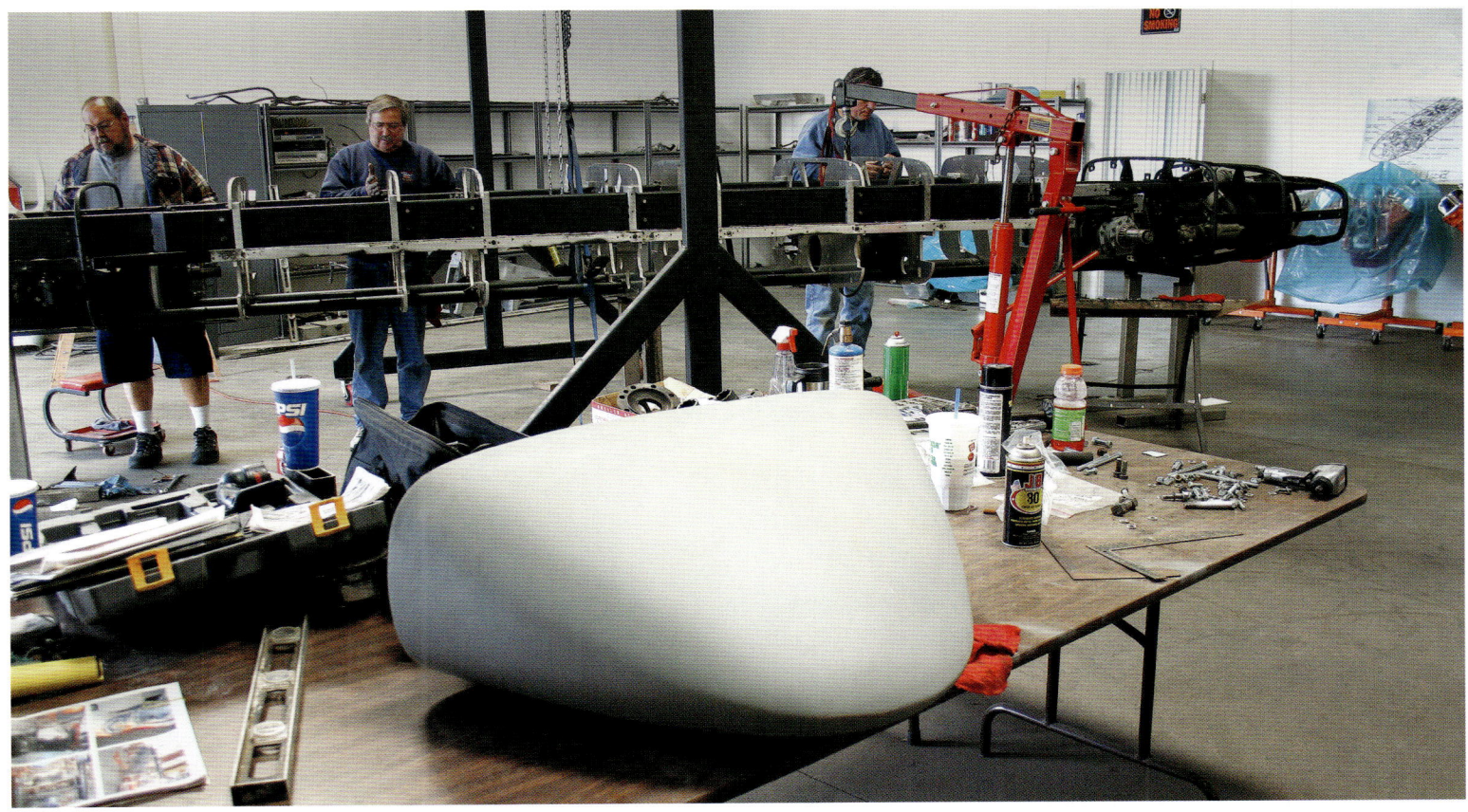

Gary Garcia, Mike Cook and Lee Hulbert aligning aluminum bulkheads prior to engine installation. The side body mount rails are already attached to the bulkheads to aid with positioning. The previously repaired dent in the front nose tank was stripped and refinished to make sure it would never need further attention. Note essential photo records on the table.

GOLDENROD

Mike Cook and Lee Hulbert positioning a transfer case between the bulkheads for engines number one and two. That's the second and third bulkhead from the front. Leaving the bolts slightly loose offered some wiggle room for accurate positioning and made it easier to start all the bolts when the engines were installed.

The eight aluminum bulkheads were marked for correct location and orientation and set in the proper spots on the lower frame rails. Then we staged a frame rail party where two groups lifted the bulky 2 x 6-inch upper frame rails into the slots on both sides of the bulkheads before digging into coffee and donuts. Once captured between the bulkheads, the engine blocks and the frame rails formed a very rigid structure capable of carrying the car's 8,465-pound weight. When the engines are locked back-to-back with a transfer case in between, the bulkheads are further secured by half-round 4-bolt tabs on the lower frame rails.

Larry Beatson checks out the frame rails they just set in place. The frame rails are firmly anchored front and back here, but the bulkheads are still loose at this point.

The bulkheads are notched to accept the large 2 x 6-inch upper frame rails. These 1-inch aluminum C-clips anchor each bulkhead in the correct position on the rails.

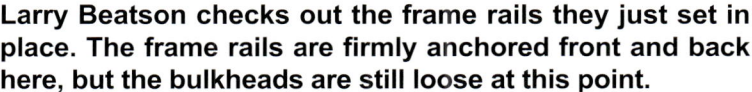

To the right, you can see how the upper and lower front frame rails bolt together via the uprights after the transmission is installed. At the left, the upper frame rail terminates at the first bulkhead and is anchored by 3/4-inch end bolts with large washers. The triangular aluminum braces lock the upper frame rail, front bulkhead, and the 2 x 6-inch side rail together to form a very rigid structure. This view also shows the front suspension layout and the anchor plates for the front gear case.

- Dummy shock replacements made from aluminum connecting rods
- Coolant feed line has one of two feed hoses Y'd in at the upper left
- Return coolant line with 3 caps connects to bung on left frame rail
- Air box bulge protruding through the bulkhead
- Feed coolant line connects to right frame rail
- Morse shifter cables attached to transmission
- Prestolite ignition box on the front bulkhead
- Solid mounted front driveshaft bearings
- Hard lines to the clutch slave cylinder
- Front disc brake on the gear case
- Throttle linkage for Engine No. 1
- Front suspension details
- Body mount framework
- Vented gear case

THE REBIRTH:
MOVING TO COOK MOTORSPORTS

Captain Billy Hodges and Mike Cook roll the Goldenrod out from the Landspeed Restorations shop for its trip to Cook Motorsports where a full crew will finish the re-assembly. A rainy day, but no incidents and the support stands fit the trailer perfectly. It caused a lot of double takes from people in other cars, but fortunately no wrecks.

Goldenrod parking only for the next few months as restoration team members prepared to swarm the project with a lot of love. At this point it was easier to work on the car supported by jack stands. The transport dollies were put away and later cut up to make individual wheel dollies for moving the car around inside the museum.

GOLDENROD

Buttoning up the front bays included aligning the body hoops and rails and starting to install the front driveline components. The recovery from its initial deteriorated state was absolutely amazing.

Rear suspension has single point upper and lower control arm links with front and rear side links for toe adjustment. Available suspension travel was slightly more than one inch total.

Rear engine fuel tank sits inside the right frame rail and projects above the transfer case in the center. The long rod passing through the bulkhead holes is the master rod for the throttle linkage.

The rear bay containing the transmission and rear drive components represents an equally impressive packaging job incorporating the hydraulic slaves for the clutch and steering mechanisms.

Throttle linkage passing the center fuel tanks is a work of mechanical and geometric art. Summers' ability to package moving parts in and around stationary components never ceased to amaze.

The dry sump tank beside the number two engine also sits on top of the frame rail and is anchored by a metal strap clamp and a support shelf that is attached to the bottom of the bulkhead.

GOLDENROD

Summers-designed center section is secured to the upper and lower frame rails with aluminum plates that also serve as mounts for the upper and lower control arms.

This view gives you a good idea of the simple, yet complex layout of the bulkheads, exhaust headers, and driveline on the left side of the car.

Flat channel (lower right) ties the body hoops together. It looks crooked because it has not yet been attached to the lower bulkhead in front of it.

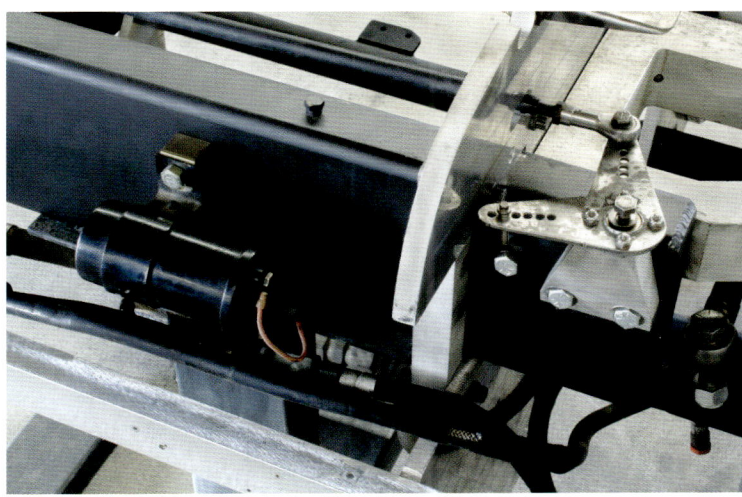

Wherever possible fluid lines, coils, linkages and other components that might require servicing are located in easily accessible locations to ensure that no small item could foil a one-hour turnaround for a record.

GOLDENROD

A young Gary Hooker did a great job of packaging the headers between the engines and the body panels while avoiding the driveline and transfer cases. Note openings in the bulkheads for the header tubes. Lower left shows the heavy-duty bearing mount on the front bulkhead. This was used in conjunction with a second rigid mount on a plate extending from the front gear case (right) to ensure front driveshaft stability and prevent whipping.

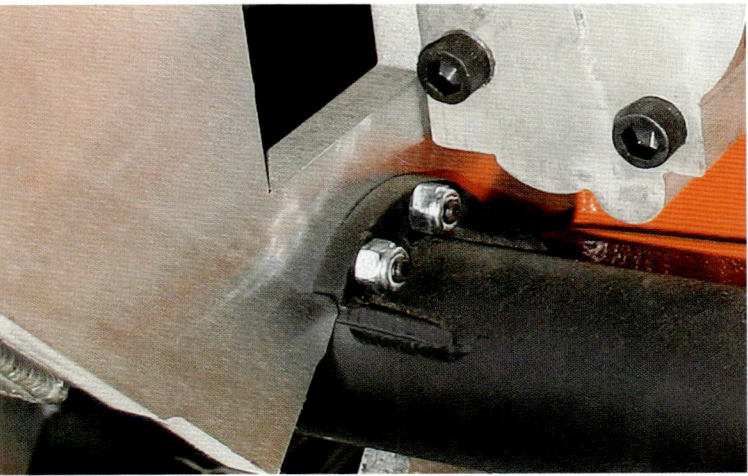

Also visible in the upper photo is one of the aluminum bottom rails for the lower body mounts and the aluminum side rail with Dzus fastener springs attached to each bulkhead. Above left shows attachment details for the lower rails and aluminum angle support for a fuel tank. An opening in the bulkhead permits direct attachment of the fuel suction line. Above right shows how the lower portion of each bulkhead is attached to half-round tabs on the lower frame rails.

GOLDENROD

This is a great view showing how the transfer case is sandwiched between two engines that both drive the transfer gears. It shows how the engine blocks are bolted directly to the bulkheads. On the right side, you can see one of the vibration dampers on the driveshaft assembly. The driveshafts are cross-bolted to ensure rigidity.

The two brass valves are a Hilborn idle check and a high-speed bypass. The idle check would be a low (2-5 psi) spring-operated relief valve to generate idle fuel pressure behind the main jet. The bypass would be an intermediate (25-60 psi) spring-operated check valve with another bypass orifice to lean the top end of the fuel delivery curve. Each engine is plumbed with these bypass valves between the fuel pump and the barrel valve.

GOLDENROD

This view shows the body mount rail attached to the bulkheads with countersunk screws. The low, compact design is evident here with the height of the bulkheads dictating the height of the body and everything contained therein. Hooker's header work is a real complement to the car.

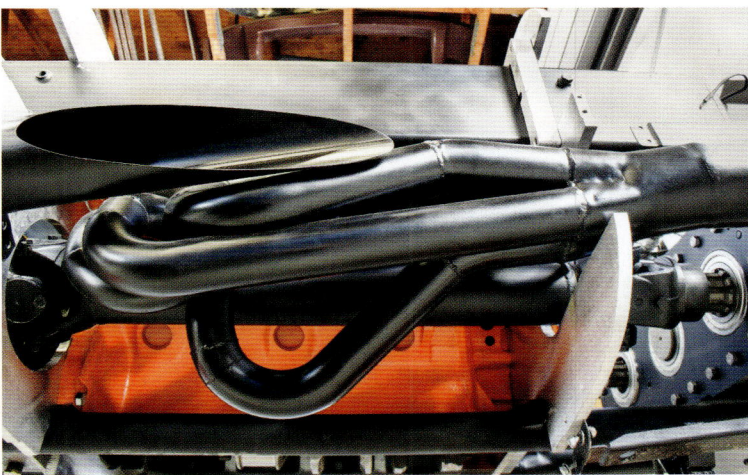

On the left is a rigid bearing mount on the rear bulkhead of the number two engine. Behind it, you can see how the bottom of the curved aluminum fuel tank arcs up and over the driveline. On the right is the rear driveshaft attached to the transfer case feeding power inboard to the clutch and transmission.

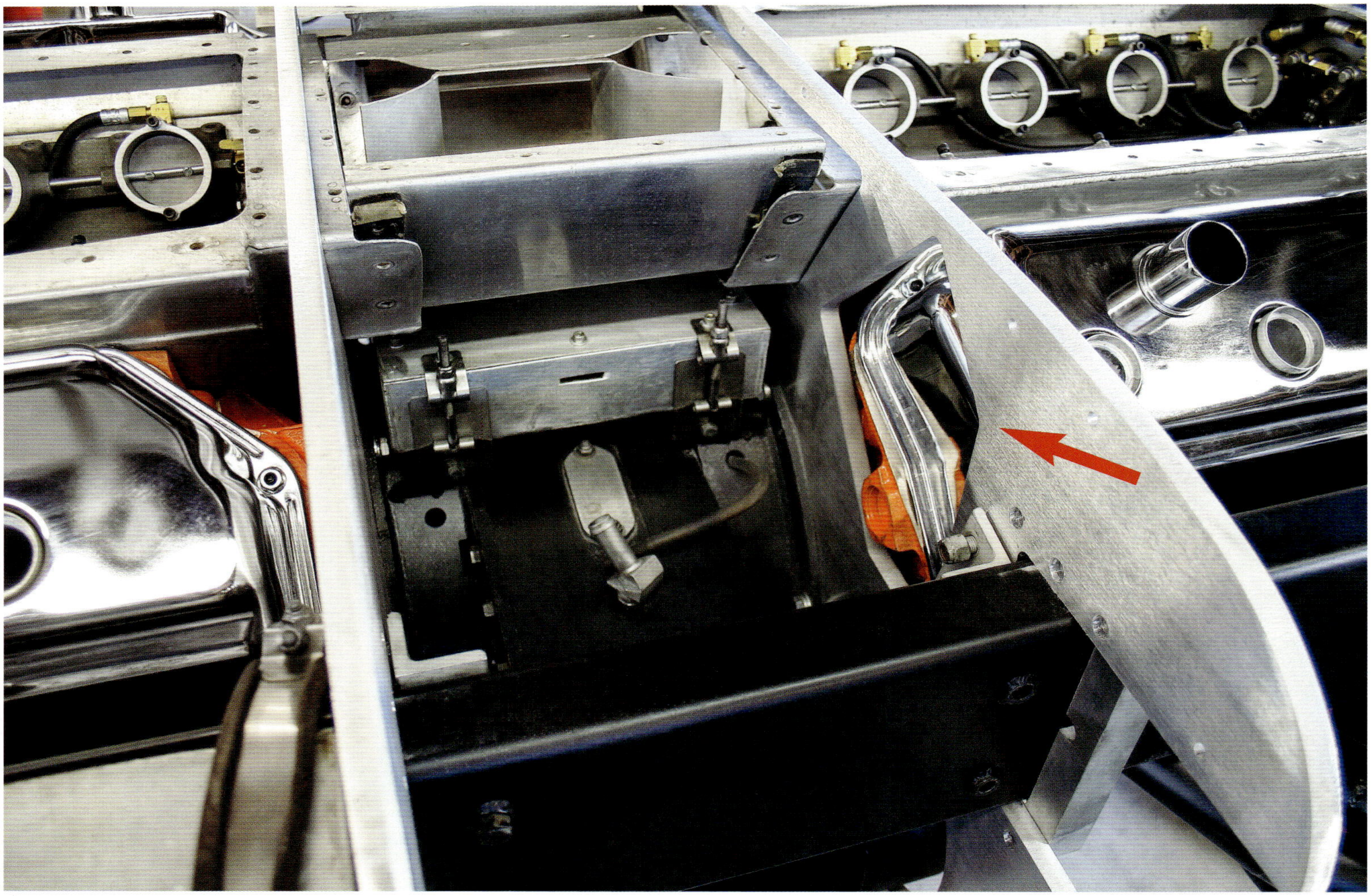

GOLDENROD

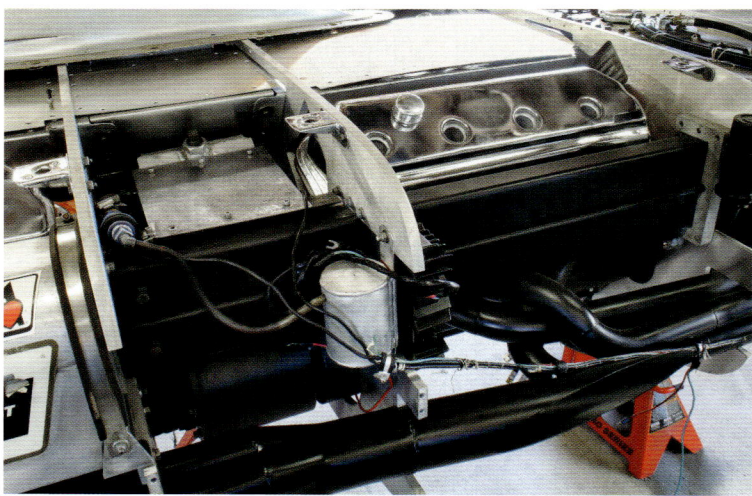

Tucked neatly beneath the scoop entry is a center mount for a fuel tank that wraps around and over the transfer case. Note the case is vented. The hole in the bulkhead (arrow) accommodates the cylinder head and valve cover, so the bulkhead mounts flush to the engine block. Bottom photos show the same space occupied by a local battery box to support the ignition system.

GOLDENROD

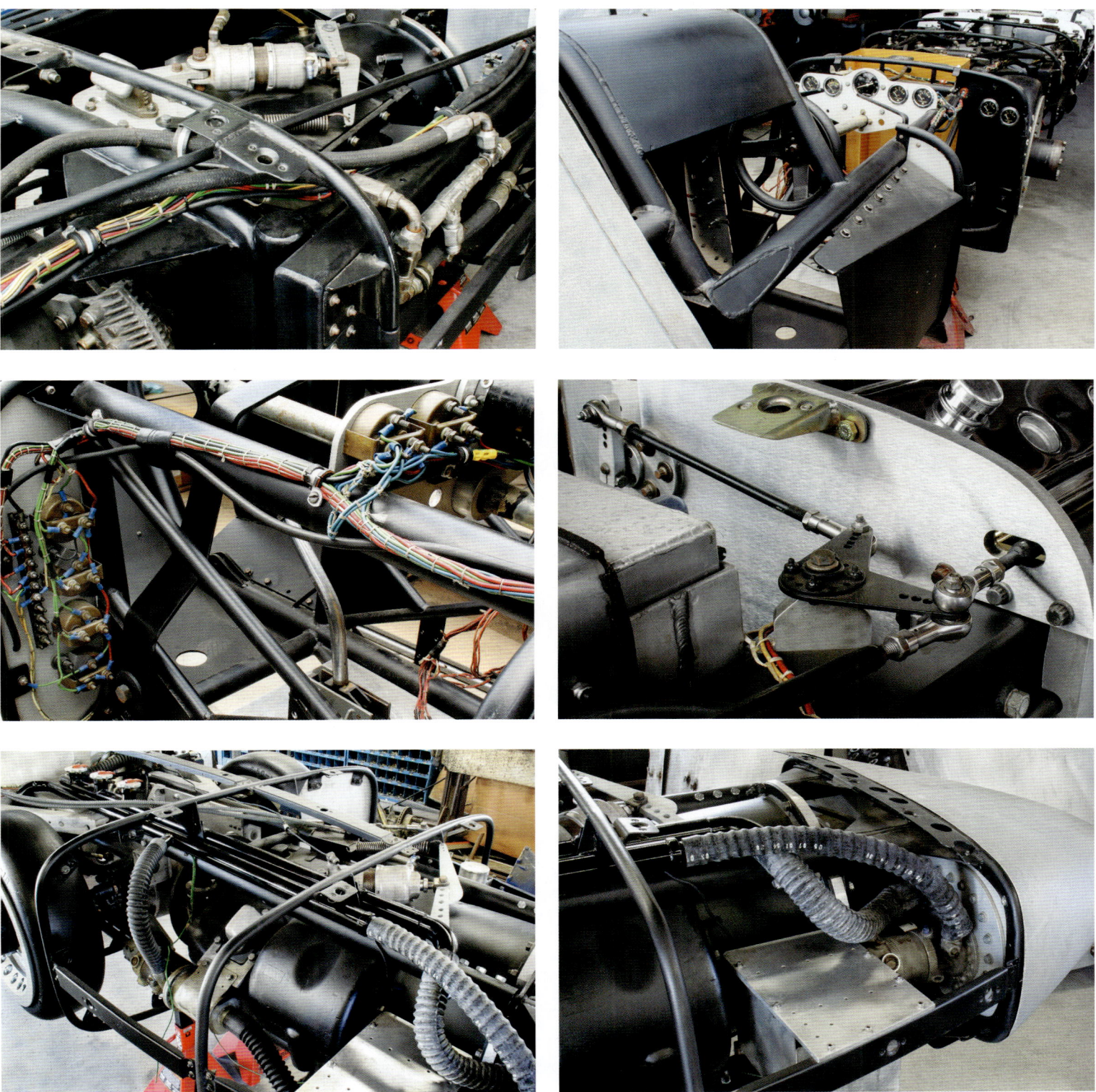

These photos show the wiring bundle consolidated down the right side of the car and the general layout of the throttle linkage rods that pass through the bulkheads and attach to bellcrank assemblies for each engine. The upper right photo shows a good view of the cockpit side and top armor. At the lower right you can see the front battery box that runs the coolant pumps and the forward hose connections for the cooling system.

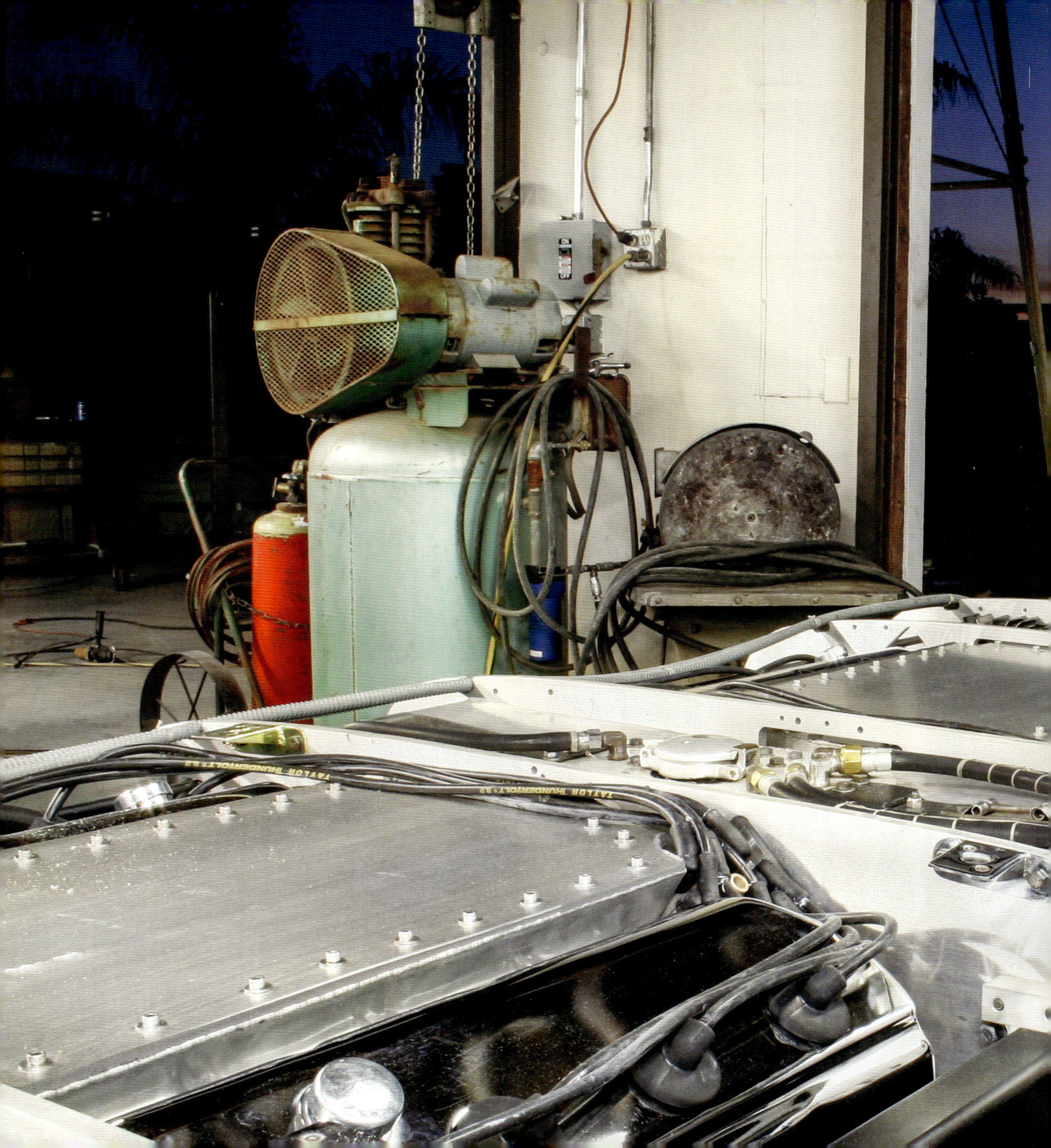

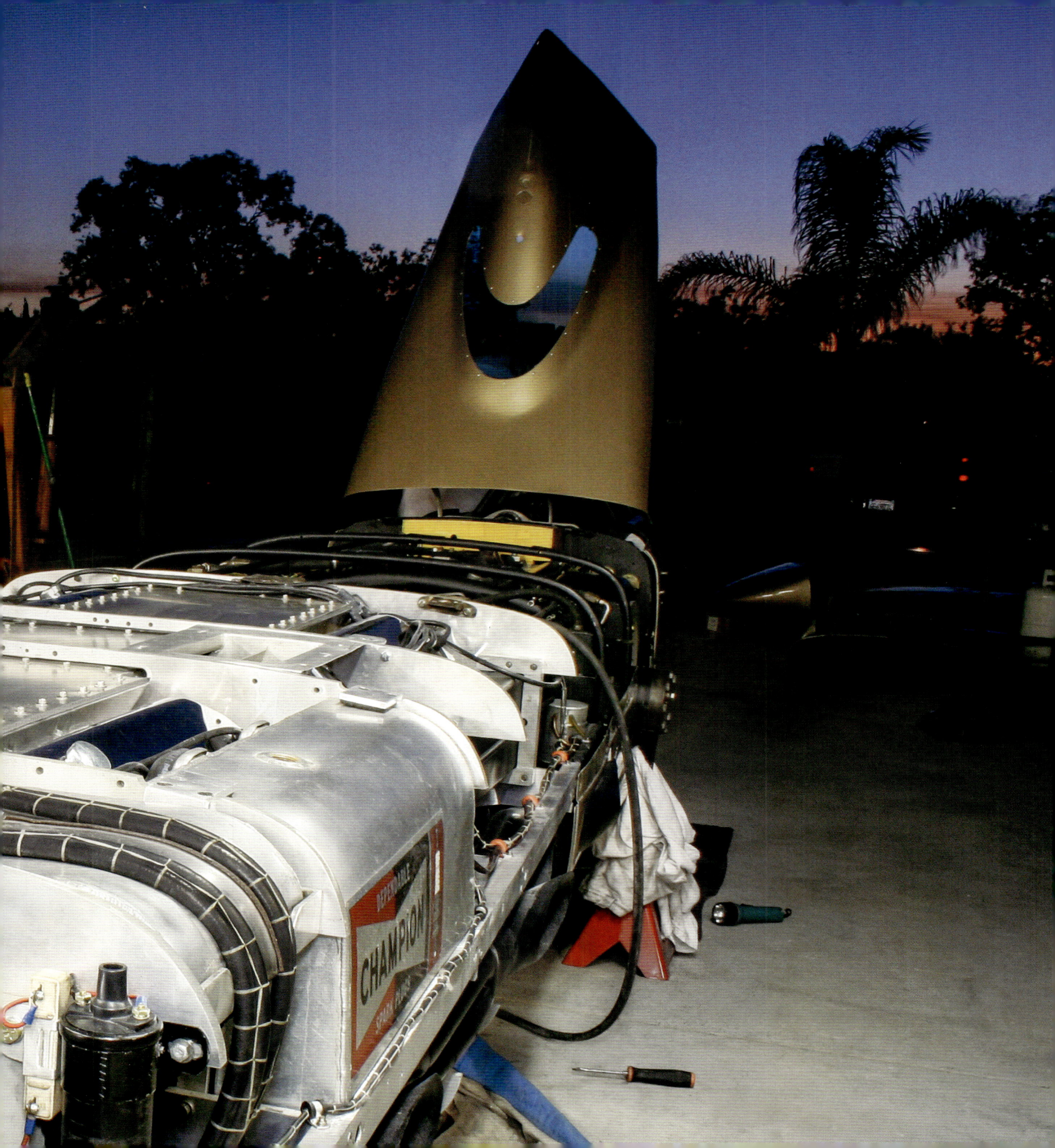

GOLDENROD

The Goldenrod is complex, yet simple from any angle. Compact construction is evident everywhere you look. A simple solution to stabilizing the body panels is seen in the channel pieces connecting the body mounting hoops. Pieces of flat steel are brake-formed with raised mounting tabs so the bolts don't interfere with the body. There are 17 of these on the car. Opposite page: Museum techs in Dearborn restored the gauge panels and wiring.

The Hurst-built reverse pattern shifter is rigidly mounted to bars beneath the cockpit floor. While the Morse cables proved difficult to adjust, the shifter worked perfectly.

Tucked away deep within the front and rear of the chassis are these Airheart disc brake calipers attached to the drive hub on each center section.

GOLDENROD

246

GOLDENROD

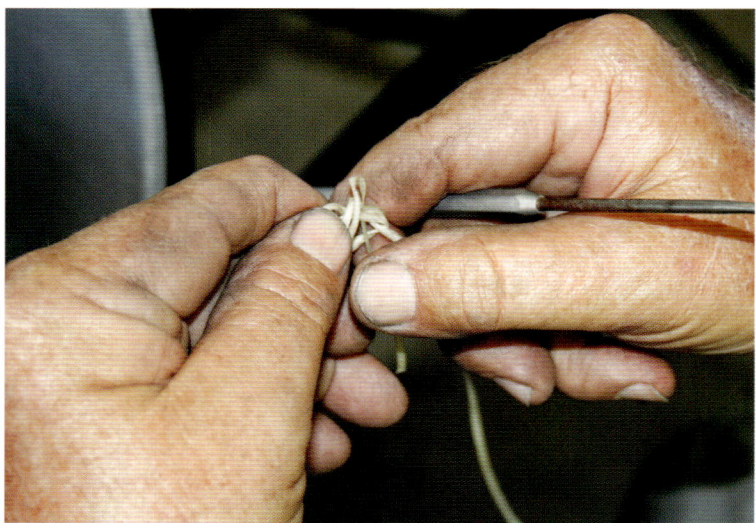

Steve Campbell proved amazingly versatile in his contribution to the effort. Besides prepping all the original bolts on the wire wheel, he also displayed a master's hand at the old aviation technique of the running string tie for wire looms and hose bundles.

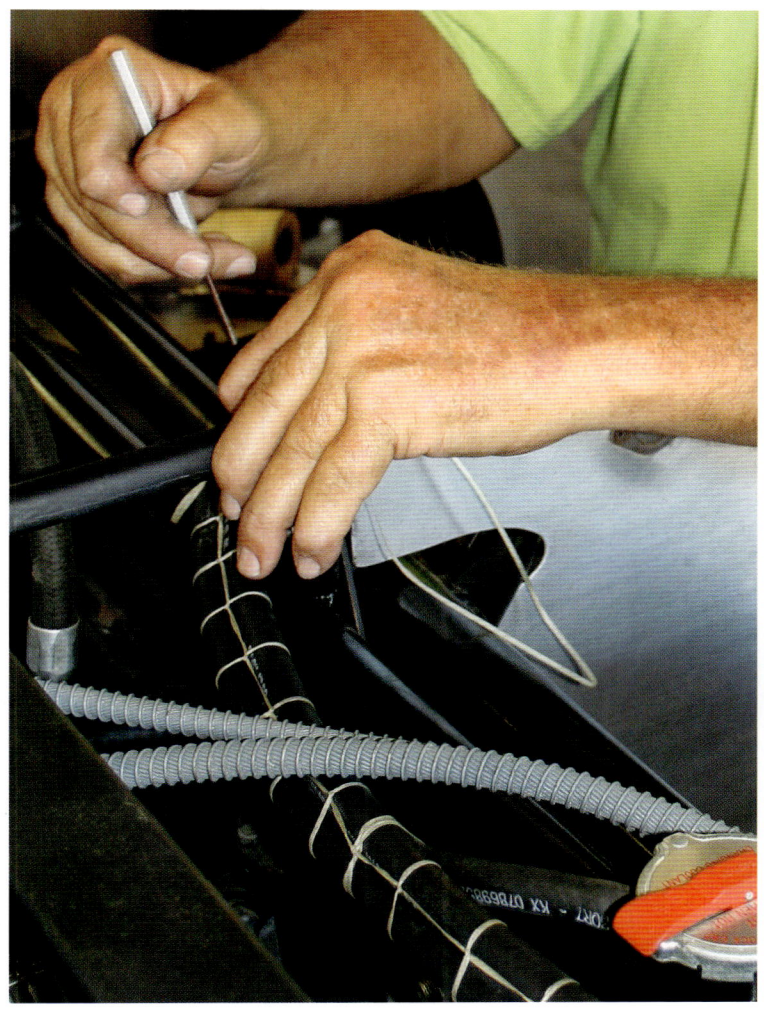
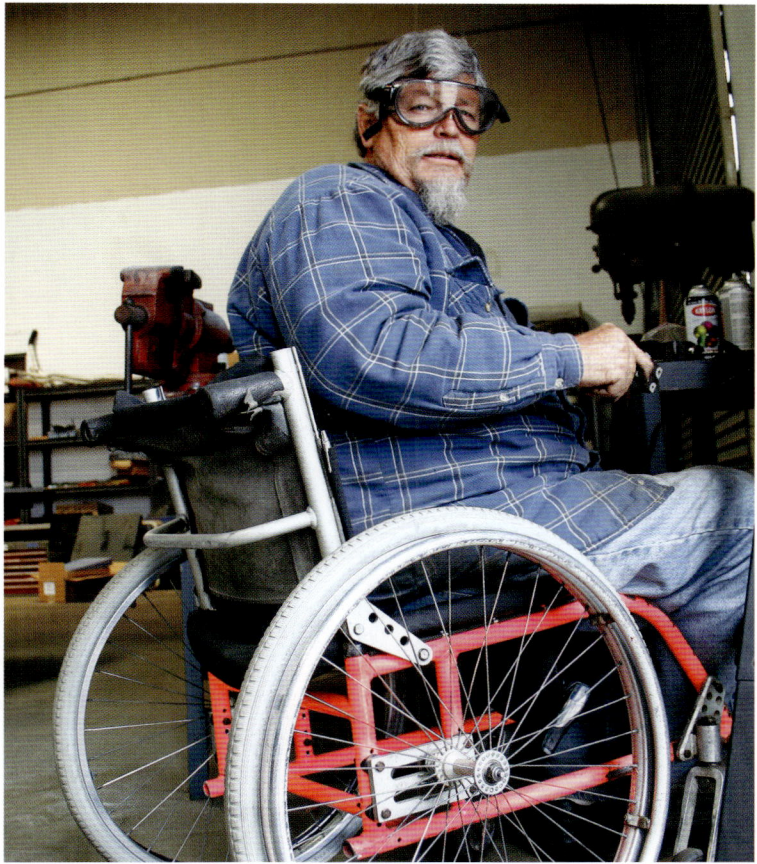

Campbell spent many long days cleaning Goldenrod bolts on the wire wheel. His contribution was essential to maintaining the authenticity of the project.

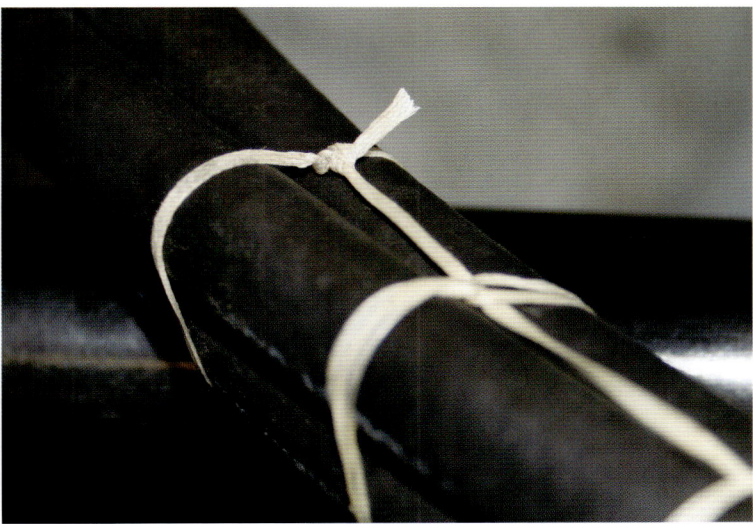

Unlike convenient tie wraps, string tie looms create a softer, more flexible means of securing wires, cables, and hoses that run adjacent to each other. The knot is smaller than the clasp on a tie wrap and is neatly tucked into a fold to create a snag-free bundle that can easily be manipulated into place.

GOLDENROD

Some panels and fasteners required a little massage work to make them fit correctly. The activity level was very high as the team pressed hard to make the museum deadline.

In addition to the high-speed tires, Firestone also designed the four specially shaped fuel bladders to accept both racing gasoline and methanol racing fuel. Note Summers' name.

With very few exceptions, all of the bolts used in the restoration are original aerospace bolts painstakingly restored and prepped by jack-of-all-trades Steve Campbell.

GOLDENROD

This photo offers a good view of the body mounting side rail and the way in which the body attaches to it. It is formed to allow quick and easy removal of the upper panels for servicing. Note how the underbody fits around the lower bulkhead and how tightly the oil reservoir is packaged within the body shell.

Body mounts also served as supports that allowed a small degree of flex while helping to maintain the rigidity needed to support the aerodynamic body shell.

Look closely at the black hose coming in from the left and the hose below it coming out of the front of the block. Those are coolant entry and discharge hoses.

GOLDENROD

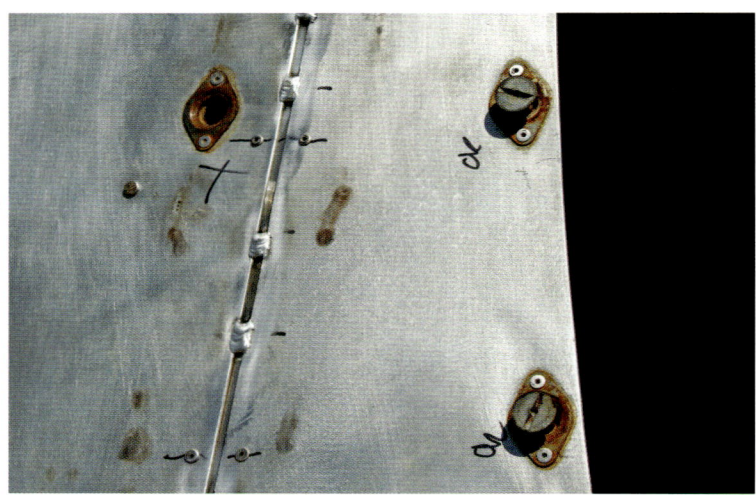

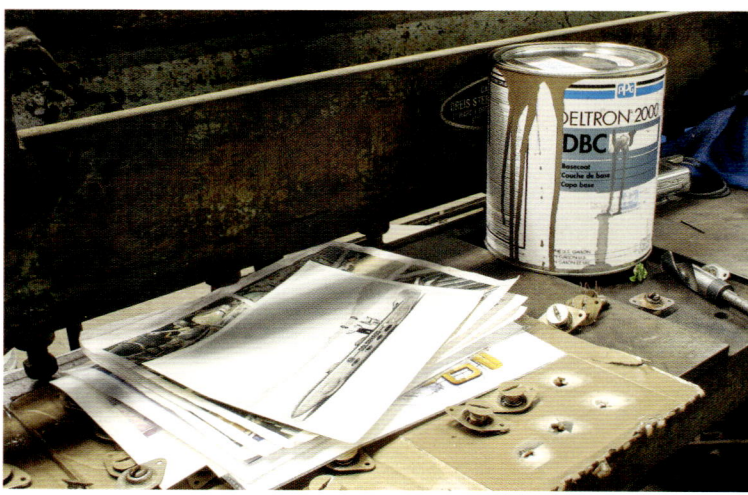

Bill Summers had cut the engine covers lengthwise to display the engines. A support stringer was welded on the bottom side, and body man Tony Fabozzi (upper right) ground the stitch welds flat in preparation for body filler to complete the repairs. The panels and Dzus fasteners were sprayed and polished by Tim Fite's West Coast Collision Center.

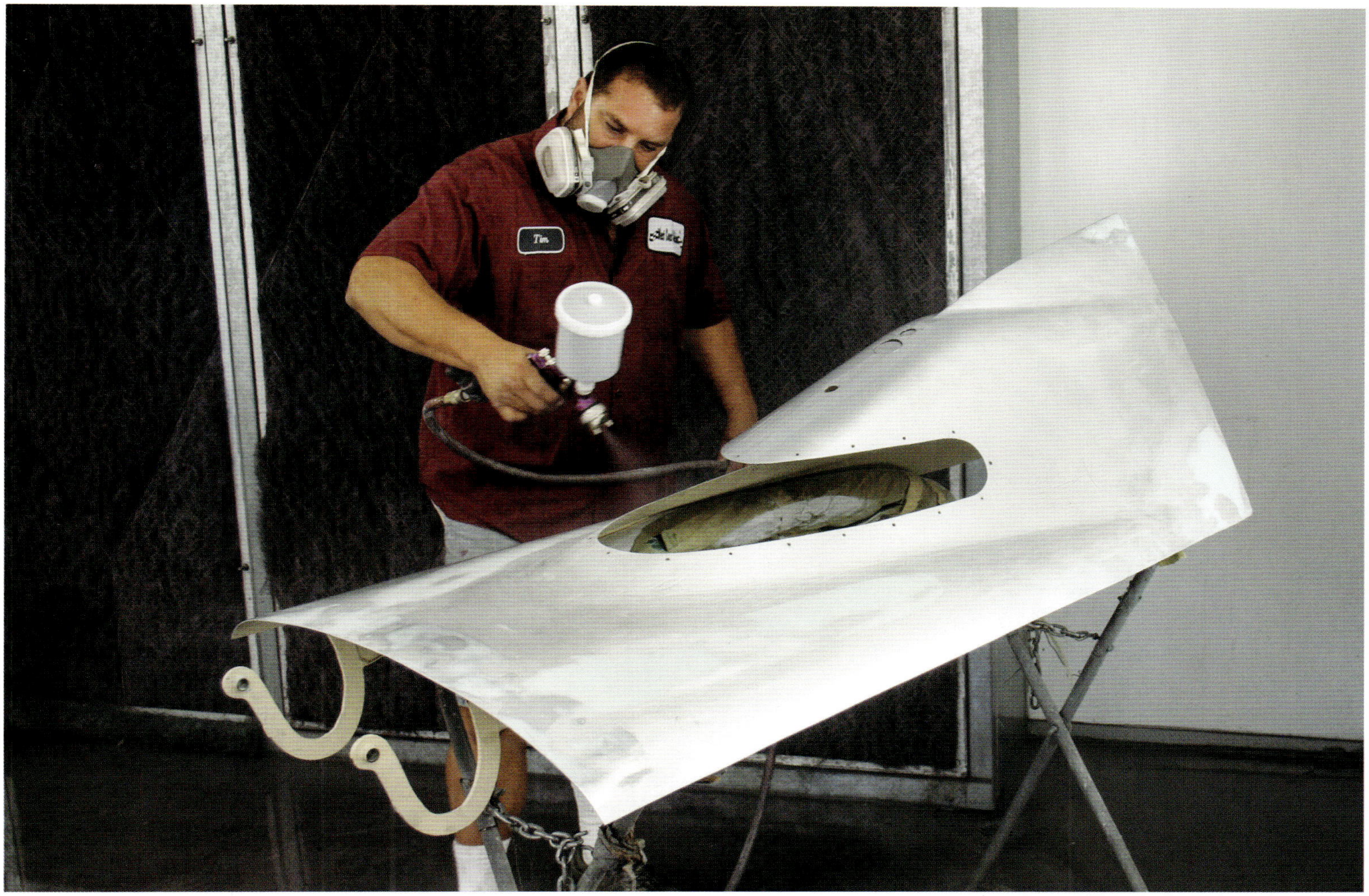

GOLDENROD

Painter Tim Fite put a high gloss, museum-quality finish on the body panels after extensive repair and preparations had restored their original quality.

Here are the mixing codes to replicate the original 1957 Chevrolet Fiesta Gold color chosen by the Summers Brothers to make the Goldenrod stand out on the salt.

GOLDENROD

Willie Sutton's bodywork fits the bulkhead shapes like a glove. There is no wasted space anywhere. Note the opening in the top of the bulkhead (top center) to accommodate the shape of the fuel injection air box.

Freshly-painted droop nose tank and front underbody awaiting installation. This nose shape was the slickest of those evaluated by Walter Korff.

Bill Summers' friend Bruce Mercer in Arizona returned all the missing access doors and fasteners so fabricating new ones became unnecessary.

GOLDENROD

An exciting milestone in any project is the point of final assembly and checking for problems. After many months of intensive labor, restoration crew members begin fitting body panels for the final time. When it all comes together the satisfaction level rises considerably, no matter how tired you are. Pictured here, Aaron Hebert, Mike Cook, Jr., and Skip Banks button up the nose section prior to roll out the next day.

Characters stamped on the left frame rail just ahead of the cockpit read SBGR 111265 for the car and the date of the record. Summers Brothers Goldenrod, 11/12/65.

Sign painter Tom Clarke adds finishing touches to the car by striping the Summers Brothers' logo with the original shade of orange.

THE REBIRTH: OVERVIEW

Goldenrod has unique features on each side of the car depending on the components and available packaging space. In addition to the central fuel tanks between the two pairs of engines, there are engine oil dry sump storage tanks on both sides. The one visible here with the original Champion decal is for engine number two. A tall, square tank for engine number four is barely visible behind the last bulkhead.

Wiring looms, fuel lines and hydraulic lines are distributed appropriately along the outside of the main frame rails. To preserve authenticity, we worked around the original Champion and Hurst decals on the oil supply tanks. The fuel tank filler cap for the front engine is seen just under the scoop.

In addition to the complex driveline tucked neatly away beneath the main frame rails, we see here the dry sump supply tanks for the number one and number three engines. Arranged against the block wall in the background are significant remnants that include (left to right) record scoops, spare fuel bladder and windscreen, original floor pan and several of the decayed bulkheads. The museum retained and stored all these pieces.

The dual pump cooling system and feed line arrangement are seen below. Both pumps draw from the nose tank and tee into the same feed line just before entering the right side frame rail where coolant is distributed to each engine via individual bungs in the frame rails adjacent to each engine.

THE REBIRTH:
OVERVIEW

GOLDENROD

The original parachutes had long since disappeared, so our friends at DJ Safety stepped forward to help replicate the missing pieces. The covers were installed with tie wraps because they are permanent for display purposes. Note the large bearing at the rear of the frame for the push car. The tow line anchors are seen directly above each parachute cannister. At the top is the opening for the shotgun shell used to blow the streamlined rear cover off when deploying the chutes.

THE REBIRTH:
FIRESTONE TIRE RESTORATION

Roger Marble, a career Firestone tire engineer, read the original article in *Hot Rod Magazine* when it was first announced that we were beginning the restoration. He immediately thought of the tires and volunteered to have Firestone restore them to as near original condition as possible. We couldn't have been happier and I shipped them off to him immediately. The task was formidable, but Roger was equipped to handle it. He even found the original mold drawings to consult.

One of the critical tasks involved removing the tires from the two-piece wheels without causing further damage. The nuts and bolts required a thorough pre-cleaning before the nuts were removed. Some of the bolts were seized in the wheels and had to be carefully broken loose and driven out with a special tool Roger fabricated to protect the threads.

Before and after views of the left front tire illustrate how Roger's meticulous restoration brought the original tires and wheels back to life without over-restoring them.

"As a life-long car guy, I was fortunate to be able to make a career at Firestone Tire & Rubber Company. When I saw the article in Hot Rod, I just had to get involved and felt my knowledge of tires would be a definite help to the restoration effort."

- Roger Marble, Firestone

The wheel hubs were rusty but serviceable, so Roger had them bead blasted and sanded to restore their surface texture and then sprayed with approved semi-gloss black.

The inner side of the wheels was in the worst condition as they were never fully cleaned from the salt. All of the wheels were completely hand sanded prior to re-anodizing.

An outer and inner view of the unrestored wheels and tires frames one of the tires that had already been removed from another wheel. The tires were in great shape inside, but the beads had some damage caused by wheel corrosion. Roger added some silicone sealant to help seal the inner and outer wheel faces and the beads upon reassembly.

FIRESTONE TIRE RESTORATION

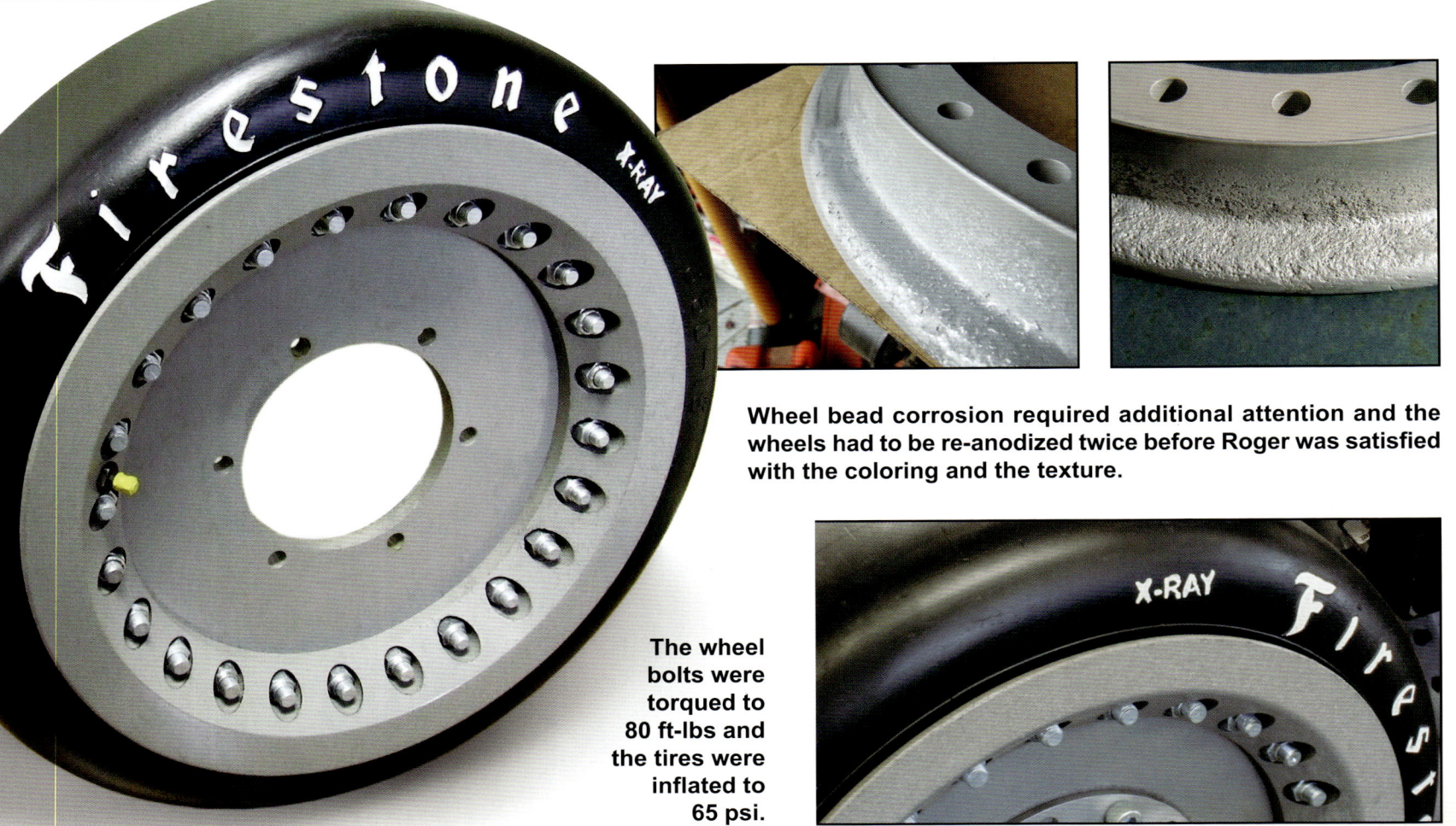

Wheel bead corrosion required additional attention and the wheels had to be re-anodized twice before Roger was satisfied with the coloring and the texture.

The wheel bolts were torqued to 80 ft-lbs and the tires were inflated to 65 psi.

The wheel halves were matched to keep them together and bead-blasted to clean them up. The surfaces were hand-sanded with 280 grit wet/dry sandpaper to the proper texture. An Akron, Ohio, shop anodized the wheels, and a clear lacquer coating was sprayed to achieve the original sheen. Some repair was done to the bead side with lab metal to ensure proper bead seal. The original O-rings between the wheel halves were in good shape, and Roger gave them a light coating of RTV silicone sealant to ensure their integrity upon reassembly. RTV was also applied to the bead surfaces because it was felt that the aged rubber might not fully conform with the minor corrosion damage to the bead surfaces. A Firestone electron microscope was used to analyze all 120 wheel bolts and nuts before hand re-tapping them and then re-plating them.

The hubs were blasted, sanded and finished with Duplicolor DA1603 Semi-Gloss Black that matched the original museum-approved color. All of the nuts and bolts are nickel-plated. Two of the wheels had spacers to increase the track width, and each wheel had a bolt washer ring that fit over the outside of the wheel around the hub. These were cad-plated.

The greatest amount of effort went into the tires with each tire consuming three to eight hours of hand sanding time to achieve the proper surface texture. Akron Paint & Varnish made the white paint for the lettering in the sixties, and Roger got them to duplicate it for the tires. They also made up a batch of the original sixties tire black paint. Roger duplicated the X-ray stampings and was able to get some period-correct Schrader tire valves with yellow caps from a Brazilian aircraft company.

Above: One of the paint samples Roger used to ensure proper coloring for the tire coating.

Tire damage from age and sitting on the same part of the tire for 40 years was minimal, but selected sections required repairs with a special blackened rubber compound that was used to patch holes.

Note the before pictures (left) and after repair pictures to the right.

THE REBIRTH:
MUSEUM BOUND

Delivering the car to the museum was further complicated when museum officials insisted on an enclosed trailer and a strict straight-through delivery schedule with stops only for fuel and food. We scrambled at the last minute to build a metal cage on Frank Silva's trailer and temporarily skin it in plywood sheeting. The trip was a severe challenge, but one happily undertaken by Billy Hodges and Pete McLeod, who delivered the car without incident.

Sadly, we were overruled on our idea to stop at the salt flats for a once-in-a-lifetime opportunity to photograph the pristine car sitting on its home ground. A special unveiling on the salt would have no doubt been a big hit with the land speed community. Curator Bob Casey liked the idea, but stodgier heads prevailed, and the Goldenrod was clandestinely delivered in a plain brown wrapper.

Scott Summers with the car in which his father had set the land speed record. Scott is holding his dad's original helmet that had been repainted gold somewhere through the years. It is clearly the real deal because it still has the original D-ring attachments that Bob Summers had installed for head restraint.

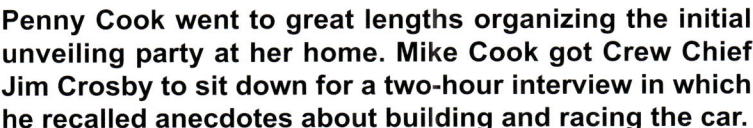

Penny Cook went to great lengths organizing the initial unveiling party at her home. Mike Cook got Crew Chief Jim Crosby to sit down for a two-hour interview in which he recalled anecdotes about building and racing the car.

Bob Summers widow, Becky (seen here with Bill), happily signed souvenir cards for the party guests. She was very pleased with the outcome of the restoration and that the car would be preserved in a prestigious museum for posterity.

THE REBIRTH:
MUSEUM BOUND

Captain Billy Hodges and Steve Campbell constructed the special transport dollies required to move the Goldenrod around in the museum's tight aisles. They suspended the car from its four wheel hubs for easy mobility.

Four padded supports were built to support the car's weight on the museum floor and prevent it from sagging in the center. They are spaced evenly front to back under alternating bulkheads. This also takes the load off the tires.

The dollies were fabricated by cutting up the old stands originally used to support the car during the teardown phase. They allowed the car to be easily maneuvered by just a few people. On the transport trailer, the dollies further served as shock absorbers for the long tow to Michigan.

At the last minute museum officials required an enclosed trailer and a non-stop transportation schedule. They had already scheduled a delivery date and an unveiling celebration, so a one-off wooden protective enclosure was fabricated to fit around the car on Frank Silva's three-axle flat trailer.

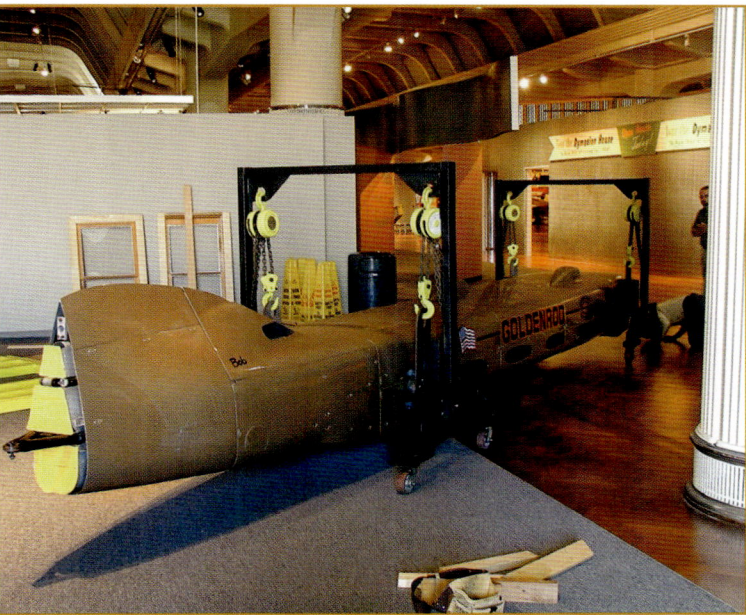

The car was delivered on schedule by Billy Hodges and Pete McLeod. Upon arrival, it was carefully unloaded and ushered into the museum using the custom transport dollies to maneuver it around obstacles and down the narrow aisles in the museum.

THE HENRY FORD:
THE LEGEND LIVES

The Summers Brothers' Goldenrod is one of the most recognizable cars in the history of motorsports. Its distinctive spearlike silhouette remains the sleekest shape ever to penetrate the rarified air where speed records lurk. As the golden centerpiece of The Henry Ford's motorsports collection, the Goldenrod is a shining example of the American hot rodder's unbridled imagination and ingenuity. The museum's choice to restore the car to its former glory assures future generations the pleasure, and indeed privilege, of seeing this remarkable thoroughbred the way it was in November of 1965 when Bob Summers established the long-standing 409.277 mph record that remained unsurpassed for decades.

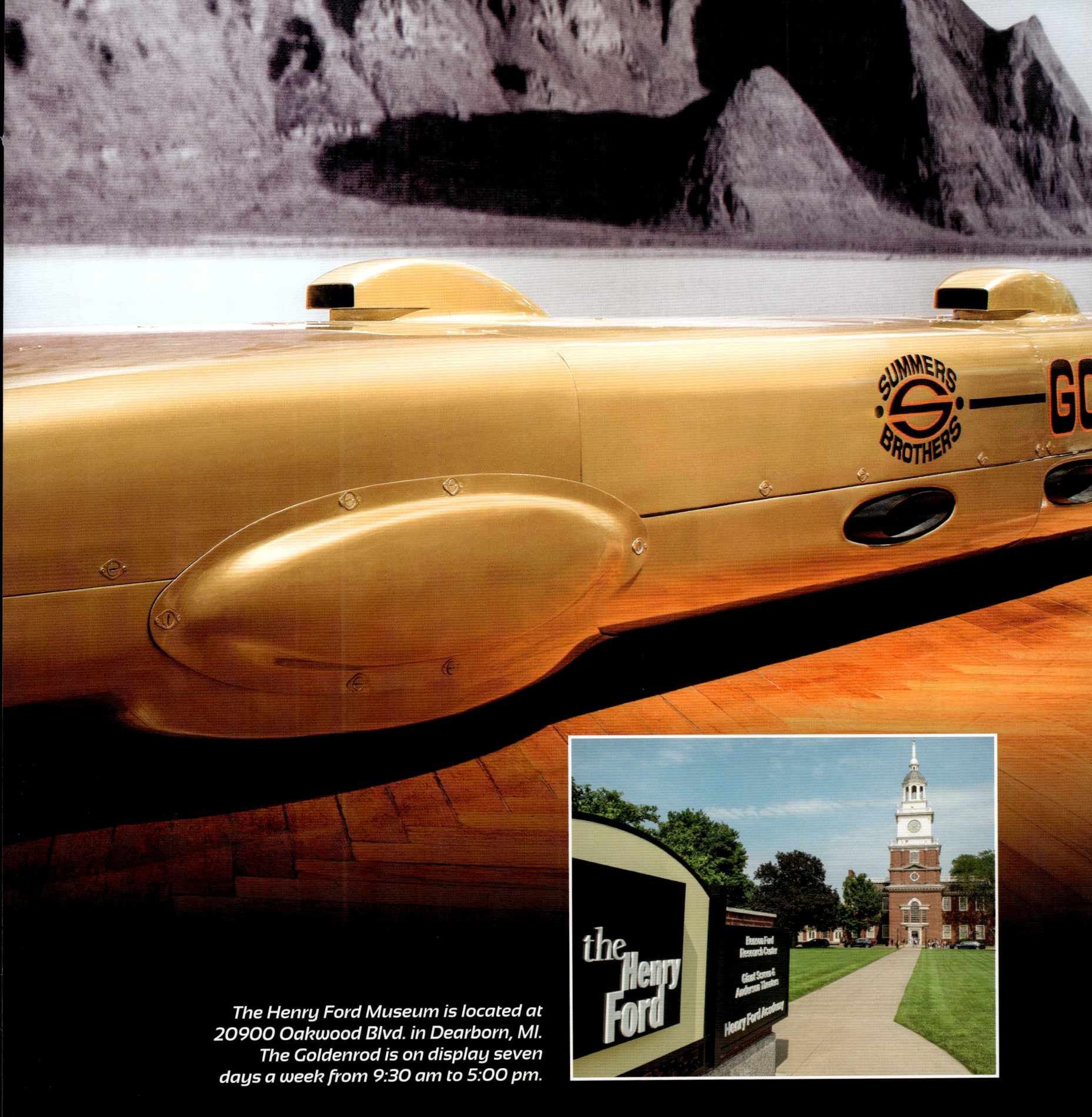

The Henry Ford Museum is located at 20900 Oakwood Blvd. in Dearborn, MI. The Goldenrod is on display seven days a week from 9:30 am to 5:00 pm.

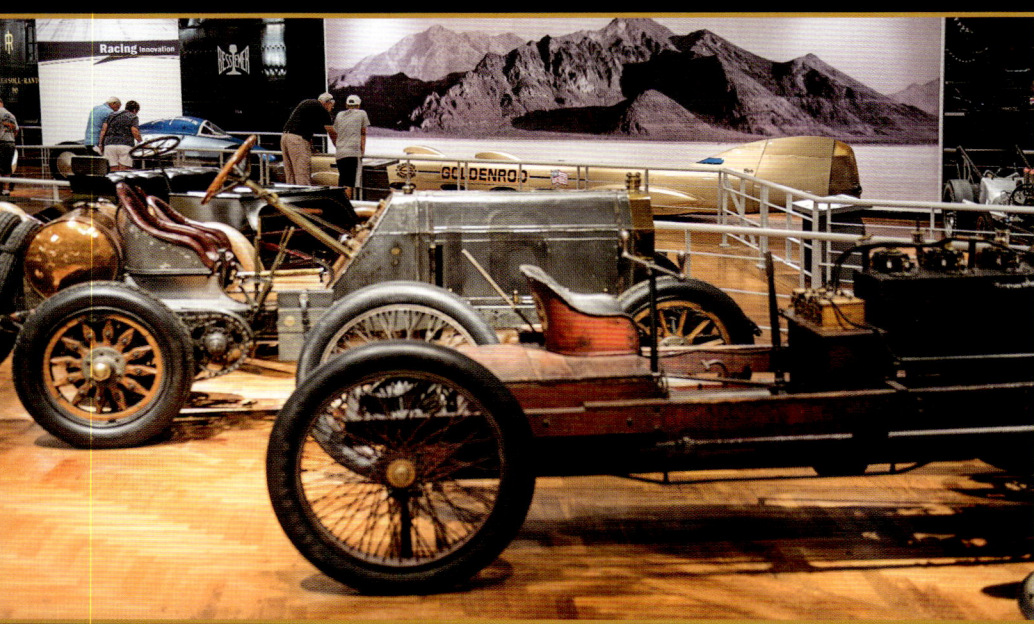

The adjacent photos show the restored cockpit and the front transmission and driveline bay which normally can't be seen. Twice each year the museum removes the engine covers so visitors can view the internals.

The center photo shows the car in context with other cars in the motorsports display, including Henry Ford's own land speed record-setting 999 car (foreground) which established a record of 91.37 mph on Lake St. Claire in 1904.

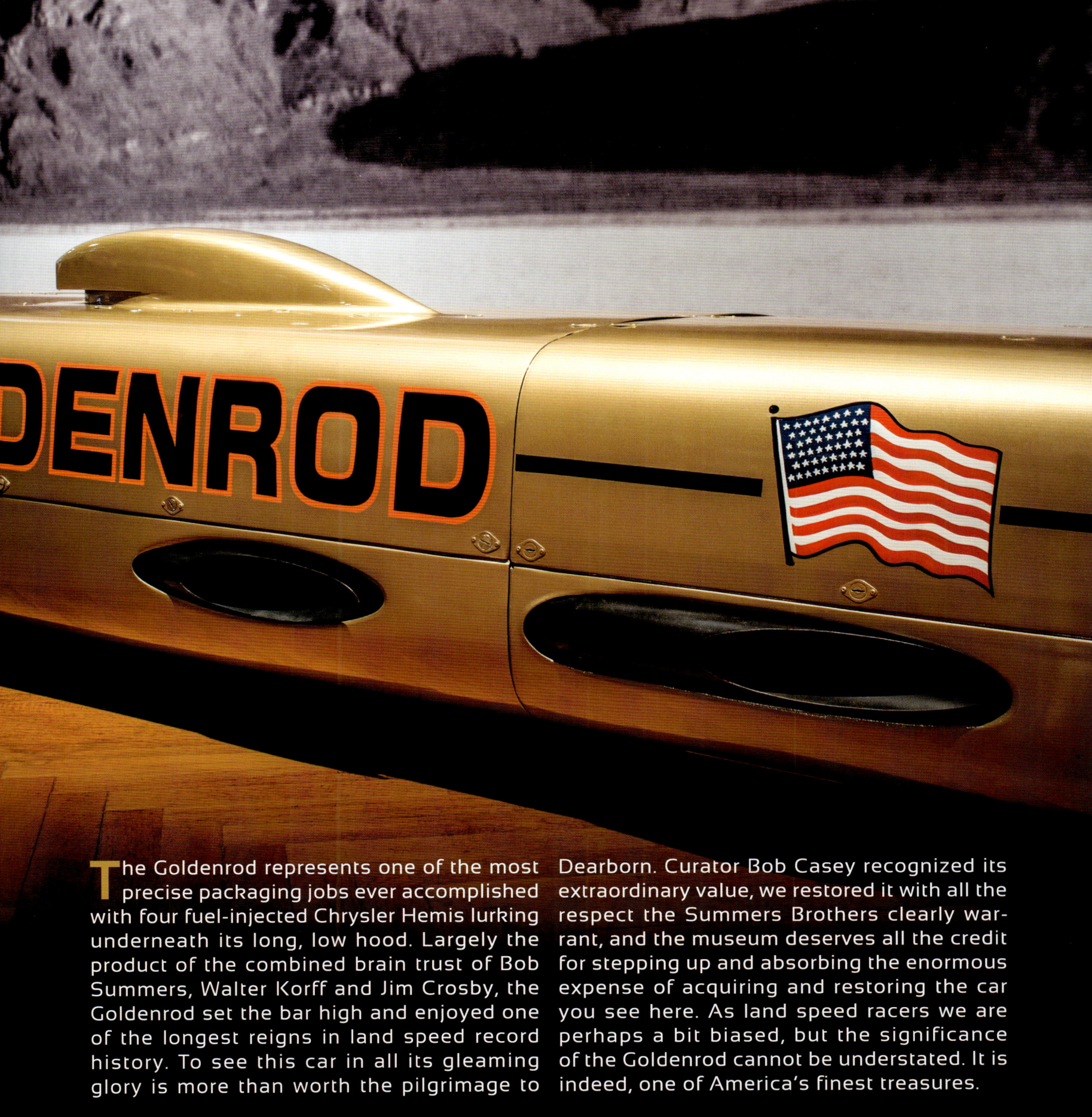

The Goldenrod represents one of the most precise packaging jobs ever accomplished with four fuel-injected Chrysler Hemis lurking underneath its long, low hood. Largely the product of the combined brain trust of Bob Summers, Walter Korff and Jim Crosby, the Goldenrod set the bar high and enjoyed one of the longest reigns in land speed record history. To see this car in all its gleaming glory is more than worth the pilgrimage to Dearborn. Curator Bob Casey recognized its extraordinary value, we restored it with all the respect the Summers Brothers clearly warrant, and the museum deserves all the credit for stepping up and absorbing the enormous expense of acquiring and restoring the car you see here. As land speed racers we are perhaps a bit biased, but the significance of the Goldenrod cannot be understated. It is indeed, one of America's finest treasures.

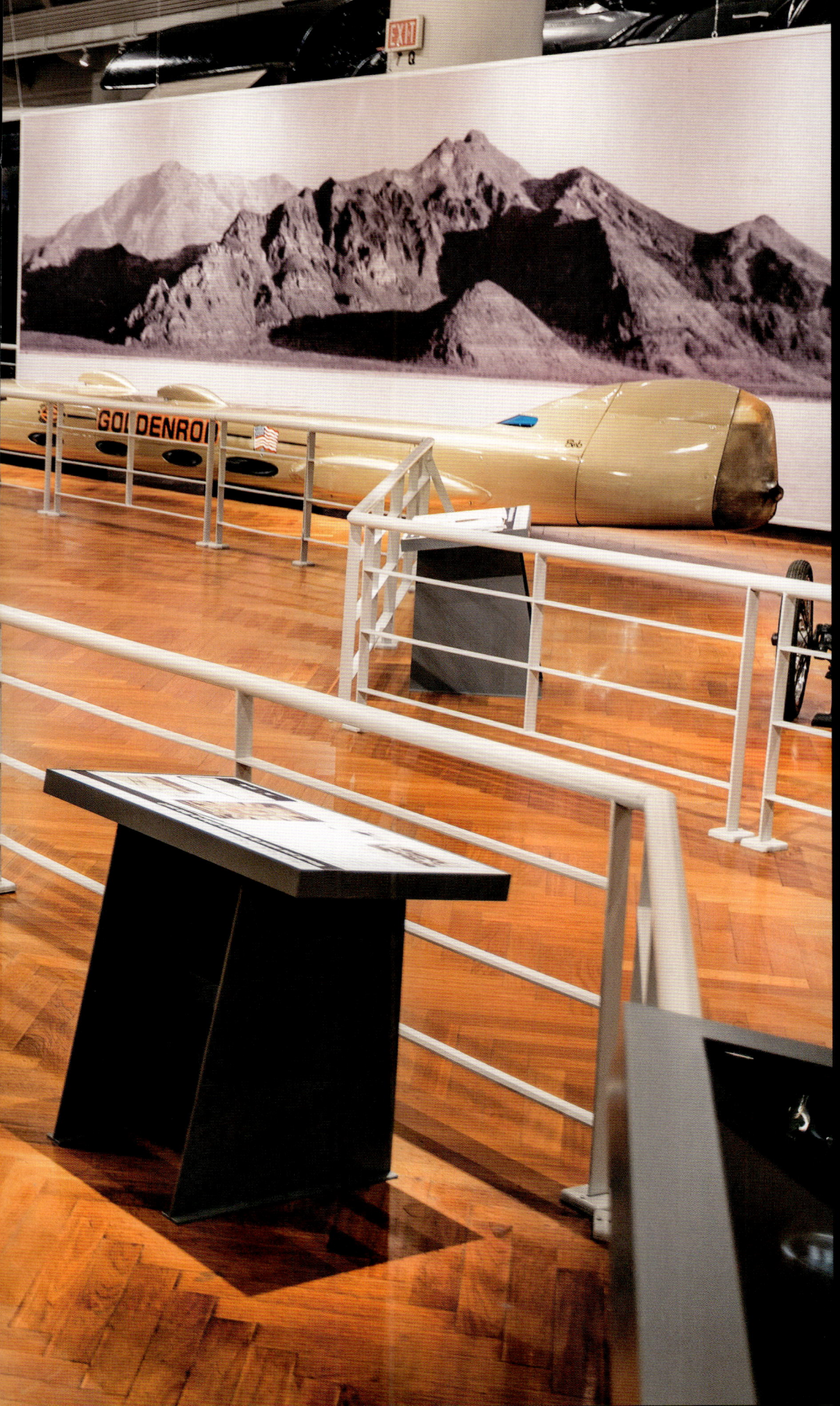

The Goldenrod is highlighted in context with other cars in the motorsports display. In addition to Henry Ford's 1907 record setter, we also see the Vanderbilt Cup winner "Old 16" Locomobile behind it, Carl Kiekhaefer's 1956 Chrysler 300-B NASCAR racer, Ford's 1962 Mustang 1 concept car, and the 1951 Tom Beatty bellytank lakester aligned around the Goldenrod.

The museum's automotive collection is quite extensive and also includes Jim Clark's original Indy-winning Lotus, the Le Mans-winning Ford GT40, the famous George Barris Ala Kart hot rod, the Malco Gasser drag car, and hundreds of other extraordinary examples of America's love for the automobile and motorsports.

Special Events

After setting the new land speed record at 409.277 mph, the Goldenrod immediately went on an extended national tour with the primary sponsors helping to foot the bill. Major events such as the New York and Chicago Auto Shows were primary venues while numerous smaller car shows and parking lot appearances at dealerships and supermarkets were also part of the program.

George Hurst took maximum advantage of his timely capital investment by making sure The Hurst Golden Girl, Linda Vaughn, was on hand for all of the Goldenrod's major appearances. The beauty and the beast proved to be a major hit, drawing large crowds wherever the car appeared. Hurst accrued considerable brand awareness and it was sometimes difficult to determine if the show attendees were drawn by the Goldenrod's speedy reputation or Linda's exuberant charm and presentation skills.

Goldenrod toured extensively after the record was set. It was displayed in various automotive venues all across Europe. Nearly forty years later, museum curator Bob Casey discovered it on display at the Meadowlands and initiated the process of purchasing it from Bill Summers.

GOLDENROD

Primagaz, a primary European supplier of propane, had the Goldenrod's paint scheme upgraded in its corporate colors for display while on tour in Europe.

Left: Cover sleeve used for insert material at the 25th anniversary of the record party at the Red Lion Inn in Ontario, CA.

Opposite: Bob Summers manning the display platform with Miss Hurst, Linda Vaughn, to answer questions and pass out Goldenrod literature at the New York Auto Show in 1966.

SPECIAL EVENTS:
GOODWOOD FESTIVAL - UNITED KINGDOM

The Goldenrod was displayed beside Donald Campbell's Bluebird CN7, both record-setting thoroughbreds with impeccable pedigrees. Different in almost every respect, the pair offered a fascinating contrast between the more formal corporate approach to land speed racing and the hot rodding approach, both uniquely successful.

When it was displayed next to Donald Campbell's Bluebird, the Goldenrod provided quite an interesting perspective to the science of land speed racing in the sixties. The Bluebird, with its powerful turbine engine, massive wheels and tires and sleek fighter plane good looks dwarfed the missile-like Goldenrod with its stealthy inline Hemi engines and pencil-thin aerodynamics.

Bill Summers proved a popular figure at the Goodwood Festival with onlookers anxious to get a closer look at the Goldenrod sitting right beside Donald Campbell's legendary 400 mph Bluebird.

Bluebird designer Ken Norris tried the Goldenrod cockpit on for size and found it remarkably confined. Summers was no small man, but his slim stature allowed him to wiggle into the tiny space with relative ease.

SPECIAL EVENTS: EUROPEAN TOUR

These are shots from an extended tour throughout Europe. Bill Summers, Jim Crosby, Royce McClintick and several friends accompanied the car on this publicity trip.

The Goldenrod's unprecedented European tour was promoted by the sponsors and heartily enjoyed by those who accompanied Bill Summers and Jim Crosby. This would not be Goldenrod's only European adventure as it returned multiple times to record crowds and admirers. The special trailer constructed for this trip later became the full-time transportation mode Bill used to display the car all over the United States. These trips eventually took a toll on the car in the form of further deterioration.

Germany was a popular venue for displaying the Goldenrod and fans flocked to see it in person. This was an old exhibition hall in southern Germany. Bob Summers did not accompany the car on this venture, so the boys told all the fräuleins that Royce McClintick was Bob. Royce is non-committal on whether this worked out to his advantage or not. Love the black California license plate on the trailer touring through Europe.

MIKE COOK

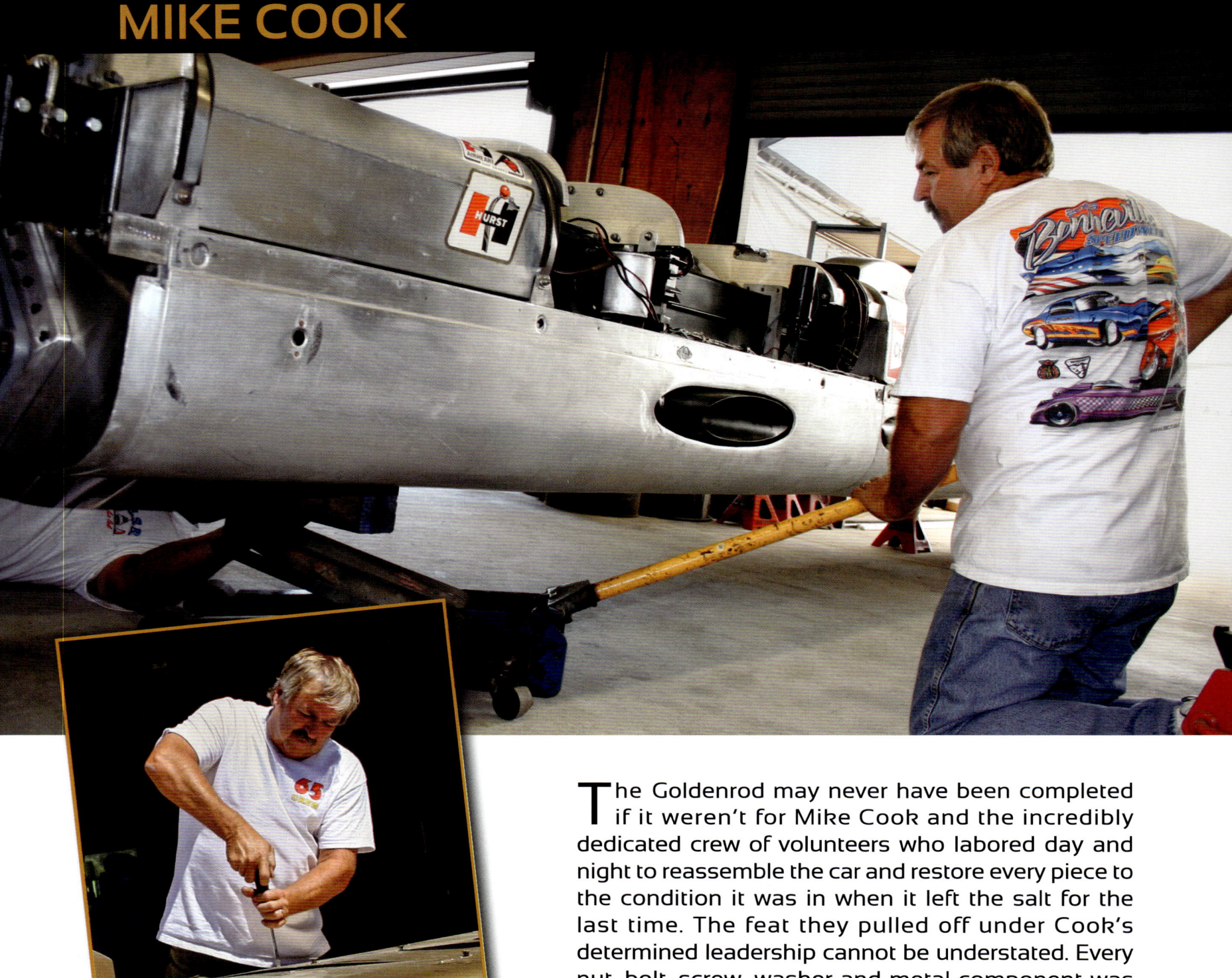

The Goldenrod may never have been completed if it weren't for Mike Cook and the incredibly dedicated crew of volunteers who labored day and night to reassemble the car and restore every piece to the condition it was in when it left the salt for the last time. The feat they pulled off under Cook's determined leadership cannot be understated. Every nut, bolt, screw, washer and metal component was massaged, restored and preserved to bring this amazing icon back to life for future generations to enjoy. The Goldenrod shines once again, a brilliant beacon of hot rod innovation and land speed racing history.

Some worked on it by day, others by night and on weekends, with Joe Pettitt faithfully recording every step in vivid photographs. Many worked on it in their

"This thing kicked our butts, but it was incredible how much everyone hung in there and saw it through to the end. It still amazes me that John took most of it apart and started the reassembly all by himself."

- Mike Cook

THE RESTORATION TEAM

Back Row: Royce McClintick, Ed Sutton, Paul Wilke, Armando Sutton, Gary Garcia, Skip Banks, Aaron Hebert, Steve Campbell, Billy Hodges, Mike Cook, Jr., Chris Hulbert, Jeff Squibbs, Stu Hilborn, Bob Robe, David Basham, Cheryl Shoemaker, John Brady, James Brown, Frank, Tim Fite, Lee Hulbert, Mike Cook, Leann Furgerson. Front, left to right: John Baechtel, Tom Habrzyk, Malcolm Collum, John Metz.

sleep as it was something you couldn't stop thinking about, especially Mike. I can't express my gratitude enough to Mike and Penny Cook and all the dedicated team members who sacrificed their time and energy to help me make this happen. Thanks also to museum curator Bob Casey and conservator Malcolm Collum for supporting this historic project and sticking with us through thick and thin. This section highlights some of our weary Goldenrod champions in action.

It took over a year for the museum to evaluate Goldenrod's condition and arrange funding. I started on it in February of 2005 and it was March 2006 before I cried uncle and asked Mike Cook for help. In the beginning, we had called for volunteers in the Hot Rod Magazine article. Some expressed interest, but there were no frequent helpers. Museum deadlines were approaching and the intricate task of reassembly loomed large. I had considered it a personal labor of love, but the pace accelerated exponentially

VOLUNTEERS & CREW

once Mike called for reinforcements. Those who answered the call shared many long days and nights reassembling a land speed racing masterpiece, as well as a once-in-a-lifetime experience. It was truly amazing how so many people, many of whom had never met each other before, merged into a seamless workforce that pushed the project through to completion with the relentless dedication it required.

Above, from the left: Aaron Hebert, Chris Hulbert, Skip Banks, Steve Campbell, Billy Hodges, Mike Cook. Foreground: Lee Hulbert. Left Top: Mike Cook, Jr., Aaron Hebert. Lower left: Billy Hodges.

Opposite Right, Top: Skip Banks. Center: Aaron Hebert, Gary Garcia, Skip Banks. Bottom: Frank Silva, who also made the crew shirts and volunteered his long trailer. Bottom Right: Lee Hulbert, Mike Cook, Gary Garcia.

GOLDENROD VOLUNTEERS

John Baechtel
Skip Banks
Larry Beatson
Steve Campbell
Bob Casey
Chrysler Motors
Tom Clarke
Duane Cole
Gary Cole
Malcolm Collum
Mike Cook
Mike Cook, Jr.
Penny Cook
David R. Cremans/PPG
James Crosby, Jr.
Jim Crosby
Lorna Crosby
Eric Dahlquist
Tom Dawson
Tony Fabozzi
Tim Fite
Leann Furgerson
Gary Garcia
Dan Goodwin
Tom Habryzk
Aaron Hebert
Stu Hilborn
Billy Hodges
Chris Hulbert
Lee Hulbert
Ed Iskenderian
Steve Kelishes
Mary Kimbrow/PPG
Doug Kruse
Roger Marble/Firestone
Royce McClintick

Bob Robe
Tommy Roberts
Greg Sharp
Frank Silva
Jeff Squibbs
Armando Sutton
Ed Sutton

BASHAM MOTORSPORTS GROUP

Dave Basham
Bob Brady
James Brown
Johnny Brown
Curtis Halverson
James Owens
Cheryl Schumacher

TRIBUTE:
400 CLUB SALUTES GOLDENROD

414.316

"I was 15 then and clearly remember when the Summers Brothers set the World Land Speed Record. It launched my fascination with Bonneville. Rett and I always dreamed about racing there, and after he died, I decided to honor him by going for big records. Thanks to Earl Wooden, many fine salt flat racers, and our tremendous team, we succeeded. September 21, 2010, was a truly magical day. Receiving congratulations from Bill Summers, George Poteet, the Nish family, and Al Teague right after breaking the 45-year-old Goldenrod record was a once-in-a-lifetime moment I am honored to be part of."

- Charles Nearburg

Photos: Car, Cook Shootout - Ray Therat. Head Shot - Thomas Graf.

Texan Charles Nearburg finally broke the actual Summers Brothers' record in 2010 with a two-way average of 414.316 mph at Mike Cook's Bonneville Shootout. Nearburg's fastest speed was 417 mph.

There are 15 men in the 400 MPH Chapter of the coveted Bonneville 200 MPH Club, six of them in jets and rockets and nine driving wheel-driven piston or turbine-powered cars like the Goldenrod and Vesco's Turbinator. They all acknowledge the truly extraordinary difficulty of achieving a 400 mph record with a vehicle that relies solely on the complicated relationship between horsepower, drag and a variable tire patch called traction. They further express great admiration and respect for Bob Summers and Donald Campbell, who both achieved this incredible feat more than 50 years ago and some 25 years before others began to match it. My thanks to "LandSpeed" Louise Ann Noeth for suggesting that I include this section with their thoughts about the Summers Brothers. Here are some of their comments.

200 MPH CLUB - 400 MPH CHAPTER

DRIVER	RECORD SPEED
Art Arfons	576.553
Craig Breedlove	600.601
Tom Burkland	417.020
Donald Campbell	403.100
Gary Gabelich	622.407
Andy Green, OBE	763.035
Tom Green	413.199
Charles Nearburg	414.316
Richard Noble, OBE	633.468
George Poteet	404.562
Bob Summers	409.277
Al Teague	409.986
Danny Thompson	406.769
Don Vesco	458.440
Nolan White	413.156

"Bob Summers was an amazing person whom I always greatly admired. Through my association with Clyde Sturdy at Associated Gear there were many stories and insights to this man's ability. The many indications that set him apart from most men were his talents as a creator, designer, builder and driver of LSR cars. The Summers Brothers' business was very helpful to the racers needs with quality products. In 1991, when we were fortunate enough to set our FIA record, the Summers Brothers sent their congratulations via Western Union. I treasure that telegram. With respect..." - Al Teague

Al Teague had numerous 400+ runs before he finally set his record in 1991. Teague's fastest exit speed exceeded 432 mph.

One of the most respected competitors to ever race at Bonneville, Don Vesco set and still holds the official unlimited land speed record at 458.481 mph in 1997. Don passed in 2002, but he left an enduring legacy that has yet to be surpassed. "Those guys were special, they were perfectionists," recalled Don's brother, Rick Vesco. "Goldenrod set a standard that was unbelievable."

"Every time I make a run over 400, I realize how impossible it was for them to achieve what they did."

- George Poteet

George Poteet has over 43 runs exceeding 400 mph. His 439.024 mph record was set in 2012, and the car has been clocked with an exit speed of 462 mph.

292

TRIBUTE:
400 CLUB SALUTES GOLDENROD

415.896

Photos: Jeffrey Conger Studio

"One of the major advancements achieved by Goldenrod and the project team was the "engineered project" nature of the development. The Summers were able to incorporate the important engineering aspects with Walt Korff's conceptual layout to achieve satisfactory weight and balance and then the aerodynamic portion including loft contours that fit around the carefully packaged parts and the wind tunnel verification of the shape prior to starting construction. This packaging aspect is often overlooked, but really good streamliner designs will use virtually all of the interior volume to minimize the aerodynamic drag caused by the frontal area and skin surfaces. As a team, they managed to translate this initial technical concept into the beautifully-completed real hardware and drive it through the timers twice inside the one-hour allotted time period for an international record that would stand for nearly 45 years." - Tom Burkland

413.156

Photos: LandSpeed Productions

"The Summers Brothers' land speed racing accomplishments were respected and admired not only by my father, Nolan (1931-2002), but by our entire Spirit of Autopower team. Trying to set a World Land Speed Record is a lofty goal - it took 25 years before their speed was matched and another 15 years before it was broken, but only by five miles an hour faster."

- Rick White

406.769

Photos: Holly Martin

"Those guys were pretty awesome going that fast in 1965. Wow, only now realizing how difficult it is."

- Danny Thompson

I knew Bill and Bob very well. They were great guys. We hunted parts and sponsors together. No one worked harder. They built a well-thought-out machine that had enough power to set the record without complicating it with superchargers. They kept the design simple. That allowed them to keep the frontal area down. The craftsmanship on the car was flawless.

- Craig Breedlove

600.601

Photo: LandSpeed Productions

293

PHOTO CREDITS & ACKNOWLEDGEMENTS

About the AUTHOR

John Baechtel served as technical editor of Car Craft Magazine in the seventies, executive editor of Hot Rod Magazine throughout the eighties and then editor of Car Craft again in the nineties. He was a GM motorsports consultant for ten years and then opened a race engine testing facility for over a dozen years before retiring early to write technical and historical automotive books and manage a growing group of automotive high-performance enthusiast websites.

He is a Bonneville racing veteran, 200 MPH Club Member, International FIA speed record holder and avid collector of land speed record memorabilia and LSR model cars. He builds his own race engines and is the author of a dozen technical books on engine building and race car construction. He enjoys researching and collecting vintage engines and speed equipment.

SPECIAL THANKS TO:

Bob Summers, Bill Summers and Jim Crosby for being the baddest hot rodders ever.

Thomas Voehringer, Archivist, The Enthusiast Network, for tireless assistance in tracking down and scanning Eric Rickman's photos.

Sidney Hidalgo, Director of Partner Development, The Enthusiast Network, for authorizing the TEN photo contributions.

Greg Sharp, Curator, NHRA Museum, for our cover photo.

Bob Casey, Former Curator of Transportation, The Henry Ford, for his vision of the project and the proposal that won the funding award from the Save America's Treasures Program.

Malcolm Collum, Former Conservator, The Henry Ford, for his many visits and insight into the preservation of materials.

Hurst Performance, Chrysler, Mobil Oil, Firestone and Champion for their visionary sponsorship and material support.

Cook Motorsports for unwavering commitment to the project.

Joe Pettitt for all his time and effort to help document the rebuild.

Steve Tremulis for assistance in acquiring John Veenstra photos.

Cover Image	Greg Sharp/NHRA Museum
Cover Insets	David Freers
Cover Insert (center)	John Veenstra
Endpapers	Joe Pettitt, Scott Lozano
Bk. Cover, T	Leann Furgerson
Bk. Cover, B, L	Joe Pettitt
Title Page	Bob Casey/The Henry Ford
Lead Page	Wayne Thoms
Publisher's Page	James Crosby
Inset	Hot Rod Magazine/TEN
TOC Intro	Eric Rickman/TEN
1	David Freers, Scott Lozano
1 Inset	Joe Pettitt
3	John Veenstra
4 Photo	Greg Sharp/NHRA Museum
4 Hurst Logo	Hurst Performance
4 Chrysler Logo	FCA US LLC
4 Firestone Logo	Bridgestone Americas, Inc.
4 Mobile Logo	Exxon Mobil Corporation
5	Eric Rickman/TEN
7	Eric Rickman/TEN
8	Royce McClintick
9-10	Eric Rickman/TEN
11-12	Wayne Thoms
13-14	Wayne Thoms/Tiffany Summers
15	Wayne Thoms
16	Wayne Thoms
17	Hurst Performance/Wayne Thoms
18 T	Royce McClintick
18 B	James Crosby
20	Eric Rickman/TEN
21	Wayne Thoms
22 TR	Joe Pettitt
22 B	Wayne Thoms
23 Illust.	C.O. LaTourette/Wayne Thoms
23 B	Wayne Thoms
25	Eric Rickman/TEN
26	Royce McClintick
27	Wayne Thoms
27 TR	Royce McClintick
28 TL	Royce McClintick
28 TR	David Fetherston
28 B	Tiffany Summers
29 T	Brisette/Landspeed Productions
29 B	Royce McClintick
30	Eric Rickman/TEN
31	Eric Rickman/TEN
32	Eric Rickman/TEN
33	Tiffany Summers
33 Illust.	C.O. LaTourette/Wayne Thoms
34	Landspeed Productions
35	Yakel/Landspeed Productions
36 T	Yakel/Landspeed Productions
36 BL, BR	John Veenstra
37-42	Eric Rickman/TEN
42 B	Bob Summers/John Veenstra
43-44 T	Bob Summers/John Veenstra
43-44 B	Eric Rickman/TEN
45-47	Bob Summers/John Veenstra
45 TL	Eric Rickman/TEN
46 BR	Eric Rickman/TEN
48-52	Eric Rickman/TEN
53 T	Royce McClintick
53 B	James Crosby Family
54	Author
55-59	James Crosby Family
61-62	David Freers
63-64 T	David Freers
63 B	Alexandre Fernandez
64 B	James Crosby
65	Joe Pettitt
66	Scott Lozano
67-68 T	Bob Summers/John Veenstra
67 B	John Veenstra
68 B	Veenstra/Landspeed Productions
69	Walter Korff Archive
70	Eric Rickman/TEN
71	Wayne Thoms
72	Royce McClintick
73	Joe Pettitt
74	Walter Korff/John Veenstra
75	Walter Korff
76	Jerry Landry
78	Wayne Thoms
80	Wayne Thoms
81-82	Walter Korff/AIAA
84	"LandSpeed" Louise Ann Noeth
85	Author
86	Joe Pettitt
89-91	Joe Pettitt
92	Eric Rickman/TEN
93	Joe Pettitt
94	David Freers
95-96	Sutton Family Archive
96 TR	Hot Rod Magazine/TEN
95 B	Christine Esquer
97-98	Author, Joe Pettitt
98 TR	Christine Esquer
99-100	Joe Pettitt
101	Lockheed Star
102	Los Angeles Times
103	Wayne Thoms
104	Chrysler Group, LLC
105	Author
107	Bob D'Olivo/TEN
108 TL	James Crosby
108 TR, B	Chrysler Group, LLC
109	Bob D'Olivo/TEN
109 B	Chrysler Group, LLC
110	Eric Rickman/TEN
111	Marc Rozeman/Chrysler Group, LLC
112 T	Chrysler Group, LLC
112 B	Geoff Stunkard
113	William Weertman
114 T	Joe Pettitt
114 B	James Crosby
115	Jim Kramer/Kramer Automotive
116	Joe Pettitt
117-118	Jim Kramer/Kramer Automotive
118 Inset	James Crosby
119	Author
120 T	Joe Pettitt
122	Scott Lozano
123	Eric Rickman/TEN
124	James Crosby
125-134	Eric Rickman/TEN
135 T, BR	Eric Rickman/TEN
135 Badges	Keith Stribling
136 B	John Veenstra
137-140	John Veenstra
141-142	Eric Rickman/TEN
143-144 T	John Veenstra
143-144 B	Eric Rickman/TEN
145 T	John Veenstra
145 B	Eric Rickman/TEN
146-149	John Veenstra
150	Batchelor/Landspeed Productions
151-152	Eric Rickman/TEN
151-152 Insets	Firestone Press Film
153-154	Eric Rickman/TEN
154 Timing Notes	Joe Petrali/Dave Petrali
155 T	James Crosby
155 BL	Eric Rickman/TEN
156	Landspeed Productions
157	FIA/Scott & Tiffany Summers
158	Lorna Crosby
159-166	USAC/Dave Petrali
167-168	Eric Rickman/TEN
169	Author
170	Bob Casey
171	Author
172-173	Author
174-175	Bob Casey
177	Randy Lorentzen
178	Author
179	Leann Furgerson
180 B	Gary Cole
180-186	Author
181 BL	Malcolm Collum
182 T	Malcolm Collum
186 CL, BR	Leann Furgerson
186 CR	Malcolm Collum
187-202	Author
187 BR	Malcolm Collum
188 TR, BR	Leann Furgerson
192 CL, BL	Malcolm Collum
196 BR	Eric Rickman/TEN
198 TR	Malcolm Collum
203	Malcolm Collum
204-214	Author
210 BR	Malcolm Collum
215	Joe Pettitt
216	Author
217 T	Leann Furgerson
217-226	Author
220 B	Joe Pettitt
227 T	Joe Pettitt
227 B	Gary Cole
228	Author
229-230	David Freers
231-266	Joe Pettitt
265 T	David Freers
265 B	Author
266-268	Roger Marble
268 T	Joe Pettitt
269-271	Joe Pettitt
272	Malcolm Collum
273-276	Cole Quinnell
275 T, B	David Freers
277-278	The Henry Ford
279	Bob D'Olivo/TEN
280-281	Royce McClintick
281 Cover	Summers Brothers
282	Bob D'Olivo/TEN
283-284	Phil Evans
285-286	Royce McClintick
287-288	Joe Pettitt
288 Crew	Mike Cook
289-290	Joe Pettitt
291	Ray Therat, Thomas Graf
292 T, C	"LandSpeed" Louise Ann Noeth
292 B	Author
293, Burkland	Jeffery Conger Studio
293, White	"LandSpeed" Louise Ann Noeth
293, Thompson	Holly Martin
293, Breedlove	Landspeed Productions

SUMMERS BROTHERS